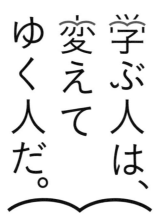

学ぶ人は、
変えて
ゆく人だ。

目の前にある問題はもちろん、

人生の問いや、

社会の課題を自ら見つけ、

挑み続けるために、人は学ぶ。

「学び」で、

少しずつ世界は変えてゆける。

いつでも、と

学ぶこと

大学入試

全レベル問題集
英語リスニング

河合塾講師 坂本 浩 著

③ 私大・国公立大レベル

はじめに

『大学入試 全レベル問題集 英語リスニング』シリーズは，レベル1〜3の3段階で構成されています。リスニングの基礎から，共通テスト・私大中堅レベル，さらには難関大に出題される問題まで，すべてのレベルの問題がそろっているので，皆さんの実力に合った1冊からリスニング対策を始めることができます。

大学入試で出題されるリスニング問題で最も多いのは，アナウンスメントやストーリー，講義などのモノローグや会話を聞いて，その内容についての質問に答える形式です。テスト用紙に質問が書いてある問題もあれば，質問はテスト用紙にはなく，音声で流れる問題もあります。いずれにしても，皆さんは，会話やモノローグを聞いて，そこに含まれる情報を正確に聞き取り，その一部を質問という形で確かめられるわけです。ですから，リスニング問題では，音声を正確に聞き取るだけでなく，聞き取った内容をメモしたり，選択肢にチェックを入れたりしながら情報を整理し，必要な項目を取捨選択する力が必要になります。音声を聞く前に質問や選択肢を読んでおくことができれば，音声を聞いてどのような情報を聞き取ればよいのかが明確になるので，そうした練習も必要になるでしょう。

音声面の習得という点から言うと，聞き取ることばかりに神経がいきがちですが，まず行っていただきたいのは，サンプル音声と同じように発音できるようになる練習です。意味を考えつつ，1つ1つの音，リズムを正確にまねて，それを何度も繰り返す練習を積んでいただきたいと思います。本シリーズに掲載された例題や練習問題は，そうした繰り返しの音読練習に向いた，英語の音声の基礎を習得でき，かつ内容的にも興味深いものを選定してあります。問題を一度解いて終わりにせずに，すでに理解した英文について，付属の音声を利用し，それに合わせて何度もシャドーイングや音読練習，ときにはディクテーションをすることで，皆さんのリスニング力がレベルアップしていくことでしょう。この問題集が皆さんの英語力向上に役立つことを心から願っています。

坂本　浩

目　次

著者紹介：**坂本　浩**（さかもと　ひろし）

河合塾講師。著書に『英文で覚える 英単語ターゲット R 英単語ターゲット 1400 レベル［改訂版］』（旺文社）など。東京外国語大学英語科卒業。東京大学大学院総合文化研究科・言語情報科学専攻博士課程単位取得退学。専門は日・英の語彙意味論。

協力各氏・各社

装丁デザイン：ライトパブリシティ

本文デザイン：内津 剛（及川真咲デザイン事務所）

校正：Jason A. Chau ／大河恭子／石川道子

録音・編集：ユニバ合同会社

ナレーション：Ryan Drees ／ Emma Howard ／ Simon Loveday ／ Jenny Skidmore ／細谷美友

編集協力：株式会社カルチャー・プロ

編集担当：赤井美樹

本シリーズの特長

『全レベル問題集 英語リスニング』には，以下の特長があります。

1. 志望校別のレベル設定

　　長年『全国大学入試問題正解 英語リスニング』（旺文社）に携わり，大学入試の
リスニング問題を分析してきた著者が，レベル別に適した問題を選び，取り組みや
すいものから順に構成しました。

2. 実践的な問題

　　問題は最新の入試過去問題から厳選，または新たに作成して掲載しています。設
問形式は各レベルの入試で頻出のものに対応しているので，効率よく対策ができま
す。

3. 丁寧な解説

　　スクリプトの中で解答の根拠となる箇所を示すなど，すべての設問をわかりやす
く，丁寧に解説しているので疑問が残りません。

4. 簡単・便利な音声

　　音声は二次元コードやアプリを使って簡単に再生することができ，ストレスなく
学習できます。

5. 音声と誌面で復習をサポート

　　全問題の英文音声を音読やディクテーションに使いやすい形に再編集した「ト
レーニング用」音声が付属しています。巻末のスクリプトと併せて復習に活用でき
ます。

志望校レベルと『全レベル問題集 英語リスニング』シリーズのレベル対応表

※掲載の大学名は活用していただく際の目安です。

本書のレベル	各レベルの該当大学
① 基礎レベル	高校基礎〜大学受験準備
② 共通テストレベル	共通テストレベル
③ 私大・国公立大レベル	**[私立大学]** 青山学院大学・国際基督教大学・南山大学・関西外国語大学　他 **[国公立大学]** 秋田大学・東京大学・東京外国語大学・一橋大学・新潟大学・大阪大学・神戸市外国語大学・福岡教育大学・熊本県立大学

本書の使いかた

1. 例題で特徴をつかむ

　リスニング試験で聞き取る英文のタイプによって章が分かれています。各章のはじめに，それぞれのタイプで頻出な設問形式を例題として取り上げています。問題を解くときのポイントなどを「こう聞く！」にまとめています。

2. 練習問題を解く

　聞き取る英文が同じタイプでも，設問形式や英文の長さなどにはバリエーションがあります。本番の入試でどんな問題が出題されても落ち着いて取り組めるよう，練習問題でさまざまなパターンに触れておきましょう。

3. 解答・解説を読む

　練習問題の解答・解説は p. 70 以降にあります。解説のうちで特に重要なところは「ここがポイント」として示しています。

4. 復習する

　巻末には，全問題の英文スクリプトだけを再掲載していま
す。「トレーニング用音声」には1文ごとにポーズを設けて
ありますので，音読やディクテーションなどに活用してくだ
さい。

復習のしかた

● **音読**

　トレーニング用音声の発音をまねて，スクリプトを声に出して読みましょう。

● **シャドーイング**

　トレーニング用音声を聞きながら，すぐあとに続いて繰り返しましょう。

● **ディクテーション**

　スクリプトを見ないでトレーニング用音声を聞き，英文を書き取りましょう。

本書で使用している記号一覧

S	……………	主語	動	……………	動詞
V	……………	述語動詞	名	……………	名詞
O, O₁, O₂	……	目的語	形	……………	形容詞
C	……………	補語	副	……………	副詞
to do	……………	不定詞	前	……………	前置詞
doing	…………	現在分詞・動名詞	接	……………	接続詞
done	……………	過去分詞			

＊すべての解答・解説・和訳は旺文社が独自に作成しました。

＊問題指示や解答のためのポーズなどは，実際の入試と異なる場合があります。

音声について

音声は 3 種類の方法で聞くことができます。音声の内容はすべて同じものです。
トラック番号 26 以降は，問題で聞き取る英文の部分だけを再編集した「トレーニング用」音声です。

●二次元コードから聞く

スマートフォンなどで，トラック番号（ ◀)) 01 など）の隣にある二次元コードを読み取ってください。

●専用ウェブサイトから聞く

パソコンから以下のサイトにアクセスし，パスワードを入力してください。

URL：https://www.obunsha.co.jp/service/zll/3.html

パスワード：zllbook3（アルファベット小文字と数字。すべて半角）

・右の二次元コードからもアクセスできます。

・音声ファイルをダウンロードするか，ウェブ上で再生するかを選べます。

> 注意▶ダウンロードについて：音声ファイルは MP3 形式です。ZIP 形式で圧縮されていますので，解凍（展開）して，MP3 を再生できるデジタルオーディオプレーヤーなどでご活用ください。解凍（展開）せずに利用されると，ご使用の機器やソフトウェアにファイルが認識されないことがあります。スマートフォンやタブレットでは音声をダウンロードできません。デジタルオーディオプレーヤーなどの機器への音声ファイルの転送方法は，各製品の取り扱い説明書などをご覧ください。▶音声を再生する際の通信料にご注意ください。▶ご使用機器，音声再生ソフトなどに関する技術的なご質問は，ハードメーカーもしくはソフトメーカーにお願いします。▶本サービスは予告なく終了することがあります。

●スマートフォンアプリで聞く

「英語の友」で検索するか，右の二次元コードからアクセスしてください。パスワードを求められたら，上と同じパスワードを入力してください。

◆ 青山学院大学

1,000 語を超える文章が流れることも

　非常に長いモノローグやダイアローグが出題されます。文学部英米文学科 A 方式の問題はすべて 4 択形式の選択問題からなり，質問と選択肢は問題紙面に示されています。放送文が長く，情報量も多いものの，選択肢は比較的短いので，音声を聞きながら答えを出していけるよう練習を積んでください。

ダイアローグは著名人へのインタビューが中心

　文学部英米文学科 B 方式や C 方式では，1 つの長いインタビュー形式のダイアローグが流れ，その中でディクテーション，記述問題，選択問題などが複合的に問われています。ディクテーションでは語レベルの書き取り，記述問題では文レベルの書き取り，選択問題では内容の正確な聞き取りが問われます。私大のリスニング問題では最も分量の多い問題の 1 つです。

◆ 国際基督教大学

ダイアローグと講義形式のモノローグ

　2 往復程度の短いダイアローグ，5 往復程度のやや長いダイアローグ，講義形式の長いモノローグなどから構成されています。すべて 4 択形式の選択問題からなり，質問と選択肢は問題紙面に示されています。ダイアローグの内容は大学生活に関連するものが中心です。

モノローグは実際の大学での講義を想定

　モノローグは講義形式になっており，放送文は 700 語を超えます。題材は大学の講義で取り上げられるような専門的な分野に及ぶこともあります。質問と選択肢の先読みに充てられる時間は非常に短く，純粋にリスニング力が問われる問題です。受験生はこのリスニング問題を通して，英語で行われる大学の講義についていけるかどうか試されていると考えるべきでしょう。

◆ 関西外国語大学

短いモノローグの聞き取り

　200 語程度のモノローグと質問 4 問が音声で流れます。選択肢は問題紙面に示されています。放送文は比較的短いですが，題材は社会・文化・政治・歴史などで，語彙レベルが高い場合もあるので，特に音声の 1 回目は細部にこだわらず，全体的な内容の聞き取りに集中しましょう。

質問は音声で流れる

　本文だけでなく質問も音声で流れます。音声は 2 回流れますが，1 回目は本文の主要な情報

を聞き取った上で，本文のあとに流れてくる質問を把握することが重要です。この時点で記憶やメモを頼りに，答えが出せるものは出しておきます。2回目では問われていることを頭に入れ，音声を聞きながら正解を選んでいきましょう。

◆ 南山大学

3つのセクションからなる

　1つ目のセクションでは，100語程度のダイアローグやモノローグ，および質問が音声で流れます。10問出題され，それぞれの質問の選択肢は問題紙面に示されています。2つ目のセクションでは，やや長いダイアローグやモノローグが2つ流れます。それぞれに2，3問の4択問題が付されています。このセクションでは質問と選択肢は問題紙面に示されています。

セクション3は真偽判定問題

　3つ目のセクションでは，やや短いダイアローグやモノローグが流れ，問題紙面に示されている文の真偽を判定します。これら3つのセクションはどれも音声が1回しか流れず，全体の分量も多いので，高い集中力の維持が要求されます。英米学科とフランス学科・アジア学科の問題は互いに類似しているので，過去問を利用して数多く練習するとよいでしょう。

◆ 秋田大学

記述問題が中心

　長いモノローグが流れ，放送文の内容に当てはまるものを問題紙面に示された選択肢から選ぶ問題，日本語で記述して答える問題，および放送文の内容に関連するトピックで書く自由英作文問題に答えます。内容は身近な話題に関して個人の意見を述べたものが多く，具体的な体験や意見の根拠を整理して聞き取ることが求められます。

自由英作文の対策も必須

　単に音声を聞き取るだけでなく，聞き取った内容を日本語や英語で表現する力も求められています。特に英作文は，放送文の内容に関連したトピックについて自分の意見が求められるので，150～200語程度の英文で自分の意見を筋道立てて表現する力を養成することが重要です。

◆ 新潟大学

ディクテーション問題

　2題からなり，問題Aは短いダイアローグの一部が空所になっており，聞こえてきた英文の一部または全部を書き取る，いわゆるディクテーション問題です。語と語の結合や，語末の子音の脱落など，英語の音声上の特質を理解して正確に聞き取る練習をする必要があります。

日本語による記述問題

　問題Bは，話者の個人的体験を語ったやや長いモノローグと，それに続けて流れる質問を聞

き，質問の答えを日本語で記述するという問題です。質問内容が分からない段階で聞く1回目は，5W1Hを中心にメモを取りながら聞き，質問が流れたあとは，質問内容に集中して聞き取るようにします。

◆ 東京大学

3題中2題は内容的に関連している

　3題からなり，うち2題は内容的に関連しています。関連した2題は，インタビュー形式または討論形式のダイアローグ（時に3人の会話）であることが多く，司会者が質問し，論者がそれに答える形をとります。内容は専門的なものが多く，1つの話題に対して対立した意見が提示されるなど，高度な内容になっています。事前に問題紙面に示された質問を把握しておくことが求められます。

選択肢を正確に理解することが重要

　もう1題は講義形式のモノローグで，500語程度からなります。講義内容にはやはり専門的な事柄が多く含まれるので，質問を先読みして事前知識を持つことが重要です。3題とも選択式の問題ですが，近年では5択形式となっています。音声理解はもちろんのこと，選択肢を素早く正確に読み取ることも，正解を導く上でカギとなります。

◆ 東京外国語大学

3択形式の選択問題

　3題からなり，うち2題は，近年では，長いダイアローグやモノローグを聞き，3択形式の選択問題を解く形が主体です。放送文は長いですが，質問と選択肢は問題紙面に示されているので，事前にどのようなトピックであるか把握することが可能です。

英文要約と自由英作文

　もう1題は，講義形式の英文を聞いて，200語程度の英文で要約する問題が出題されています。要約のヒントとなる本文のまとめメモやイラストなどが示されています。また，放送文の内容に関連したトピックについて，自分の意見を書くことが求められる自由英作文問題も出題されています。自分の意見を英語で自由に表現できるよう練習しておくことが求められます。

◆ 一橋大学

ディクテーションの力が求められる

　長年，200語程度のモノローグが2題出題され，内容に関する各3問の質問に英語で答えるという形式が主流でした。この形式では，質問文が放送文の内容をなぞる形で設定されているので，実質的にディクテーション問題であるということができます。質問を事前に把握し，該当箇所の音声が流れたら素早く書き取ることが求められます。

傾向の変化も

　近年では傾向の変化も見られます。問題数は変わりませんが，1題当たりの放送文の語数が3倍ほどに増えています。ただし，1題はやはりディクテーション問題で，聞き取った内容を正確に書き取ることが求められます。もう1題は放送文の内容に関する4択形式の選択問題で，青山学院大学文学部英米文学科A方式の問題や国際基督教大学のPart 3に近い形式です。

◆ 大阪大学

日本語による記述問題

　長めの講義形式のモノローグを2回聞き，日本語で設定された質問に日本語で答える独特の質問形式です。質問を事前に読むことで，放送文のおおまかなトピックをつかむことが可能です。ただし，書き取る分量は意外に多く，メモを取っているうちに，音声が次々に流れていくので，ノートテイクの練習を積む必要があるでしょう。

◆ 神戸市外国語大学

質問も選択肢もすべて音声

　内容的に関連した3つのセクションからなる英文を聞いて，4択形式の選択問題に答えます。放送文はダイアローグが中心ですが，最初のセクションではダイアローグにおける背景知識や事前説明などがなされます。質問も選択肢もすべて音声で流れるため，2回流れる音声のうち，1回目はメモを取りながら内容を把握することに努め，2回目は質問を念頭に置いた上で，答えを求めるつもりで聞くようにするとよいでしょう。

◆ 福岡教育大学

ディクテーション問題

　モノローグとダイアローグ（正確には3人の会話）の2題構成です。モノローグは空所を伴った英文が示され，音声を聞きながら空所を埋めていくディクテーション問題です。書き取る内容はフレーズレベルなので，急いで書き取らないと英文の該当箇所を見失う恐れがあるので，事前に十分練習を積みましょう。

独特な記述問題

　会話問題では登場人物が3人いるので，誰の発話であるかを把握することに少し戸惑うかもしれません。また，問題形式も独特で，事前に示されている英語の質問に英語で答える形式で，質問には表が設定されており，話者それぞれがどのような立場であるか，またはどのような行動を取ったかを整理して記入する形式になっています。また，50語前後で自分の意見を書く自由英作文も出題されています。

1 短いダイアローグ

短い対話を聞き，内容に関する質問の答えとして最も適切な英文を選ぶ問題を扱います。質問を先に読み，対話の中で聞き取るべき情報が何であるかを把握します。また，音声を聞きながら選択肢の情報にも目を配ります。

✔ **Check** 対話の状況と展開をとらえる

対話を聞き，それぞれの問いの答えとして最も適切なものを，①〜④のうちから1つずつ選びなさい。1回流します。

問1 Between whom is the conversation probably taking place?
① two university students planning to study in Japan
② a Japanese student and her friend living in New York
③ two Japanese students going on a study abroad program
④ a Japanese student and an international student in Japan

問2 Which is the most likely reason the woman wanted to speak to the man?
① She felt anxious about studying abroad in America.
② She was keen to know how to prepare to study abroad.
③ She was interested in having lunch with the man.
④ She was wondering if Americans speak too fast.

（国際基督教大学）

スクリプト W(1)： Chris, can I talk to you for a minute? I'm so nervous about studying abroad. I'm worried I won't be able to communicate with anyone.

M(1)： You worry too much, Hana. You speak English well.

W(2)： Yeah, but some Americans speak so fast. I don't know if I'll be able to understand them.

M(2)： But you can understand me, can't you?

W(3)： Yeah, but you speak very clearly. I don't think everyone is as easy to understand as you.

M(3)： Well, I'm having lunch with a couple of friends from New York tomorrow. Why don't you join us? You can practice with us.

12

W(4): Really? Thanks, Chris. That will make me feel better.

M(4): Sure. Meet us in the cafeteria at lunch time.

W(5): I'll be there. Thank you.

和訳　女性(1)：クリス, 少し話すことできる？　留学のことですごく緊張しているの。誰ともコミュニケーションが取れないんじゃないかって心配で。

女性(1)：

男性(1)：心配しすぎだよ, ハナ。君はきちんと英語を話しているよ。

女性(2)：うん, でもアメリカ人には話すのがとても速い人もいるから。彼らの言うことを理解できるかわからないわ。

男性(2)：でも僕の言っていることは理解できているだろう？

女性(3)：そうだけど, あなたはすごくはっきりと話してくれるじゃない。みんながあなたみたいにわかりやすいとは思えないの。

男性(3)：そうか, 明日, ニューヨーク出身の友だち2人と昼食をとる予定なんだ。一緒に来ない？　僕らと練習できるよ。

女性(4)：本当？　ありがとう, クリス。そうしてもらえたら気が楽になるわ。

男性(4)：いいよ。昼食時間にカフェテリアで会おうよ。

女性(5)：カフェテリアに行くわね。ありがとう。

解説　問1　会話はおそらく誰の間で行われているか。

① 日本に留学を計画している2人の大学生

② 日本人学生と, ニューヨークに住んでいる彼女の友人

③ 留学プログラムで海外に行こうとしている2人の日本人学生

④ 日本人学生と, 日本にいる留学生

　選択肢から,「話者は日本人か外国人か」「日本から海外への留学か, 日本への留学か」などが聞き取りのポイントになります。女性の1・2番目の発話から, 女性は「これからアメリカに留学する」ことがわかります。そして留学することに不安を感じている女性に, 男性は, 最初の発話で You speak English well.「君はきちんと英語を話しているよ」と言っていることから, 女性は英語に不安を抱える日本人学生であると考えることができます。また,「アメリカ人には英語を話すのが速い人もいる」と不安がる女性に対して, 男性は, 2番目の発話で But you can understand me, can't you?「でも僕の言っていることは理解できているだろう？」と言って不安を和らげようとしていることから, 男性は英語のネイティブスピーカーであると考えられます。また男性は3番目の発話で, I'm having lunch with a couple of friends from New York tomorrow. Why don't you join us? と昼食に女性を誘い, 次の発話でカフェテリアを場所に指定していることから, 男性も女性と同じ大学内にいることがわかります。したがって, 正解は ④ です。

　　　① 彼女はアメリカに留学することに不安を感じていた。

　　　② 彼女は留学のためにどのような準備をすべきか知りたがっていた。

　　　③ 彼女は男性と昼食をとることに関心があった。

　　　④ 彼女はアメリカ人があまりに速く話すのかどうか気になっていた。

　女性の1～3番目の発話より，女性は留学してアメリカ人との会話について いけるかということに不安を感じており，英語のネイティブスピーカーである クリスという男性に相談していると考えることができるので，正解は ① です。 女性は，留学準備として何をすればよいかというようなことは質問していませ んし，some Americans speak so fast と言っていますが，そのことを男性に尋 ねたわけではありません。また，昼食は男性からの提案です。

正解　問1　④　　問2　①

語句　cafeteria 图「カフェテリア，学食」

────────────────────────────────

🎧 こう聞く！　　質問を先に読もう

質問を先に読んで，**対話からどのような情報を引き出せばよいか**について，あら かじめ理解しておきましょう。また，聞いている間に選択肢の情報を素早く読み 取り，対話文を聞きながら，答えを特定できるように練習していきましょう。

────────────────────────────────

 **練習問題**　解答・解説▶ pp.70 ～ 77

1 対話を聞き，それぞれの問いの答えとして最も適切なもの
を，① ～ ④ のうちから 1 つずつ選びなさい。1 回流しま
す。

◀))02

問 1 How do the man and the woman usually get to college?
① The man and the woman take the bus.
② The man rides his bicycle and the woman takes a taxi.
③ The man rides his bicycle and the woman takes the bus.
④ The man takes the bus and the woman rides her bicycle.

問 2 What can be inferred from the man's suggestion?
① The woman should live on campus.
② The woman should get more exercise.
③ The woman should use money wisely.
④ The woman should be on time for class.

（国際基督教大学）

短いダイアローグ

2 対話を聞き，それぞれの問いの答えとして最も適切なもの
を，① 〜 ④ のうちから 1 つずつ選びなさい。1 回流しま
す。

問1 Who is the man talking to?
① his friend
② a counselor
③ his professor
④ a writing tutor

問2 What time will the woman's last available appointment end?
① 2:10 p.m.
② 2:40 p.m.
③ 3:10 p.m.
④ 3:40 p.m.

問3 Why does this session finish so quickly?
① The man does not have enough time.
② The woman has another appointment.
③ The woman refuses to correct his writing.
④ The man does not have his paper with him.

(国際基督教大学)

3 対話を聞き，それぞれの問いの答えとして最も適切なもの ◀))04
を，① ～ ④ のうちから1つずつ選びなさい。1回流しま
す。

問1 How does the man know that the woman is on the new meal plan?
　① Most of his friends changed plans.
　② His friend informed him.
　③ She had already told him.
　④ He saw her changing to it.

問2 Which of the following is true about the woman's new meal plan?
　① She changed it a week ago.
　② She can still eat on weekends.
　③ She is spending less money.
　④ She uses the cafeteria more.

問3 Which of the following is a reason the man gives for staying on his current
　meal plan?
　① He can eat any time of the day.
　② The plan is reasonably priced.
　③ The plan includes breakfast.
　④ His teammates are on the plan.

（国際基督教大学）

2 短いモノローグ

短いニュース記事や説明文を聞き，内容に関する質問の答えとして最も適切な英文を選ぶ問題を扱います。事前に選択肢に軽く目を通して，話題に関連すると思われる表現をチェックするようにしましょう。

Check　細部の情報を聞き取る

英語と問いを聞き，それぞれの問いの答えとして最も適切なものを，① 〜 ④ のうちから１つずつ選びなさい。１回流します。　◀))05

問1　① Because it contains such pure gold.
　　② Because it has a special maple leaf on it.
　　③ Because it is so famous.
　　④ Because it is the largest coin in the world.

問2　① Because the case was bulletproof and impossible for a normal person to break.
　　② Because the coin is too heavy for an ordinary person to carry.
　　③ Because the security camera recorded weightlifters leaving the museum.
　　④ Because the window the thieves entered through was too heavy to open.

(青山学院大学)

スクリプト　※下線部は解答の根拠に当たる箇所です。

The Bode Museum in Germany is known for its collection of rare coins. But on March 27, 2017, the collection's largest coin was stolen. Known as the "Big Maple Leaf," it weighs 100 kilograms and is 53 centimeters wide. 問1 The face value of the coin is $1 million, but experts say it may be worth up to $4 million because its gold is so pure. It had been kept behind bulletproof glass since it was loaned to the museum in 2010. Berlin police believe the thieves climbed in through a window, broke the case and took the coin in just 25 minutes. 問2 People question how the thieves got such a large and heavy coin out of the museum. One person guessed that the thieves must all be weightlifters.

Questions:

1. Why did some experts think the coin might be worth up to $4 million?

2. Why did some people believe that the thieves were weightlifters?

和訳 ドイツにあるボーデ博物館は希少な硬貨が収蔵されていることで有名です。しかし，2017年3月27日，収蔵品の中で最大の硬貨が盗まれました。「ビッグメープルリーフ」として知られるその硬貨は，重さ100キログラム，直径は53センチメートルあります。問1 硬貨の額面の価値は100万ドルですが，金の純度が非常に高いため，400万ドルに上る価値があるかもしれないと専門家は言います。それは2010年にボーデ博物館に貸し出されて以来，防弾ガラスケースに保管されていました。ベルリン警察は，窃盗団はわずか25分間で，窓によじ登って侵入し，ケースを破り，コインを盗んだものと見ています。問2 人々は窃盗団がどのようにしてそのような巨大で重い硬貨を博物館から盗み出したのか疑問を感じています。窃盗団は全員ウエイトリフティングの選手にちがいないと考える人もいました。

質問

1. その硬貨に400万ドルに上る価値があると考えた専門家がいるのはなぜか。

2. 窃盗団がウエイトリフティングの選手であると考えた人がいるのはなぜか。

解説 問1　① 非常に純度の高い金を含んでいるから。

　　　　② 表面に特別なカエデの葉が刻まれているから。

　　　　③ 非常に有名だから。

　　　　④ 世界最大の硬貨だから。

　事前に選択肢に目を通し，Because から始まる選択肢であることからなんらかの理由や根拠を尋ねる質問であることを確認します。また，選択肢に含まれる語句は話の内容と関連するので，それぞれの語句がどのような文脈で用いられているのかに注意するとよいでしょう。ここでは，第4文 experts say it may be worth up to $4 million because its gold is so pure「金の純度が非常に高いため，400万ドルに上る価値があるかもしれないと専門家は言います」で，pure gold「純度の高い金」が，硬貨の価値を高める根拠として取り上げられているので，正解は ① です。その他の選択肢に出てきた語句（またはその同意表現）も聞こえてきますが，選択肢それぞれの内容が「硬貨に400万ドルの価値がある理由」としては当てはまらないことに注意してください。

問2　① ケースが防弾性で普通の人が破るのは不可能だったから。

　　　② 硬貨は重すぎて，普通の人には運べないから。

　　　③ 防犯カメラが，ウエイトリフティングの選手たちが博物館を出て行くのを記録していたから。

　　　④ 窃盗団が入り込んだ窓は，開けられないほど重いものだったから。

　問1と同様にどれも Because から始まる文であることを確認します。また本

問のように選択肢が長い場合も，時間の許す限り事前に語句をチェックします。実際の試験では，音声を聞きながら選択肢の意味を把握する必要も出てきます。①「ケースが防弾性だった」，②「硬貨が重すぎた」，③「防犯カメラが記録した」，④「窃盗団が侵入した窓」のように部分的でもいいので，内容を素早く把握して，正誤の判断に生かしましょう。本問では，最後から2番目の文 People question how the thieves got such a large and heavy coin out of the museum. において，100キログラムもある硬貨を窃盗団はどのように運んだのかに関して疑問が提示されています。その1つの答えとして，続く最終文 One person guessed that the thieves must all be weightlifters.「窃盗団は全員ウエイトリフティングの選手にちがいないと考える人もいました」で，「その硬貨は普通の人には運べないけれどもウエイトリフティングの選手であれば運べるにちがいない」という推測が紹介されたので，正解は②になります。③の選択肢は，音声では全く触れられていない内容なので，質問に関係なく消去できます。

> 正解 問1 ① 問2 ②

> 語句 collection 名「収蔵品」，weigh 動「〜の重さがある」，face value「額面価値」，bulletproof 形「防弾の」，loan 動「〜を貸す」，thieves ＜ thief 名「窃盗犯」，weightlifter 名「ウエイトリフティング［重量挙げ］の選手」

🎧 こう聞く！ 事前に選択肢をざっと読んでおこう

・質問が紙面に書かれておらず，音声で流れる問題の場合には，音声を聞く前に選択肢にざっと目を通して，扱われる語や表現に注目します。それぞれがどのような文脈で扱われているかに注意を向けましょう。

・放送文の内容と事実関係が異なる内容を含む選択肢は，あとから流れてくる質問に関係なく正解にはならないことが多いので，それがわかった時点で消去することもできます。

1　英語を聞き，それに対して，それぞれの問いの文の内容が　◀))06
　正しければ **T**（TRUE）と，正しくなければ **F**（FALSE）
　と答えなさい。1回流します。

2

短いモノローグ

問1　Ham and butter baguette sandwiches are the most popular fast food in France.

問2　In 2017, people in France bought more burgers than ham and butter baguette sandwiches.

問3　In 2017, the sales of baguette sandwiches dropped in France by 1.3%.

問4　In 2017, burger sales in France fell more than the sales of baguette sandwiches.

問5　In recent years, burger sales at McDonald's in France have not increased.

問6　Some famous French restaurants put hamburgers on their menus 10 years ago.

（南山大学）

2 英語と問いを聞き，それぞれの問いの答えとして最も適切 ◀)07
なものを，① ～ ④ のうちから1つずつ選びなさい。2回
流します。

問1　① Because they got married in London.
　　　② Because they attracted media interest.
　　　③ Because they escaped from a bombed city.
　　　④ Because they remained in London during the war.

問2　① High moral standards.
　　　② Imperfect family lives.
　　　③ Interest in the media.
　　　④ Criticism of the public.

問3　① They have kept their family problems private.
　　　② They have lived more public lives.
　　　③ They have had no family problems.
　　　④ They have attracted no media interest.

問4　① It began to rise gradually.
　　　② It remained the same.
　　　③ It started to fall.
　　　④ It disappeared completely.

（関西外国語大学）

3 英語と問いを聞き，それぞれの問いの答えとして最も適切
なものを，① ～ ④ のうちから1つずつ選びなさい。1回
流します。

◀)) 08

問1　① A gene.
　　② A hormone.
　　③ A region of the brain.
　　④ A type of cancer.

問2　① They are less anxious in their relationships with family and friends.
　　② They are more intelligent.
　　③ They find it easy to recognize facial expressions.
　　④ They have more difficulty with social interactions.

（青山学院大学）

4 英語と問いを聞き，それぞれの問いの答えとして最も適切
なものを，① ～ ④ のうちから1つずつ選びなさい。1回
流します。

◀)) 09

問1　① Most of them have been demolished.
　　② People are eager to buy them.
　　③ Their number is decreasing.
　　④ Their number is growing.

問2　① Because they can become targets of illegal waste dumping.
　　② Because they might catch on fire during demolition.
　　③ Because they might collapse when a typhoon or an earthquake occurs.
　　④ Because wild animals might occupy them.

（青山学院大学）

長いダイアローグ

長い対話を聞き，対話の内容に関する質問に答える問題を扱います。設問は
選択式と記述式があります。音声を聞く前に質問を確認し，必要な情報が何
であるか，あらかじめ頭に入れてから音声を聞くようにしましょう。

Check 対話の流れを追いながら即座に解答する

これからある男性へのインタビューを聞きます。その内容に合う
ように，それぞれの問いの文を完成させるのに最もよくあてはま
るものを，それぞれ ① ～ ③ のうちから1つずつ選びなさい。1
回流します。

■))10

問1 John Shaw has been living in Tokyo for about (　　　).

① one year

② two years

③ three years

問2 As a young boy, he found some places he visited (　　　).

① boring

② enjoyable

③ memorable

問3 On his first trip to Japan, Mr. Shaw was fascinated by the (　　　) there.

① shops

② train rides

③ TV programs

問4 When Mr. Shaw said, "the apple didn't fall very far from the tree," he was
referring to the fact that he had become a (　　　).

① book writer

② train driver

③ university graduate

問5 The source of inspiration for his new work was (　　　).

① a piece of information on the Internet

② a toy that fell off a shelf

③ an old souvenir from Japan

問6 John's decision to visit Japan this time was (　　　).

① made after two months of consideration

② made suddenly

③ planned a long time ago

問7 Mr. Shaw says that he has yet to visit (　　　).

① Hiroshima

② Kagoshima

③ Osaka

問8 The writer has just finished writing a (　　　).

① collection of short stories

② guide for riding trains in Japan

③ thriller based in Japan

問9 He found out that his preferred place to write was (　　　).

① in a café

② in his bedroom

③ on a train

問10 For John Shaw, the biggest problem on the train is the (　　　).

① crowdedness during rush hours

② expensive fares

③ time it takes to commute

(東京外国語大学)

スクリプト　※下線部は解答の根拠に当たる箇所です。

(**A**: Interviewer　**B**: Interviewee)

A(1): Good morning and welcome to the "Japan Life" podcast. Today I'm speaking with John Shaw. 問4John is a young writer and currently lives right here in Tokyo. John, welcome to the podcast.

B(1): Glad to be here. Thanks for having me.

A(2): So, tell me, how long have you been living in Japan?

B(2): Well, 問1 I came to Japan just over two years ago. I lived in Osaka for about a year before relocating to Tokyo.

A(3): OK. So, what brought you to Japan?

B(3): It's kind of a long story, but I guess it all started when I first visited Japan when I was seven years old. You see, 問4 my parents are travel writers and they used to drag me along with them on their trips all over the world. By the time I turned eight, I had been to over ten countries.

A(4): Did you like traveling that much as a child?

B(4): Well, I didn't always enjoy those trips because I couldn't really appreciate the new places I was visiting. 問2 I remember finding some places quite boring, but my trip to Japan was different.

A(5): How so?

B(5): Well, I grew up in a pretty rural area of the US where people get around almost entirely by car. I had seen trains on TV and in movies, but I had never actually ridden on one. 問3 So, when I came to Japan, I rode a train for the first time in my life. And according to my parents, I absolutely loved it. I wasn't interested in doing anything other than riding on the trains during my trip here.

A(6): It must have been hard for you when it was time to go back home.

B(6): Maybe it was, but my parents bought me a toy train from a shop in Kyoto before we left Japan. It instantly became my favorite toy and one of my prized childhood possessions.

A(7): That's great. So, did your interest in trains continue once you were back home?

B(7): For a little while, yes, but over time I found new hobbies and interests. And in high school I realized I had a skill and a passion for writing.

A(8): Just like your parents.

B(8): Yeah, the apple didn't fall very far from the tree, I guess. In university I studied creative writing and decided to make writing my career. So, one day, after graduation, I was having some trouble trying to come up with an idea for my next project. 問5 As I was sitting at my computer in my bedroom I looked up and noticed my old toy train that I got in Japan sitting on a shelf, and it hit me. My next book will be based in Japan and involve trains, and I should go to Japan to write this book.

A(9): Had you considered coming to Japan again before this moment?

B(9): Not at all. 問6 The idea came to me totally out of the blue. And I moved here within two months from that day.

A(10): Wow! That's pretty fast for such a big decision.

B(10): Yeah, it was, but I'm glad I did it.

A(11): So, have you been traveling a lot on the trains here?

B(11): Of course! I've spent a lot of time riding the trains in and around Osaka and Tokyo, of course, and I've taken the bullet train across most of the country to cities like Nagoya, Kyoto, and Hiroshima. And 問7 I'd really like to go to Kagoshima. I've heard it's really beautiful there.

A(12): And how is your writing process going?

B(12): Great! 問8 I've just finished my final manuscript.

A(13): So, can you tell me what the book is about?

B(13): 問8 It's a suspense novel about a young man who while visiting Japan on vacation gets into a pretty unusual situation while riding a train late at night in Osaka.

A(14): That sounds interesting.

B(14): I've really enjoyed writing it, and I'm already working on the next book in the series. 問9 I've also learned something about myself during my time here.

A(15): What's that?

B(15): 問9 I can actually write better while riding on a train. Back home I always did my writing alone in my bedroom or in a café, but I've been writing on my laptop while riding the trains here and it's great. I'm more creative. I'm more focused. And I can come up with better ideas for characters and stories.

A(16): That's great. So, the train is now your writing space!

B(16): Exactly. 問10 It can be difficult at times, like if the train is crowded, but that's not the biggest challenge I've encountered with my new writing technique.

A（17）: What challenge is that?

B（17）: 問10 Using the train as your office isn't cheap!

A（18）: John, what a story. Thank you for sharing it on the podcast. Best of
luck with your book and have fun riding all those trains!

B（18）: Thanks for having me.

和訳 （A：インタビューアー　B：インタビューを受ける人）

A（1）: おはようございます。そして『ジャパンライフ』ポッドキャストへようこそ。本日
はジョン・ショーさんをお迎えします。問4 ジョンさんは若手の作家で，現在はここ
東京にお住まいです。ジョン，当ポッドキャストへようこそ。

B（1）: 出演できてうれしいです。お招きいただきありがとうございます。

A（2）: では，伺いますが，日本にはどれくらい住んでいるんですか。

B（2）: ええ，問1 日本にはほんの2年ちょっと前に来たんです。大阪に1年ほど住んで，そ
のあと東京に引っ越しました。

A（3）: なるほど。で，日本に来たきっかけはどういうことで？

B（3）: 話せば長いのですが，おそらく，7歳のときに日本に初めて来たのがすべての始ま
りですね。というのも，問4 両親が旅行作家をしていて，昔は彼らが世界中旅行に行
くときによく一緒に連れられて行ったんです。8歳になるころには10カ国以上まわ
っていましたよ。

A（4）: 子供のころ，そんなにたくさん旅行することはお好きでしたか？

B（4）: まあ，そうした旅行をいつも楽しんだわけではないです。訪れている見知らぬ場所
のことを本当に理解することなどできていませんでしたから。問2 場所によっては退
屈しましたが，日本への旅行は違いました。

A（5）: どう違ったんですか。

B（5）: まあ，私はアメリカの中でも，人々がほとんどいつだって車で移動するようなかな
り田舎の地域で育ったんです。テレビや映画で列車を見たことはありましたが，実
際に乗ったことはありませんでした。問3 ですから，日本に来たとき，生まれて初め
て列車に乗りました。それに両親の話によれば，私はそれをすっかり気に入ってし
まったようです。日本を旅行しているときには列車に乗る以外のことには一切興味
を持ちませんでした。

A（6）: 家に帰るとき，あなたにはつらかったに違いありませんね。

B（6）: そうだったかもしれませんね。ですが日本を離れる前に，両親が京都のお店で列車
のおもちゃを買ってくれたんです。それがすぐにお気に入りのおもちゃになりまし
たし，子供時代の大切な持ち物の1つとなりましたね。

A（7）: すてきですね。それで，帰国したあとも列車への興味は続いたんですか。

B (7)：ええ，少しの間は。でも，やがて新しい趣味や興味を見つけました。そして高校生になると，私は文章を書くのがうまいことと，それが大好きであることに気づきました。

A (8)：ご両親と全く同じですね。

B (8)：ええ，リンゴの実はリンゴの木からそんなに遠く離れた所には落ちなかったんですね，たぶん。大学では文芸創作を勉強しまして，文筆を自分の仕事にしようと決めました。それで，卒業後のある日，次の企画のアイデアを見つけるのに，少し苦労していました。問5自分の寝室のコンピューターの前に腰かけて上を見たところ，日本で買った古い列車のおもちゃが棚の上にあるのに気づいて，それでひらめいたんです。私の次の本は日本を舞台にして，列車に関するものにしよう，そしてこの本を書くために日本に行かなきゃって。

A (9)：その瞬間までに，日本に再び来ようと考えたことはあったんですか。

B (9)：いや，全く。問6その考えは本当に突然浮かびました。そして，その日から2カ月もたたないうちに日本にやって来たんです。

A (10)：へえ！　そんな大きな決断をするのに，ずいぶんと早かったですね。

B (10)：ええ，確かに。でもそうしてよかったですよ。

A (11)：それで，こちらではかなり列車で旅をされたんですか。

B (11)：もちろんですよ！　大阪と東京やその周辺では当然かなりの時間を列車に乗ることに充ててきましたし，新幹線に乗って国内の大半の場所をめぐり，名古屋や京都や広島などの都市に行きました。それに問7鹿児島にも本当に行きたいんですよ。ずいぶん美しいと聞いていますので。

A (12)：執筆作業の進み具合はいかがですか。

B (12)：すばらしいですよ！　問8最終稿を書き終えたところなんです。

A (13)：それで，その本は何に関する本ですか。

B (13)：問8休暇で日本を訪れている若い男性に関するサスペンス小説です。彼は夜遅く大阪で列車に乗っているときに，非常に奇妙な状況に巻き込まれるんです。

A (14)：おもしろそうですね。

B (14)：書いていて楽しかったですし，もうこのシリーズの次の作品に取り組み始めているんです。問9また，ここにいる間に自分自身についても発見がありました。

A (15)：それは何です？

B (15)：問9列車に乗っている間のほうが実際よく書けるんです。自分の国ではいつも寝室やカフェでひとりで書いていましたが，日本では列車に乗りながらノートパソコンで書いていまして，それがいいんです。より創造的になります。より集中します。それに人物や物語についてよりよい考えを思いつけるんです。

A (16)：すごいですね。とういうことは，今は列車が書斎なんですね！

B（16）：そのとおりです。_{問10}列車が混んでいるときなど, 時に難しい場合もありますが, そ
れは私の新しい執筆方法において私が直面してきた最大の難問ではありません。

A（17）：それはどんな難問ですか？

B（17）：_{問10}列車をオフィスとして使うのはすごくお金がかかるんですよ！

A（18）：ジョン, おもしろいお話でした。このポッドキャストで話をしてくれてありがとう
ございました。本の成功を祈るとともに, そうした列車すべてに楽しく乗れますよ
う！

B（18）：お招きいただきありがとうございました。

解説　長い対話文では質問が対話の順になっている場合が多いので, 聞きながら選択
肢を眺め, わかった段階で答えを選んでいきましょう。聞き漏らしても, それ
にはこだわらず次へ進み, 対話の流れを追うことが重要です。

問1　ジョン・ショーは東京に約（　　）間住んでいる。

① 1年

② 2年

③ 3年

　ジョン（＝ B）の2番目の発話 I came to Japan just over two years ago. I
lived in Osaka for about a year before relocating to Tokyo.「日本にはほんの2
年ちょっと前に来たんです。大阪に1年ほど住んで, そのあと東京に引っ越し
ました」より, 東京にいるのは約1年間ということになるので, 正解は ① で
す。「日本に何年間住んでいるか」という質問ではないので注意が必要です。

問2　彼は子供のころ, 訪れた場所のいくつかは（　　）と思った。

① 退屈だ

② 楽しい

③ 忘れられない

　ジョンの4番目の発話 I remember finding some places quite boring「場所
によっては退屈しました」より, 正解は ① です。

問3　ショー氏が日本に初めて来たとき, 日本の（　　）に魅了された。

① お店

② 列車に乗ること

③ テレビ番組

　ジョンの5番目の発話 So, when I came to Japan, I rode a train for the first
time in my life. And according to my parents, I absolutely loved it.「ですか
ら, 日本に来たとき, 生まれて初めて列車に乗りました。それに両親の話によ
れば, 私はそれをすっかり気に入ってしまったようです」より, 正解は ② で
す。

問4　ショー氏が「リンゴの実はリンゴの木からそんなに遠く離れた所には落ちなかった」と言ったとき，彼は自分が（　　）になった事実を指して言っていた。

① 作家

② 列車の運転士

③ 大学の卒業生

　ジョンは7番目の発話で，高校時代に自分の文筆の才能を自覚したという話をしています。それを受けてインタビューアーが「ご両親と全く同じですね」と言うと，ジョンは "The apple doesn't fall far from the tree." 「リンゴの実はリンゴの木から遠く離れた所には落ちない」ということわざを引用して返答しています。このことわざには「子供はたいてい，親と似た性格や才能を示すものだ」という意味があるので，「両親の才能が自分にもあるのだ」とジョンは言っていることになります。ジョンは3番目の発話で「両親が旅行作家」と言っています。そしてインタビューアーは最初の発話で，ジョンを「若手の作家」と紹介していますし，会話の後半では最新作を書き終えたという話も出てきますので，ジョンの職業が両親と同じ作家であることは明らかです。したがって，正解は ① です。ことわざの意味が正確にはわからなくても，質問と文脈から推測できるでしょう。

問5　彼の新しい作品のインスピレーションの源になったのは（　　）だった。

① インターネット上のある情報

② 棚から落ちてきたおもちゃ

③ 日本の昔のおみやげ

　ジョンの8番目の発話の後半に noticed my old toy train that I got in Japan sitting on a shelf, and it hit me. My next book will be based in Japan and involve trains「日本で買った古い列車のおもちゃが棚の上にあるのに気づいて，それでひらめいたんです。私の次の本は日本を舞台にして，列車に関するものにしようと」とあります。ここから，ジョンが取り組むことになる新しい作品のインスピレーションは，昔日本で両親に買ってもらった列車のおもちゃから得たものだとわかるので，③ が正解です。この発話内に it hit me とありますが，これは棚からおもちゃが落ちてきて自分に当たったと言っているのではなく，「それから着想を得た」という意味です。

問6　今回ジョンが日本を訪れることにしたのは（　　）決断だった。

① 2カ月考えた末の

② 突然の

③ ずいぶん前から計画していた

　ジョンの9番目の発話 The idea came to me totally out of the blue. And I

moved here within two months from that day. 「その考え（＝日本に再び来よ
うと考えたこと）は本当に突然浮かびました。そして，その日から 2 カ月もた
たないうちに日本にやって来たんです」より，正解は ② です。out of the blue
「突然，出し抜けに」という熟語の理解がポイントです。

問 7　ショー氏によれば，彼はまだ（　　）を訪れていない。

   ① 広島

   ② 鹿児島

   ③ 大阪

　ジョンの 11 番目の発話 I'd really like to go to Kagoshima「鹿児島にも本当
に行きたいんですよ」より，② が正解です。この直前でジョンは，大阪はもち
ろん，広島にも新幹線で行ったことがあると言っています。

問 8　この作家は（　　）を書き終えたところだ。

   ① 短編小説集

   ② 日本の列車乗車案内

   ③ 日本を舞台としたスリラー物

　ジョンは 12 番目の発話で「最終稿を書き終えたところ」だと言い，インタ
ビューアーが本の内容を尋ねると，ジョンは It's a suspense novel about a
young man who while visiting Japan on vacation gets into a pretty unusual
situation while riding a train late at night in Osaka.「休暇で日本を訪れてい
る若い男性に関するサスペンス小説です。彼は夜遅く大阪で列車に乗っている
ときに，非常に奇妙な状況に巻き込まれるんです」と答えています。「サスペ
ンス小説」はハラハラドキドキさせる物語を含むものなので，「スリラー物」と
言い換えることができます。したがって，正解は ③ です。

問 9　彼は，自分が執筆するのに好きな場所は（　　）だと気づいた。

   ① カフェの中

   ② 自分の寝室の中

   ③ 列車の中

　ジョンが 14 番目の発話で「また，ここにいる間に自分自身についても発見
がありました」と言って，インタビューアーにそれは何かと聞かれると，I can
actually write better while riding on a train.「列車に乗っている間のほうが実
際よく書けるんです」と言っているので，正解は ③ です。カフェや寝室は，ア
メリカで執筆に利用していた場所だと，このあとで説明しています。

問 10　ジョン・ショーにとって列車での最大の問題は（　　）だ。

   ① ラッシュアワーの混雑

   ② 高い運賃

③　通勤にかかる時間

　インタビューアーが17番目の発話で,「列車で書くことの最大の難問は何か」と尋ねると, ジョンは Using the train as your office isn't cheap!「列車をオフィスとして使うのはすごくお金がかかるんですよ!」と答えているので, ② が正解です。① についてもジョンは16番目の発話で触れていますが,「それは最大の難問ではない」と言っているので, 正解にはなりません。

正解　問1　①　　問2　①　　問3　②　　問4　①　　問5　③
　　　問6　②　　問7　②　　問8　③　　問9　③　　問10　②

語句　fascinate 動「〜を魅了する」, have yet to *do*「まだ…していない」, podcast 名「ポッドキャスト (インターネット上の音声コンテンツ)」, relocate 動「移住する」, drag 動「〜を無理やり連れて行く」, appreciate 動「〜を真に理解する」, absolutely 副「すっかり, 完全に」, instantly 副「即座に」, prized 形「大切な」, possession 名「(複数形で) 所有物」, come up with 〜「〜を思いつく」, out of the blue「突然」, manuscript 名「原稿」, suspense novel「サスペンス小説」, challenge 名「難問」, encounter 動「〜に出くわす」

🎧 こう聞く!　　先に質問を読み, 対話の流れについていこう

あらかじめ質問に目を通し, 聞き取るべき情報が何であるかを頭に入れてから聞くようにしましょう。聞きながら選択肢を見ていき, わかった段階で答えを選びます。聞き漏らしても, それにはこだわらず次へ進み, 対話の流れを追うことを心がけましょう。

練習問題

解答・解説 ▶ pp.87 〜 109

1 これから英国（UK）のテストについて Richard と Jackie
の対話を聞きます。その内容に合うように，それぞれの問
いの文を完成させるのに最もよくあてはまるものを，それ
ぞれ ① 〜 ③ のうちから1つずつ選びなさい。1回流しま
す。

◀))11

問1　To earn Portuguese citizenship, Jackie had to (　　　　).
　① pass a language exam
　② pay 250 pounds
　③ work in Portugal for six years

問2　The Life in the UK Test must be taken by people who want to (　　　　) in
the UK.
　① become a citizen
　② study
　③ work

問3　As a way to prepare for the Life in the UK Test, Richard and Jackie mention
(　　　　).
　① buying a guide at a bookshop
　② taking a course
　③ visiting a website

問4　To pass the test, people must get a minimum of (　　　　).
　① 16 correct answers out of 24 questions
　② 18 correct answers out of 20 questions
　③ 18 correct answers out of 24 questions

問5　Richard passed the test (　　　　).
　① once
　② twice
　③ three times

問6 People who fail the test can (　　　).

① get a refund of 50 pounds

② pay to take the test again

③ retake the test for free

問7 The chapter Richard and Jackie find most difficult is titled (　　　).

① "A long and illustrious history"

② "The UK government and your role"

③ "The values and principles of the UK"

問8 Some of the questions are difficult because (　　　).

① the multiple choices are similar

② they are not in the handbook

③ they are not multiple-choice questions

問9 Jackie believes the test's questions should focus on British (　　　).

① economics and politics

② history and society

③ law and customs

問10 A test like the Life in the UK Test is NOT given in (　　　).

① France

② Portugal

③ Spain

(東京外国語大学)

これから ESS クラブの催しについて 2 人の日本人学生と 1 人の留学生の会話を聞きます。問 1・問 2 には英語で，問 3 には日本語で答えなさい。2 回流します。 ◀)) 12

問 1 What did the following students present for the annual ESS events in the past?

students	presentation
a Mexican student	A
B	The student sang his or her national anthem.
a Spanish student	C

問 2 The following ideas have some problems. What are they?

ideas	problems
singing a song on the stage	X
a magic trick	Y
cooking something on the stage	Z

問 3 「宿題」についての冗談を日本語で説明しなさい。

（福岡教育大学・改）

3 これから 3 人の大学生 (Axel, Mei, Barry) の会話を聞きます。それぞれの問いに英語で答えなさい。2 回流します。 ◀)) 13

問 1　What is the main topic of their conversation?

問 2　Which of the characters do you think is Nami's best friend?　Support your opinion with details from the conversation.

問 3　What theories do the speakers have to explain Nami's disappearance?　Why are those theories rejected?　Please fill in the gaps in the table below.

	Theories	*Reasons for rejecting*
1	She's at work.	A
2	B	Her boots are still in the closet.
3	She's at her parents' place doing laundry.	C
4	D	E
5	F	G

（福岡教育大学・改）

4 長いモノローグ

500 語を超える講義を聞き, 示された質問に答える問題に取り組みます。これまでと同様, 音声を聞く前に質問を読み, 聞き取るべき内容を把握しておきましょう。講義に特有の文章の組み立て方を知っておくことも有効です。

 Check 講義の流れを予測する

講義を聞き, それぞれの問いの答えとして最も適切なものを, ① ~ ④ のうちから1つずつ選びなさい。1回流します。 ◀))14

問1 Which of the following is one of the three common beliefs about children's lies?

① Adults usually cannot identify children's lies.

② Children's lies can reveal aspects of human nature.

③ Children begin lying before entering elementary school.

④ Young children who lie have problems with their character.

問2 According to the lecture, which is true about the first experiment?

① The examiner excused the children who did not peek at the cards.

② The examiner created an opportunity for children to look at the cards.

③ The children asked the researcher if they could see the cards to win rewards.

④ The children wanted to be alone in the room to check the numbers on the cards.

問3 How many 2-year-old children admitted that they looked at the cards?

① about 30%　② about 50%　③ about 70%　④ about 80%

問4 What did Lee discover about the adult subjects in his follow-up study?

① Parents often lie to their children.

② Adults cannot spot children's lies.

③ Parents can detect half of children's lies.

④ Adults lie once or twice a day on average.

問5 According to the lecture, which is the best definition of theory of mind?

① the ability to understand the emergence of lying

② the ability to control the situation around oneself

③ the ability to function more appropriately in society

④ the ability to distinguish one's knowledge from that of others

(国際基督教大学)

スクリプト ※下線部は解答の根拠に当たる箇所です。

[1]　Have you ever lied to anybody? No? Then I'm afraid you're lying. In fact, lies are a part of our daily life. For instance, you might have made up an excuse for being absent from a class or you might give a compliment to a friend about a bad haircut. In fact, a key study in 1996 by a social psychologist, Bella DePaulo, and her colleagues, revealed just how often we tell lies. They found that their adult subjects lied on average once or twice a day. While most lies were not offensive, they also found later that adults tell one or more serious lies at some point in their life. How about children? Another researcher, Kang Lee, a psychologist at the University of Toronto, more recently conducted interesting studies about children's lies. Today we're going to explore lies by looking at Doctor Lee's child development studies. They can reveal a fascinating and surprising aspect of human nature.

[2]　When you were little, did your parents tell you not to deceive others? I guess so, because most parents worry if their children lie to them. 問1 Lee said that there are three common beliefs about children's lies. First, preschool children don't lie. Second, children are bad liars, so it's easy to detect their lies. Third, if children lie when they are very young, they must have a character defect. Lee's research suggests that these three beliefs are wrong.

[3]　The research was based on an experiment, in which children play the guessing game with an examiner. 問2 If they correctly guessed the numbers on cards, they would get rewards. But during the game, the examiner left the room with an excuse, telling the children not to peek at the cards. There were hidden cameras in the room to record the children's reactions. Surprisingly or perhaps not, more than 90% of the children looked at the cards. Then, when the examiner came back into the room, she asked the

children if they had looked. No matter what their gender, nationality and religion was, 問3 about 30% of 2-year-olds lied, saying that they hadn't looked at the cards. At 3 years of age, about 50% lied. And at 4, more than 80% lied. Thus, the common belief that preschool children don't lie was disproved.

[4]　Lee conducted a follow-up study by showing some of the videos of the research to adults of different backgrounds. In these videos, half of the children were lying, and the other half were telling the truth. The adults were tested on whether they could tell when the children were lying. 問4 The results showed that adults such as social workers, who work closely with children, couldn't detect the children's lies. Others, such as judges or police officers, who often deal with liars, couldn't either. Even parents of the children in the videos couldn't recognize their own kids' lies. Therefore, the second common belief that children are poor liars was not supported.

[5]　How about the third belief? The children who lie at an early age have a character defect. Lee says that parents should actually celebrate the emergence of lies in their children because it's a sign that the children's cognitive development is right on track. According to him, one of the requirements of lying is a development of theory of mind. 問5 Theory of mind is the ability to understand that our knowledge about the situation is different from the knowledge of others. Lee says, "I can lie because I know you don't know what I know." According to Lee, theory of mind is fundamental for us because we need to understand other people's knowledge and intentions to function well in society. So, as lies seem to reflect an important stage in our cognitive development, the third common belief also seems to be rejected.

[6]　However, other researchers are not so optimistic. For instance, Victoria Talwar and her fellow researchers say children's frequent or inappropriate use of lies could be problematic. If children lie often, that might indicate poor development of conscience.

[7]　Today we looked at lies through child development studies. Studies of lying would reveal more features of this complex and interesting behavior. In the future, for example, we might be better detectors of children's lies and better able to understand their behaviors. So, based on what you have learned in today's lecture, do you think we should discourage children from lying?

(728 words)

和訳

[1] 今まで誰かに嘘をついたことはありますか。ない？　では残念ながらあなたは嘘をついていることになりますね。実際，嘘は私たちの日常生活の一部なのです。例えば，あなたは授業を休むときの言い訳を考えたことがあるかもしれませんし，友だちにひどい髪型なのに褒め言葉を言ってしまうことがあるかもしれません。事実，社会心理学者のベラ・デパウロと彼女の共同研究者による1996年の重要な研究は，私たちがどれくらいの頻度で嘘をつくのか明らかにしました。成人の被験者は平均して1日に1,2回嘘をついていることがわかりました。大半の嘘は人をおとしめるようなものではないものの，成人は一生のうちのどこかの時点で最低でも1つは重大な嘘をつくということもそのあとわかりました。子供はどうでしょうか。別の研究者，トロント大学の心理学者のカン・リーは，子供の嘘についての興味深い研究を近年行いました。今日私たちはリー博士の子供の発達に関する研究を見ることで，嘘について学びます。この研究は人間性の魅力的で驚くべき側面を示すことができるのです。

[2] 子供のころ，人に嘘をつくなと親から言われませんでしたか。言われたと思います。ほとんどの親は自分の子供が他人に嘘をつくのでないかと心配しているからです。_{問1}リー博士は子供の嘘についての通説が3つあると言いました。まず，就学前の子供は嘘をつかないということ。次に，子供は嘘をつくのが下手なので，彼らの嘘を見抜くのは難しくないこと。3つ目に，子供が非常に幼いときに嘘をつくような場合，性格上欠陥があるにちがいないということです。リー博士の研究は，この説は3つとも誤りであることを示唆しています。

[3] この研究は，子供たちが実験担当者と当てっこゲームをするという実験に基づいていました。_{問2}子供たちはカード上の数字を正確に言い当てたら，ほうびがもらえることになっていました。しかしゲーム中に実験担当者が何か口実を作って部屋を出ていくのです。そのとき子供たちにはカードを盗み見ないように言いました。子供の反応を記録するために部屋には隠しカメラが設置されていました。意外なことに，あるいは意外なことでもないのかもしれませんが，90パーセントを超える子供がカードを見たのです。そして実験担当者が部屋に戻ってきて，子供たちに見たかどうかを尋ねました。性別，国籍，宗教に関係なく，_{問3}2歳児のおよそ30パーセントがカードを見なかったと言って嘘をつきました。3歳児は，およそ50パーセントが嘘をつきました。4歳児では80パーセントを超える子供が嘘をつきました。こうして，就学前の子供は嘘をつかないという通説は誤っていることが証明されました。

[4] リー博士は，この研究の録画ビデオの一部をさまざまな経歴を持つ成人に見せることで，追加調査を行いました。これらのビデオでは，子供の半数が嘘をついていて，残りの半数は本当のことを言っていました。被験者の成人は，子供が嘘をついている場合に見抜くことができるかどうか試されました。_{問4}この結果わかったのは，子供と密接にかかわる仕事をしているソーシャルワーカーのような成人が，子供の嘘を見抜くことができないということでした。嘘をつく人間と接することの多い裁判官や警察官などの成人も，やはり見抜くことはできませんでした。ビデオに出ていた子供の親ですら自分の子供の嘘を見分けることがで

きませんでした。したがって，子供は嘘をつくのが下手であるという，2つ目の通説も裏づけられなかったことになります。

[5]　3つ目の説はどうでしょうか。幼いときに嘘をつく子供には性格上の欠陥があるという考えです。リー博士は，子供が嘘をつくようになったら，それは子供の認知の発達が順調に進んでいる兆候なので，実は祝福すべきことだと言います。博士によると，嘘をつくのに必要な条件の1つは心の理論の発達です。問5 心の理論とは，ある特定の状況に関して自分の知っていることと他人の知っていることが異なっているということを理解する能力のことです。リー博士は，「私が嘘をつくことができるのは，私の知っていることをあなたは知らないと私がわかっているからです」と言います。リー博士によれば，私たちが社会できちんと役割を果たすためには他人が何を知っていてどんなことをやろうと思っているかを理解する必要があるので，心の理論は私たちに必須のものとなります。ですから，嘘は私たちの認知の発達上重要な段階を反映しているように思われるので，3つ目の通説も否定されるように思われます。

[6]　しかしそれ程楽観的ではない研究者もいます。例えば，ビクトリア・タルワールと仲間の研究者は，子供が頻繁にあるいは不適切な形で嘘を利用するのは問題になりうると言います。子供が嘘をつくことが多い場合，それは善悪の観念が十分に発達していないことを示しているかもしれないというのです。

[7]　今日は，子供の発達の研究を通して嘘というものを見てきました。嘘をつくことに関するさまざまな研究が，この複雑で興味深い行動のより多くの特徴を明らかにしていくことでしょう。例えば，将来，私たちは子供の嘘をよりよく発見できるようになり，彼らの行動をよりよく理解できるようになるかもしれません。さて，今日の講義で学んだことを基にすると，私たちは子供に嘘をつかないようにさせるべきだとあなたは思いますか。

解説　本問は700語を超える英文を聞いて5つの選択問題に答える問題です。音声を聞く前に質問を頭に入れて，何を聞き取るべきかを把握します。質問はたいてい放送文の出現順に設定されているので，聞き取りながら，可能な限り答えを特定していきましょう。また，講義形式の文章は，「主題の導入」，「通説の提示」，「（それを覆す）仮説の提示」，「仮説の検証（実験，調査）」，「結果の分析」，「結論」，「今後の課題」などからなるので，展開を予測しながら聞くことも重要です。本問は「子供が嘘をつくこと」を主題とし，「子供の嘘に関する3つの通説」，「それを検証するための実験と追加調査」，「それらによる3つの通説の否定」，「反論の提示」，「まとめ」などからなっています。こうした大きな流れを把握しながら，質問で問われる細部へと注意を向けましょう。実際の講義を聞くように，論理展開を追い，メモを取りながら聞くことが重要です。

問1　子供の嘘に関する3つの通説のうちの1つは次のどれか。

　　① 大人はたいてい子供の嘘を嘘だと見抜くことができない。

② 子供の嘘は人間の本性のさまざまな側面を明らかにすることができる。

③ 子供は小学校に入学する以前から嘘をつき始める。

④ 嘘をつく幼い子供は性格に問題がある。

第2段落第3文以降で「子供の嘘に関する3つの通説」が紹介されています。それによれば，1つ目は preschool children don't lie「未就学児は嘘をつかない」，2つ目は children are bad liars, so it's easy to detect their lies「子供は嘘をつくのが下手なので嘘を見抜きやすい」，3つ目は if children lie when they are very young, they must have a character defect「幼い子供が嘘をついたらその子供は性格に欠陥がある」というものです。④ はこの3つ目の説と一致するので，これが正解となります。① と ③ はこの通説と矛盾した記述になっています。② は第1段落最終文に関連しますが，「3つの通説」の説明ではないので，正解にはなりません。

問2 講義によると，最初の実験について当てはまるものはどれか。

① 実験担当者はカードをこっそり見なかった子供たちを大目に見た。

② 実験担当者は子供たちがカードを見る機会を作った。

③ 子供たちは研究者に，ほうびをもらうためにカードを見てもいいかと尋ねた。

④ 子供たちはカードの番号を確認するために部屋の中でひとりになりたがった。

　最初の実験に関して，第3段落第2文で実験の概要が述べられます。それによると，子供たちはカードの数字を言い当てるとほうびがもらえるということです。続く第3文では during the game, the examiner left the room with an excuse, telling the children not to peek at the cards「ゲーム中に実験担当者が何か口実を作って部屋を出ていくのです。そのとき子供たちにはカードを盗み見ないように言いました」とあり，実験担当者が部屋を出ていくことで，子供たちにこっそりカードを見る機会を与え，そのことに関して嘘をつくかどうかを調べようとしていることがその後の話からわかります。したがって，正解は ② になります。① は講義中に聞こえてくる excuse や peek などの単語を使った文ではありますが，講義の内容とは全く関係のない意味内容です。③ と ④ も講義で話されていない内容なので，正解にはなりません。

問3 カードを見たことを認めた2歳児はどれくらいいたか。

① およそ30パーセント

② およそ50パーセント

③ およそ70パーセント

④ およそ80パーセント

　第3段落第7文 about 30% of 2-year-olds lied, saying that they hadn't looked at the cards より，2歳児の30パーセントが嘘をついたことがわかるの

で、カードを見たことを認めた、つまり正直に答えたのは70パーセントとなります。したがって、正解は ③ です。「嘘をついた2歳児の割合」を聞かれているのではないということに注意してください。数値の聞き取りは重要です。簡単な計算を伴うことも多く、問われ方によって解答が変わってくるので、質問をよく確認しましょう。

問4 リー博士は成人の被験者に関する追加調査においてどのようなことを発見したか。

    ① 親は子供にしばしば嘘をつく。

    ② 大人は子供の嘘を見抜くことができない。

    ③ 親は子供の嘘の半分を見抜くことができる。

    ④ 大人は平均すると1日に1, 2回嘘をつく。

　第4段落第4文以降で語られたように、追加調査でわかったことは、大人は、子供のことをよく知っている職業の人であろうと親であろうと、子供の嘘を見抜けないということでした。したがって、② が正解です。① と ③ のようなことは講義で話されていません。④ は第1段落で話されていますが、1996年のベラ・デパウロらの研究の成果であって、リー博士の研究によって得られたものではありません。

問5 講義によると、心の理論の定義として最も適切なものはどれか。

    ① 嘘が発せられたことを理解する能力

    ② 自分の置かれた状況をコントロールする能力

    ③ 社会でより適切に機能する能力

    ④ 自分の知っていることと他人の知っていることを区別する能力

　第5段落第5文 Theory of mind is the ability to understand that our knowledge about the situation is different from the knowledge of others.「心の理論とは、ある特定の状況に関して自分の知っていることと他人の知っていることが異なっているということを理解する能力のことです」より、正解は ④ です。① は第5段落第3文に関連しますが、ここでは「子供が嘘をつくようになったらむしろ親は喜ぶべきだ」という意味で用いられているので、① は内容的に異なります。② は講義の中で話されていません。③ は第5段落第7文に関連しますが、ここは「社会で適切に機能するには、心の理論が必須だ」ということを言っており、「社会で適切に機能する能力」＝「心の理論」と説明しているわけではないので、③ も正解とはなりません。

正解 問1 ④ 問2 ② 問3 ③ 問4 ② 問5 ④

語句 excuse for ～「～に対する言い訳」, compliment 图「褒め言葉、お世辞」, reveal 動「～を明らかにする」, subject 图「被験者」, offensive 形「人を不快にする」, conduct 動「～（実験など）を行う」, explore 動「～を調べる、探る」, human nature「人間の

本性，人間性」，deceive 動「〜に嘘をつく，〜をだます」，preschool 形「就学前の」，detect 動「〜を突きとめる」(≒ identify, recognize, spot)，character 名「性格」，defect 名「欠陥」，reward 名「ほうび」，follow-up study「追跡調査，追加調査」，celebrate 動「〜を祝福する」，emergence 名「出現」，cognitive 形「認知の」，intention 名「意思，意向」，inappropriate 形「不適切な」，indicate 動「〜を示す」，conscience 名「良心，善悪の観念」，feature 名「特徴」，detector 名「発見者」，discourage ～ from *doing*「〜に…する気にさせない」

🎧 こう聞く！ 講義の流れを予測しつつ，細部を聞き取ろう

・講義は，「主題→通説→仮説→検証→分析→展望」など，一定の流れを持つものが多いので，こうした**展開を予測しつつ**，実際の講義を聞くように，**メモを取りながら聞く**ようにしましょう。講義の展開については冒頭部で説明されることもよくあります。

・問われるのは講義の**細部の情報**であることが多いので，先に質問を頭に入れて，必要な情報をこちらからつかみ取るような気持ちで聞きましょう。

   解答・解説 ▶ pp.110 ～ 127

1 講義を聞き，それぞれの問いの答えとして最も適切なもの ◀)) 15
を，①～④のうちから1つずつ選びなさい。1回流します。

問1 Which of the following is given as a reason for the increased use of technology
in the recruitment process?
① to save applicants' time
② to develop candidates' skills
③ to hire more suitable candidates
④ to reduce the number of applicants

問2 According to the lecture, how many job applicants did one multinational
investment bank receive in 2016?
① 100,000 ② 250,000 ③ 750,000 ④ 1,000,000

問3 According to the lecture, what does AI do during video interviews?
① It identifies the most relevant keywords in applicants' résumés.
② It allows applicants to record their answers on their computers.
③ It evaluates elements of the applicants' non-verbal communication.
④ It enables companies to adapt questions based on the content of
responses.

問4 Which of the following is the main reason companies think that computer
games can be a useful tool for selecting candidates?
① Candidates enjoy role-playing in the games.
② Candidates behave more naturally in the games.
③ Candidates change facial expressions in the games.
④ Candidates show their computer skills in the games.

問5 According to the lecture, how can the use of AI in recruitment reduce
diversity in the workplace?
① by evaluating applicants based on unrealistic expectations
② by removing human input from the decision-making process
③ by making the process of selecting candidates more subjective
④ by selecting candidates whose traits resemble those of current staff

(国際基督教大学)

問 1 In what year did Boeing Airplane Company begin operations under that name?

① 1903　② 1914　③ 1916　④ 1917

問 2 The builder of Smith Tower made his fortune by manufacturing (　　　　).

① aircraft

② needles

③ seaplanes

④ typewriters

問 3 About how much taller is the Space Needle than Smith Tower?

① 15%　② 25%　③ 35%　④ 50%

問 4 How long did it take to complete the Space Needle?

① Less than one year

② One year

③ Three years

④ More than three years

問 5 Which of these things can be seen from the Space Needle?

① Jets flying by

② Flying saucers

③ Lake Rainier

④ The Boeing Tower

問 6 What is sold in all three of these places: Space Needle, Smith Tower and Columbia Center?

① Airplane tickets

② Food and drink

③ Jewelry

④ Real estate

次のページに続く▶

問 7　Which of these is the tallest, according to the narrator?

① 　Columbia Center

② 　Seattle-Tacoma International Airport

③ 　Smith Tower

④ 　Space Needle

問 8　Seaplanes（　　　）.

① 　can travel underwater

② 　have enough fuel capacity to fly overseas

③ 　have floats instead of wheels

④ 　are usually parked in the B&W building next to Lake Union

問 9　If a Kenmore Air seaplane flight is full, how many people, including the pilot, are expected to be on board?

① 　9　　② 　10　　③ 　11　　④ 　12

問 10　What is the purpose of this passage?

① 　To explain that tourist activities in Seattle all center around seaplanes

② 　To show that Seattle is an attractive tourist destination

③ 　To convince the reader to go eat and drink at Seattle restaurants

④ 　To argue that Seattle is not worth visiting

（青山学院大学）

3

講義を聞き，それぞれの問いの答えとして最も適切なもの　◀)) 17
を，①～⑤のうちから1つずつ選びなさい。1回流します。

問1 Which scientific advance made the recent progress in speed breeding possible?

① Better space flight technology.

② Developments in LED technology.

③ Improvements in climate control technology.

④ More efficient methods of harvesting.

⑤ The invention of the carbon arc lamp.

問2 When did scientists in China achieve their breakthrough in making one of the world's vital food crops resistant to a disease?

① 2002　② 2004　③ 2008　④ 2012　⑤ 2014

問3 Which of the crops listed below is NOT used to illustrate how gene editing has protected plants from disease?

① Bananas　② Barley　③ Rice　④ Soybeans　⑤ Wheat

問4 Which of the following is NOT mentioned as a location where research projects are currently carried out?

① Australia

② China

③ Europe

④ India

⑤ South Korea

問5 According to Hickey, meeting the future challenges of food security will require (　　　).

① continuing advances in speed breeding

② efforts to control population growth

③ new breakthroughs in gene editing

④ the application of all available technologies

⑤ the development of new tools

（東京大学）

5

複合問題

1つのテーマに関して語られた複数のモノローグやダイアローグを聞き，内容に関する質問に答えます。テーマに関連するトピックとその説明を捉えるようにしましょう。質問が書かれている場合は先に読みましょう。

 Check　トピックごとに説明をつかむ

問題は3つのパートに分かれています。英語を聞き，それぞれの問いの答えとして最も適切なものを，① 〜 ④ のうちから1つずつ選びなさい。各パート2回流します。

Part 1　◀))18

問1　①　②　③　④
問2　①　②　③　④
問3　①　②　③　④

Part 2　◀))19

問1　①　②　③　④
問2　①　②　③　④
問3　①　②　③　④

Part 3　◀))20

問1　①　②　③　④
問2　①　②　③　④
問3　①　②　③　④
問4　①　②　③　④

（神戸市外国語大学）

Part 1

　※下線部は解答の根拠に当たる箇所です。

Interviewer:

Hello everyone and welcome to 'Libertytown Today', bringing you the latest news from our wonderful city. As you all know, 問1 <u>the election for Mayor of Libertytown is only a week away</u>, and joining us later on today's show are the two leading candidates, Mr Brad Peterson and Mrs Laura Hopkins. Mr Peterson is the present mayor of Libertytown and has held the position for the last fifteen years, winning four elections. His opponents, like Mrs Hopkins, accuse him of being conservative and out of touch with the needs of a modern city. 問2 <u>Most of his support comes from older people, and from voters in suburban and rural districts.</u> Mrs Hopkins, on the other hand, has only recently entered politics. 問3 <u>She is a businesswoman, and runs a successful TV advertising agency.</u> But, she says, she is angry with the conservatism of Mr Peterson's administration, and has promised 'to drive Libertytown into the 21st century'. Her policies have made her popular among younger, university-educated voters. But critics point out that she has no experience of political life, and argue that many of her policies would be unworkable in practice.

(187 words)

Questions:

1. When will the election for mayor be held?
   ① A week from now.
   ② Later today.
   ③ After four other elections.
   ④ In fifteen years.

2. What kind of people likely vote for Mr Peterson?
   ① Younger people.
   ② Popular people.
   ③ People who need a modern city.
   ④ People who live in rural areas.

3. What kind of business does Mrs Hopkins run?
   ① Education.
   ② Administration.
   ③ Advertising.
   ④ Driving.

和 訳 インタビューアー：
皆さん，こんにちは，そして私たちのすばらしい町から最新のニュースをお届けする『リバティータウン・トゥデイ』にようこそ。ご存じのとおり，問1 リバティータウンの市長選挙がわずか1週間後にせまっておりまして，本日の番組では，後ほど，2人の主要候補者である

51

ブラッド・ピーターソンさんとローラ・ホプキンズさんにご登場いただきます。ピーターソンさんはリバティータウンの現市長で、これまで4度の選挙に当選し、15年にわたって市長を務めておられます。ホプキンズさんをはじめとした彼に対抗する立候補者は、彼が保守的であり、現代都市の要請に応えていないと非難します。問2 彼の支持者の大半は高齢者や、郊外および農村地区の有権者からなります。それに対して、ホプキンズさんが政治の世界に入られたのはつい最近のことです。問3 彼女は実業家であり、テレビ広告の代理業で成功しておられます。しかし、彼女はピーターソン行政の保守主義に怒りを感じており、「リバティータウンを21世紀へいざなう」ことを約束したと言っています。彼女はその政策によって、より若年層の、大学教育を受けた有権者の間で人気が出ています。しかし批評家は、彼女に政界での経験がないことを指摘し、彼女の政策の多くが実際には実行不可能だろうと主張しています。

質問

1. 市長選挙はいつ行われるか。
　　① 今から1週間後。
　　② 本日後ほど。
　　③ 他の4つの選挙の後。
　　④ 15年後。

2. ピーターソンさんに投票する人はどのような人である可能性が高いか。
　　① 若年層の人々。
　　② 人気のある人々。
　　③ 現代都市を必要とする人々。
　　④ 農村地区に住む人々。

3. ホプキンズさんはどのような事業を営んでいるか。
　　① 教育。　　② 行政。　　③ 広告。　　④ 運転。

解説 番組の大きなテーマである「市長選挙の2人の主要立候補者」をつかんだうえで、トピックごとに内容を整理しながら聞きましょう。質問を聞いた後は、問われている内容を聞き取ること、または答えを確認することに集中します。本文の概要は次のようになります。

問い	トピック	説明
問1	市長選挙の日程	今日から1週間後

問2	立候補者1：ピーターソン	現市長，当選4回，在任15年
		保守的
		高齢者，農村の有権者から支持
問3	立候補者2：ホプキンズ	政治家経験なし
		広告代理業を営む
		市の現代化を目指す
		若年層，大卒者からの支持

問1　第2文 the election for Mayor of Libertytown is only a week away「リバティータウンの市長選挙がわずか1週間後にせまっております」より，正解は ① です。

問2　第5文 Most of his support comes from older people, and from voters in suburban and rural districts.「彼の支持者の大半は高齢者や，郊外および農村地区の有権者からなります」より，正解は ④ です。

問3　第7文 She is a businesswoman, and runs a successful TV advertising agency.「彼女は実業家であり，テレビ広告の代理業で成功しています」より，正解は ③ です。

正解　問1　①　　問2　④　　問3　③

語句　leading 形「主要な，先導する」，candidate 名「立候補者」，opponent 名「対抗馬」，accuse 〜 of ...「〜を…のことで非難する」，conservative 形「保守的な」，out of touch with 〜「〜とかけ離れて，〜に理解がなくて」，voter 名「有権者」，suburban 形「郊外の」，rural 形「田舎の」，district 名「地区，地域」，politics 名「政治」，agency 名「代理業」，conservatism 名「保守主義」，administration 名「行政，政権」，drive 〜 into ...「〜を…へと駆り立てる」，policy 名「政策」，critic 名「批評家」，point out that SV「…と指摘する」，political life「政界，政治生活」，unworkable 形「実行不可能な」，in practice「実際に（は）」

Part 2

スクリプト　※下線部は解答の根拠に当たる箇所です。

(I: Interviewer　P: Peterson　H: Hopkins)

I(1): First, we'll talk to you, Mr Peterson. What are your main policies?

P(1): The key to our city's future is law and order. 問1 Young people today are increasingly out of control. They have wild parties that disturb the sleep of honest working citizens, they drink alcohol and engage in vandalism, they attend political meetings where dangerous views are freely discussed .... What I'm saying is that it is vitally important that our police be given the powers and resources to deal effectively with this increase of youthful disorder.

I (2): Let's turn to economic policy. Mr Peterson, what is your position on this?

P (2): That's easy. My policies are the policies of what I call 'small government'. In my opinion, for far too long governments have been taking money from good, productive people, and wasting it on unnecessary public projects, and on help for the lazy. All of this must stop! And for too long businesses have not wanted to invest in our city because of unnecessary and expensive environmental regulations. 問2 We must reform these regulations, to encourage investment.

I (3): Over to you, Mrs Hopkins. I think it's fair to say you disagree strongly with Mr Peterson.

H: Well, what Mr Peterson calls law and order is the right of the police to arrest teenagers for hanging around outside convenience stores, and fire tear gas at students protesting against overcrowded classrooms. And 問3 relaxing environmental regulations will allow factories to dump lots of poisonous chemicals in our rivers. So yes, I disagree with Mr Peterson. (248 words)

Questions:

1. What does Mr Peterson NOT say about young people?
    ① They are out of control.
    ② They commit vandalism.
    ③ They are honest workers.
    ④ They go to political meetings.

2. Which of the following is a policy of 'small government'?
    ① Providing help for lazy people.
    ② Changing environmental regulations.
    ③ Taking money from productive people.

④ Spending on public projects.

3. Which of the following is a reason Mrs Hopkins disagrees with Mr Peterson?
　① The police will protest about tear gas.
　② There will be less investment in Libertytown.
　③ Too many teenagers will hang out at convenience stores.
　④ Libertytown's rivers will become full of poisonous chemicals.

和訳 （I：インタビューアー　P：ピーターソン　H：ホプキンズ）

I (1)：まず，ピーターソンさんにお話をうかがいます。あなたの主要政策は何ですか。

P (1)：わが市の未来へのカギは法と秩序です。問1今の若者はどんどん制御を失っています。彼らはどんちゃん騒ぎのパーティーをして誠実な働く市民の睡眠を妨げたり，酒を飲んで破壊行為をしたり，政治集会に参加して，そこで危険な思想を自由に語り合ったり……。つまり，若者のこの増大する無秩序に効果的に対処するため，警察に権力と予算を与えることが極めて重要であると申しているのです。

I (2)：経済政策についてうかがいます。ピーターソンさん，これについてのあなたの立場はいかがですか。

P (2)：それは簡単なことです。私の政策は，私が「小さな政府」と呼んでいる政策です。私見では，市はあまりに長きにわたり，善良で生産力を有する人々からお金を取り，それを不要な公共事業や，怠惰な人々を救済することに浪費してきました。このようなものはすべて止めなければなりません！　そして，あまりに長きにわたり，企業は不要でお金のかかる環境規制があるために，わが市に投資をしたがらなかったのです。問2私たちは投資を促すために，このような規制を改革しなければなりません。

I (3)：ではホプキンズさん，お願いします。ピーターソンさんに対して大いに異論があると言っても差し支えないと思いますが。

H：ええ，ピーターソンさんの言うところの法と秩序は，警察がコンビニの周辺をたむろしているティーンエージャーを逮捕し，定員オーバーの教室に抗議する学生に催涙ガスを噴射する権利のことですね。そして，問3環境の規制を緩和することで，工場が大量の有毒化学物質を私たちの河川に捨てるのを許すのですね。というわけで，はい，私はピーターソンさんには同意できません。

質問

1. ピーターソンさんは若者について何を言っていないか。
　① 彼らは制御を失っている。
　② 彼らは破壊行為を行う。
　③ 彼らは誠実な労働者である。

④　彼らは政治集会に参加する。

2.　「小さな政府」の政策は次のうちどれか。

①　怠惰な人々を救済すること。

②　環境規制を変更すること。

③　生産力のある人々からお金を取ること。

④　公共事業に費用をかけること。

3.　ホプキンズさんがピーターソンさんに反対する理由は次のうちどれか。

①　警察が催涙ガスについて抗議するから。

②　リバティータウンへの投資が減るから。

③　あまりに多くの若者がコンビニにたむろするから。

④　リバティータウンの川に有毒化学物質があふれるから。

解説　このパートでは立候補者の1人が主要政策と経済政策について語り，もう1人がそれに反論しています。内容を整理すると次のようになります。

問い	トピック	説明
問1	ピーターソンの主要政策	法と秩序→警察権力強化
		若者問題・大騒ぎのパーティー
		・酒を飲んで破壊行為
		・政治集会参加
問2	ピーターソンの経済政策	「小さな政府」
		・不要な公共事業とりやめ
		・環境規制の緩和→投資の促進
問3	ホプキンズの反論	警察権力肥大化への危惧
		環境への悪影響（河川の汚染）

問1　ピーターソンの1つ目の発話第2・3文 Young people today are increasingly out of control. ... they drink alcohol and engage in vandalism, they attend political meetings ... 「今の若者はどんどん制御を失っています。…彼らは酒を飲んで破壊行為をしたり，政治集会に参加して…」より，ピーターソンは ①，②，④ については述べていることがわかります。③ は，若者によって睡眠を妨げられている人として言及しているにすぎません。したがって正解は ③ です。

問2　ピーターソンは2つ目の発話で「小さな政府」政策について説明しています。彼は，その最終文で We must reform these regulations 「このような規制（＝環境規制）を改革しなければなりません」と述べているので，

正解は ② です。①，③，④ はすべてピーターソンが見直したい政策です。

問3　ホプキンズの発話第2文 relaxing environmental regulations will allow factories to dump lots of poisonous chemicals in our rivers「環境の規制を緩和することで，工場が大量の有毒化学物質を私たちの河川に捨てるのを許すのですね」より，正解は ④ です。①，②，③ に似た表現が放送文中に出てきますが，引っかからないように注意。

正解　問1　③　　問2　②　　問3　④

語句　law and order「法と秩序」，wild 形「騒々しい」，disturb 動「～を妨げる，～（の心）を乱す」，vandalism 名「破壊（行為）」，resource 名「資金，財源」，deal with ～「～に対処する」，effectively 副「効果的に」，disorder 名「無秩序」，productive 形「生産力を有する」，invest in ～「～に投資する」，regulation 名「規制」，reform 動「～を改革する」，investment 名「投資」，arrest 動「～を逮捕する」，hang around「うろつく」，fire ～ at ...「～を…めがけて発射する」，tear gas「催涙ガス」，protest against ～「～に抗議する」，overcrowded 形「超満員の」，dump 動「～を投棄する」，poisonous 形「有毒の」，chemical 名「（複数形で）化学物質」

5

複合問題

Part 3

スクリプト　※下線部は解答の根拠に当たる箇所です。

（I: Interviewer　H: Hopkins　P: Peterson）

I (1): Mrs Hopkins, what do you believe in?

H (1): I believe in the future, and the future is youth! What, at this moment, does Libertytown have to offer young people? Nothing. Go into Old Town on a Saturday night, and it's dark, quiet, empty. A few people walking in the parks with their dogs, and the sound of soft music from expensive restaurants — restaurants only Peterson and his friends can afford to eat in. So, 問1 the first policy of my government will be the encouragement of businesses that cater to youth. Bars, nightclubs, Internet cafés, hamburger joints, youth theatres .... 問2 The young will flock to the town, and then tourists will flock after them. Because that's what tourists want to see: beautiful, spirited people having fun, being creative, not boring people wearing slippers, drinking weak beer, and complaining about their illnesses ....

P (1): For Mrs Hopkins everybody over the age of 30 might as well not exist.

I(2): Yes, Mrs Hopkins, that reminds me of one of your most controversial polices, the ending of the city pension scheme. Won't this make life very difficult for old people, who often have no income other than their city pension?

H(2): Who cares if a few pensioners have to cancel their vacations or can no longer afford to keep pets? Remember: my concern is with the future, and the old people will all be dead by the time that arrives ....

I(3): I'm afraid I'll have to stop you there Mrs Hopkins. Our time is up. But if I might just summarize your positions. Mr Peterson, you think teenagers should be arrested for standing outside convenience stores. Mrs Hopkins, you are looking forward to a time when all the old people are dead. Do I understand you both correctly?

P(2): That's outrageous. Obviously not all teenagers should be arrested. Only the delinquent ones ....

H(3): And in fact some of my best friends are old. My parents for example. But as for 問3 <u>the fogies who vote for Peterson</u>, well ....

I(4): 問4 <u>I'm wondering, and I think our viewers will also be wondering, whether either of you is fit to be mayor of Libertytown.</u>

P(3): Well, if not one of us, who else could it be ...?

H(4): Exactly ....

(371 words)

Questions:

1. Which of these businesses does Mrs Hopkins NOT want to encourage?
   ① Nightclubs.
   ② Internet cafés.
   ③ Youth theatres.
   ④ Expensive restaurants.

2. What, according to Mrs Hopkins, will attract tourists to Old Town?
   ① Dogs in the park.
   ② City pensions.
   ③ Creative people.
   ④ Warm beer.

3. What does Mrs Hopkins mean by the word 'fogies'?

   ① Old, conservative people.

   ② Her best friends.

   ③ People who vote for her.

   ④ Delinquent people.

4. What is the interviewer's opinion of Mr Peterson and Mrs Hopkins?

   ① He thinks Mr Peterson is a better candidate than Mrs Hopkins.

   ② He thinks Mrs Hopkins is a better candidate than Mr Peterson.

   ③ He thinks neither of them is a good candidate.

   ④ He thinks they are both good candidates.

和 訳 （Ｉ：インタビューアー　Ｈ：ホプキンズ　Ｐ：ピーターソン）

Ｉ(1)：ホプキンズさん，あなたが信じているものは何ですか。

Ｈ(1)：私は未来を信じていますし，未来とは若者のことです！　今，リバティータウンが若者に提供できるものに何がありますか。何もありません。土曜の夜，オールドタウンに行ってごらんなさい。そこは暗く，物音がせず，閑散としていますよ。公園で犬を連れて歩いている少数の人と，高級レストラン ― ピーターソンさんと彼のお仲間しかそこで食べる金銭的余裕のある人はいないような高くつくレストラン ― から聞こえてくる静かな音楽だけです。ですから，_{問1}私が市を統治するときの第1の政策は，若者の要求に応える店を奨励することになるでしょう。バー，ナイトクラブ，インターネットカフェ，ハンバーガーレストラン，ユースシアター…などです。_{問2}若者が町に集まり，そしてその後を追って観光客が集まるでしょう。それこそが観光客の見たいものなのです。楽しんで，創造的になっている，美しくはつらつとした人々の姿です。サンダルを履いて，ライトビールを飲んで，病気の愚痴を言っている退屈な人々ではありません…。

Ｐ(1)：ホプキンズさんにとって，30歳を超える人は全員存在していないも同然ですな。

Ｉ(2)：ええ，ホプキンズさん，それで思い出すのは，あなたの政策で最も議論の分かれるものの1つ，つまり市の年金制度の打ち切りです。これによって，市の年金以外に収入を持たないことも多い高齢者は，生活がかなり大変になりませんか。

Ｈ(2)：少数の年金生活者が休暇をキャンセルしなければならなかったり，ペットがもはや飼えなくなったりすることを誰が気にしますか。忘れていただきたくないのは，私の関心は未来にあるということです。高齢者はそのころまでには全員亡くなって……。

Ｉ(3)：申し訳ありませんが，ホプキンズさん，そこで止めさせていただきます。時間切れです。しかしお二人の立場を簡単に要約させていただければと思います。ピーターソンさん，あなたはティーンエージャーがコンビニの周辺にうろうろしていたら逮捕した

ほうがよいとお考えです。ホプキンズさん，あなたは高齢者全員が亡くなるときを待ち望んでいます。お二人のお話を私は正確に理解していますか。

P (2)：それは言いすぎです。もちろん，ティーンエージャー全員を逮捕すべきとは言いませんよ。法を犯しているものだけを……。

H (3)：そしてですね，実際のところ，私の最良の友人の何人かは高齢です。例えば私の両親ですね。しかし，_{問3}ピーターソンさんに投票する時代遅れの人に関しては，つまり……。

I (4)：_{問4}私は疑問を感じているんです。そして視聴者も感じるだろうと思います，あなた方お二人のうちのどちらがリバティータウンの市長にふさわしいのだろうかと。

P (3)：で，私たち二人がだめなら，他に誰がその地位に値すると……？

H (4)：おっしゃるとおりです……。

質問

1. ホプキンズさんが奨励したくないと思う店は次のうちどれか。

   ① ナイトクラブ。

   ② インターネットカフェ。

   ③ ユースシアター。

   ④ 高級レストラン。

2. ホプキンズさんによると，オールドタウンに観光客を引き寄せるものは何か。

   ① 公園の犬。

   ② 市の年金。

   ③ 創造的な人々。

   ④ ぬるいビール。

3. ホプキンズさんは 'fogies' という語で何を言いたいのか。

   ① 高齢で保守的な人々。

   ② 彼女の最良の友人。

   ③ 彼女に投票する人々。

   ④ 法を犯す不良。

4. ピーターソンさんとホプキンズさんに対するインタビューアーの見解はどれか。

   ① 彼はピーターソンさんがホプキンズさんよりよい候補者だと思っている。

   ② 彼はホプキンズさんがピーターソンさんよりよい候補者だと思っている。

   ③ 彼はどちらもよい候補者だと思っていない。

   ④ 彼はどちらもよい候補者だと思っている。

解説 パート3では，ホプキンズの政策が具体的に述べられています。最後にインタ
ビューアーが2人の意見に対して，見解を述べて終わります。内容を整理する
と次のようになります。

問い	トピック	説明
	ホプキンズの政策	若者を盛り立てる未来
	ホプキンズの見る市の現状	暗く，静かで閑散（少数の人が犬を連れて散歩し，高級レストランがあるだけ）
問1	ホプキンズの描く市の未来	若者が町に集まる場所の招致（バー，ナイトクラブ，インターネットカフェ，ハンバーガーレストラン，ユースシアターなど）
問2		楽しく元気で創造的な人々のいる町→観光客が集まる
	ホプキンズの物議を醸す政策	市の年金打ち切り
問4	インタビューアーの見解	この2人が市長にふさわしいか疑問

問1 ホプキンズの最初の発話の第6・7文 the first policy of my government
will be the encouragement of businesses that cater to youth. Bars,
nightclubs, Internet cafés, hamburger joints, youth theatres「私が市を
統治するときの第1の政策は，若者の要求に応える店を奨励することにな
るでしょう。バー，ナイトクラブ，インターネットカフェ，ハンバーガー
レストラン，ユースシアター」で，①，②，③ が奨励したい店として挙げ
られています。高級レストランは「ピーターソンさんとお仲間しか行けな
い店」として言及しているだけです。したがって，正解は ④ です。

問2 ホプキンズの最初の発話の第8・9文 The young will flock to the town,
and then tourists will flock after them. Because that's what tourists
want to see: beautiful, spirited people having fun, being creative「若者
が町に集まり，そしてその後を追って観光客が集まるでしょう。それこそ
が観光客の見たいものなのです。楽しんで，創造的になっている，美しく
はつらつとした人々の姿です」より，正解は ③ です。①，②，④ は観光
客を引き寄せるという文脈の中で述べられていません。

問3 ホプキンズの3番目の発話の最終文 the fogies who vote for Peterson よ
り，fogies とはピーターソンを支持する人々を指していることがわかりま
す。パート1より，ピーターソンは保守的で，彼を支持しているのは主に
高齢者なので，正解は ① です。このように，ひと続きの会話などでは，最

5 複合問題

61

初のほうで語られた前提を基に設問が作られている場合があるので注意が必要です。fogy とは「時代遅れの（老）人」という意味の名詞です。

　問4　インタビューアーの4番目の発話 I'm wondering, and I think our viewers will also be wondering, whether either of you is fit to be mayor of Libertytown.「私は疑問を感じているんです。そして視聴者も感じるだろうと思います，あなた方お二人のうちのどちらかがリバティータウンの市長にふさわしいのだろうかと」より，正解は ③ です。これに続くピーターソンの発話 Well, if not one of us, who else could it be ... ?「で，私たち二人がだめなら，他に誰がその地位に値すると……？」からもそれがわかります。

正解　問1　④　　問2　③　　問3　①　　問4　③

語句　Old Town「オールドタウン（ある地区の最も古くからある地域）」, can afford to *do*「…する（金銭的）ゆとりがある」, cater to ～「～の要求を満たす」, joint 名「安レストラン」, flock to ～「～に集まってくる」, spirited 形「はつらつとした，元気な」, weak beer「アルコール度数の低いビール」, might as well *do*「…するも同然だ，…するほうがましだ」, remind ～ of ...「～に…を思い出させる」, controversial 形「物議を醸す」, ending 名「終止」, pension scheme「年金制度」, my concern is with ～「私の関心は～にある」, summarize 動「～を要約する」, look forward to ～「～を楽しみに待つ」, outrageous 形「行きすぎていて受け入れられない」, delinquent 形「不良の，法を犯した」, fogy 名「時代遅れの（老）人」, vote for ～「～に投票する」, *be* wondering whether *SV*「…かどうか疑問に思う，悩ましい気持ちである」, *be* fit to *do*「…するのに適任である」

こう聞く！　テーマ＋トピック＋説明をとらえよう

・設問や選択肢が紙面に示されていない場合は，1回目の音声で内容を整理しながら聞き，質問が流れた段階で答えが出せるものは出しておきます。2回目の音声では**質問の答えを確認することに集中**しましょう。質問が流れていない段階では，話のテーマ，付随する小トピック，その具体的説明などに分けて聞くとよいでしょう。**聞き役が質問を出すことによってトピックを提示することが多い**ので，それを基に整理するとよいでしょう。

・設問が紙面に示されている場合には，音声を聞く前にそれらに目を通し，聞き取るべき内容を頭に入れてから音声に集中するようにしましょう。

解答・解説 ▶ pp.128 ～ 160

1 対話を聞き，それぞれの問いに答えなさい。

Part 1 対話を聞き，① ～ ⑩ の空所に入る英単語を書きなさい。　🔊21
2回流します。（音声は2分後に流れます。）

Jake Jenkins: Hello. I'm Jake Jenkins. A sculpture called *The Orbit* is Britain's largest piece of public art. It was _____①_____ by one of the country's most ____②____ artists. *The Orbit*, which can be seen in London's Olympic Park, is twice the _____③_____ of New York's Statue of Liberty and it stands at 115 meters in height. Made of approximately 2,000 tons of steel, it also includes the world's tallest and longest tunnel slide. It was built as a ____④____ reminder of the 2012 Olympic and Paralympic games, and was completed in May 2012. Since then, it has raised eyebrows of fans and ____⑤____ alike. And this is just one example of what Anish Kapoor considers art. Known for ____⑥____ form and perspective, the Mumbai*-born British artist has ____⑦____ the public with his bean-shaped sculpture in Chicago's Millennium Park, turned New York's Rockefeller Center upside down with his 10 meter *Sky Mirror*, and astonished art fans with his ____⑧____ installation of *Giant*, in London. This week, on our show, we meet Anish Kapoor in Seoul, as he ____⑨____ his eye-catching pieces to the East. Anish Kapoor, welcome to the show.

Anish Kapoor: Hello. Thank you for inviting me.

Jake Jenkins: You are one of the most famous sculptors in the world, and many believe that you are ____⑩____ for changing the way that people view sculpture. How do you think you've done this?

(Note* The city of Mumbai used to be called Bombay until 1995. Today, Mumbai and Bombay refer to an identical city in India.)

Part 2 対話を聞き，それぞれの問いに英語で答えなさい。2回 ◀))22
流します。（音声は1分後に流れます。）

問1 How does Anish Kapoor think his sculpture helps people?

問2 What did Anish Kapoor think he would become when he was a child?

問3 How did Anish Kapoor feel when he moved to London and started art school?

問4 How does Anish Kapoor feel about India now?

問5 Why was the Venice Festival a time that Anish Kapoor will never forget?

Part 3 対話を聞き，それぞれの問いの答えとして最も適切なも ◀))23
のを，① ～ ④ のうちから1つずつ選びなさい。2回流
します。（音声は3分後に流れます。）

問1 Why did Kapoor decide to use mirrors in his work?
① He wanted viewers to see themselves reflected from circles.
② He wished to give viewers a sense of being pulled into outer space.
③ He is interested in how art relates to spaces around art.
④ He is interested in how sculpture separates itself from the space around it.

問2 After Kapoor made the first *Sky Mirror*, he made another one that was
(   ).
① 6 meters in diameter and installed in Nottingham
② 6 meters in diameter and installed at Rockefeller Center
③ 10 meters in diameter and installed at Rockefeller Center
④ 10 meters in diameter and installed above the New York skyline

問 3　Along with its size what is Kapoor's work, *Giant*, known for?
① Being one of the most visited sculptures in the world.
② Using almost one third of the great hall at the Tate Modern Art Museum.
③ Making people feel crazy when they see this enormous work of art.
④ Helping the Tate Modern Art Museum expand the size of its great hall.

問 4　What does Jenkins, the interviewer, say about the size of *Giant*?
① It looks like an enormous ant that has been stretched out.
② It is over 150 meters high.
③ It makes people seem antlike.
④ It is too big to be meaningful.

問 5　Even though the basic theme for *Giant* is human suffering, Kapoor feels that the sculpture (　　　).
① also evokes great human sympathy
② is too big to be meaningful
③ still shows respect to the God Apollo
④ is less cruel than the painting by Titian

問 6　What is one of the potential problems that Kapoor faces when starting a new large sculpture?
① There is no way to know how the sculpture will turn out.
② The model for the large art object is often better than the finished sculpture.
③ The public sees the sculpture even before the artist does.
④ The public never sees the model, so they may not understand the larger work.

次のページに続く ▶

問7 To start a new project Kapoor works (　　　).

　① alone, with small models of the large sculpture

　② with a team with drawings that determine the outcome of the large sculpture

　③ alone, usually with materials from his studio

　④ with a team, sometimes just making something, anything

問8 *Cloud Gate* is a large sculpture that (　　　).

　① pleases Kapoor and the people of Chicago, but not city leaders

　② city leaders in Chicago approved after seeing only a small drawing

　③ Kapoor renamed "The Bean" after he saw the finished product

　④ pleases Kapoor, because he had full control over how people interpreted it

問9 What were two unintended outcomes of *Cloud Gate*?

　① People began to call it "The Bean," and it was far more expensive than planned.

　② People began to call it "The Bean," and it turned out to be cheaper than planned.

　③ It was a little more expensive than planned, but it became a large tourist attraction.

　④ It was officially renamed "The Bean," and tourists love it more than even the people of Chicago.

問10 What might we conclude about *Cloud Gate* from this interview?

　① It is a beautiful sculpture that is loved more by the people of Chicago than by tourists.

　② It is a beautiful sculpture that cost over 33 million dollars.

　③ Though an expensive work of art, people are still allowed to touch it.

　④ Though an inexpensive work of art, it is loved and cared for daily.

（青山学院大学）

対話を聞き，それぞれの問いに答えなさい。

Part 1 これから心理学者 Gopnik 博士の著書 *The Gardener and the Carpenter*（『庭師と大工』）に関するインタビューを聞きます。それぞれの問いの答えとして最も適切なものを，① 〜 ⑤ のうちから 1 つずつ選びなさい。2 回流します。

問 1　Which of the following statements does NOT match the carpenter concept of parenting?

① It assumes parenting is like shaping basic materials into a particular form.

② It includes a clear idea of the final goal of parenting.

③ It involves following a specific plan for raising children well.

④ It is the dominant model of parenting in the developed world today.

⑤ It requires cooperation between parents and other active agents.

問 2　Which of the following changes in human society has been more important for producing the dominant model of parenting in the developed world?

① The development of an industrial economy.

② The emergence of higher education.

③ The reduced experience of caring for children before having one's own.

④ The rise of large, extended families.

⑤ The shift from hunting and gathering to settled agricultural society.

問 3　Which of the following statements is NOT mentioned in the interview?

① In modern society, people often start a family without first having the experience of caring for children.

② Parenting began to change in the 20th century.

③ Parenting has been viewed as similar to going to school or working.

④ Parenting will go more smoothly if you first have a successful career.

⑤ Some parents look for the right manual in order to bring up their children well.

次のページに続く ▶

問 4 Which of the following does Gopnik mention as a reason why humans have an especially long childhood?

① It allows them to acquire language.

② It allows them to become more flexible and adaptable.

③ It allows them to develop a larger brain.

④ It allows them to experience life more fully.

⑤ It allows them to protect their surrounding environment.

問 5 Based on this conversation, which of the following statements best describes the views of Gopnik and the host, Vedantam?

① Gopnik and Vedantam both prefer the carpenter model.

② Gopnik and Vedantam both prefer the gardening model.

③ Gopnik and Vedantam find much to appreciate in both models.

④ Gopnik prefers the carpenter model, but Vedantam prefers the gardening model.

⑤ Gopnik prefers the gardening model, but Vedantam prefers the carpenter model.

Part 2 これから司会者 (Vedantam) と Gopnik 博士，Webb 博 ◀))25
士の 3 人による，Part 1 と内容的に関連した会話を聞き
ます。それぞれの問いの答えとして最も適切なものを，
① ～ ⑤ のうちから 1 つずつ選びなさい。2 回流します。

問 1 According to Gopnik, what is a likely outcome of the carpenter model of parenting?

① Children will achieve more by taking chances.

② Children will be better able to deal with uncertainty.

③ Children will be more likely to be cautious.

④ Children will be well-balanced in their later life.

⑤ Children will benefit from greater freedom.

問2　According to Vedantam, what does Gopnik argue?

① Children learn valuable lessons by taking risks.

② Children need to develop specialized skills from an early age.

③ Parents need to have specific goals for their children.

④ The carpenter model is designed to increase the child's sense of freedom.

⑤ The current culture of parenting needs only minor adjustments to be successful.

問3　What objection does Webb raise to Gopnik's argument?

① Giving children a lot of freedom can limit their future opportunities.

② If you are going to be free of anxiety, you need a structured life.

③ If you are going to succeed, you need to try a lot of things before choosing one.

④ In order to be an Olympic athlete, you must start taking lessons before the age of fourteen.

⑤ Success in life is based on a child's natural ability.

問4　What does Gopnik think about the problem Webb describes?

① Children should be encouraged to trust their parents.

② Children should not be expected to work that hard in order to succeed.

③ Parents in a competitive culture should make great demands of their children.

④ Parents should give children every advantage possible to help them succeed.

⑤ We should feel sympathy for parents in this situation.

問5　What conclusion does Webb finally draw from this discussion?

① Life is like an unfair competition.

② Most models of parenting do not prepare children well enough for life.

③ Not enough parents understand how to help their children succeed in life.

④ Parenting can be a very unrewarding activity.

⑤ The real problem lies in society.

（東京大学）

1 **正解** 問1 ③ 問2 ③

〜〜〜

スクリプト　M(1)： Hi, Reiko.

W(1)： Oh, hi, Taka.　I didn't know you took this bus from the station to campus.

M(2)： No, I usually ride my bicycle from here.　The bus is too expensive. But it's raining so hard today.

W(2)： Oh, I never ride my bike.　The campus is too far from the station.　I normally get the bus.

M(3)： But it only takes 20 minutes by bike.　And when you have to wait for the bus, it takes ages.

W(3)： Well, yeah, the buses are pretty infrequent.　But the worst thing is when it's too crowded to get on.

M(4)： What do you do then?

W(4)： I try to share a taxi so I won't be late for class.

M(5)： I think you should get a bike.　It would be much cheaper in the long run.

W(5)： Oh, that sounds like too much exercise to me.　Maybe the best thing would be a dorm room on campus.

和訳　男性(1)：やあ，レイコ。

女性(1)：あら，こんにちは，タカ。駅から大学までこのバスを使っているなんて知らなかったわ。

男性(2)：いや，いつもはここから自転車で行くんだ。バスは高すぎるよ。でも今日は雨の降りが激しいからさ。

女性(2)：あら，私は自転車には全く乗らないわね。大学は駅からすごく離れているじゃない。普通はバスに乗るわ。

男性(3)：でも自転車で20分しかかからないよ。それに，バスを待たなければならないとなると，ものすごく時間がかかるじゃない。

女性(3)：うん，そうね，バスの本数はちょっと少なすぎるわ。でも最悪なのは，混みすぎて乗れないときよ。

男性⑷：そういうときはどうするの？

女性⑷：授業に遅れないようにタクシーに相乗りしようとするけど。

男性⑸：自転車を手に入れたほうがいいと思うよ。結局はずっと安上がりになるから。

女性⑸：だめ、私には体力的にきつすぎると感じるわ。ひょっとすると一番いいのは学内の
　　　　寮に部屋を借りることかもね。

解説　問1　男性と女性はたいていどのような交通手段を使って大学に行くか。

　　①　男性も女性もバスを利用する。

　　②　男性は自転車で行き、女性はタクシーを利用する。

　　③　男性は自転車で行き、女性はバスを利用する。

　　④　男性はバスを利用し、女性は自転車で行く。

　質問と選択肢から、それぞれの話者が自転車／バス／タクシーのどれで通学するかを聞き取ります。男性は、2番目の発話で、I usually ride my bicycle from here と言っているので、大学まで自転車を使っていることがわかります。女性は、2番目の発話で I normally get the bus. と言っているので、大学までバスを使っていることがわかります。したがって、正解は③です。

問2　男性の助言からどのようなことが推測できるか。

　　①　女性は大学構内に住むべきだ。

　　②　女性はもっと運動すべきだ。

　　③　女性はお金を賢く使うべきだ。

　　④　女性は授業に間に合うようにすべきだ。

　質問に the man's suggestion とあり、選択肢はすべて The woman should ... となっているので、男性が女性の行動について何と言うかに注意します。女性は、3・4番目の発話で、「バスが混みすぎて乗れないときは、授業に遅れないためにタクシーに乗る」と説明しています。男性はこの発言を受けて、I think you should get a bike. It would be much cheaper in the long run. と言って、タクシーに乗ってお金を使うより、自転車を買ったほうが「結局は安上がりだ」と説明しています。したがって、男性は、女性のお金の使い方について助言を与えたと考えられるので、③が正解になります。

語句　it takes ages「非常に時間がかかる」, infrequent 形「頻度が少ない」, share a taxi「タクシーに相乗りする」, in the long run「結局は、ゆくゆくは」, dorm 名「寮」(= dormitory)

ここがポイント　質問は音声が流れる前に必ず読んでおきます。できれば選択肢にもざっと目を通し、**選択肢間のおおよその違い**について意識しておきましょう。音声を聞きながら、選択肢の情報が拾えるようになることが目標となります。

~~~~~~

スクリプト

M (1): Hello? Is this the Writing Center?

W (1): Yes. Hi, have a seat.

M (2): My name is Yoshi.

W (2): Nice to meet you, Yoshi. Welcome to the Writing Support Desk. I'm Wendy. Is this your first time here?

M (3): Yes. I feel very nervous.

W (3): Well, it's great that you've come. Okay, each session is only half an hour, so we need to decide how we're going to use the time. Can you tell me what you'd like to work on today?

M (4): Yeah. It's my English literature paper.

W (4): I see.

M (5): Can you fix it for me?

W (5): Well, we aren't supposed to correct your writing.

M (6): Oh no, I'm going to fail.

W (6): But we can work together to improve your paper. Can you tell me what problems you are having with it?

M (7): Well, my professor said I needed more evidence to support my ideas. But I'm more worried about my grammar mistakes.

W (7): Okay. So evidence and grammar. Do you have your work with you?

M (8): Yes. My essay is in my bag. Ah, oh no, where is it? I must have left it in one of my morning classes.

W (8): Okay. In that case, it would be better if you booked another appointment and came back with your essay.

M (9): But the deadline's tomorrow.

W (9): It's all right. My last free appointment this afternoon starts at 2:40. Why don't you make another appointment with me then?

M (10): Okay. I'll make an appointment and come back later.

和訳

男性 (1)：すみません。ここはライティングセンターですか。

女性 (1)：はい。こんにちは，おかけください。

男性 (2)：ヨシと申します。

女性(2)：はじめまして，ヨシさん。ライティングサポートデスクへようこそ。私はウェンディです。ここに来るのは初めてですか。

男性(3)：はい，とても緊張しています。

女性(3)：まあ，でもここに来たのはすばらしいことですよ。さあ，1回の面談は30分しかないので，その時間をどのように使うか決める必要がありますね。今日はどんなことに取り組みたいのか教えてくれますか。

男性(4)：はい，僕の英文学のレポートのことなんです。

女性(4)：なるほど。

男性(5)：直してもらうことはできますか。

女性(5)：実は，私たちは書いたものを添削しないことになっているんです。

男性(6)：困ったな，落第しちゃいます。

女性(6)：でも，あなたのレポートをよくするために協力することはできますよ。どんな問題があるか教えてくれますか。

男性(7)：その，教授が言うには，僕の意見を支える根拠がもっと必要だということなんです。でも，僕は文法の間違いのほうが心配でして。

女性(7)：わかりました。ということは根拠と文法ですね。書いたものは持って来ていますか。

男性(8)：はい。レポートはカバンの中にあります。あれ，おかしいな，どこいった？　午前中のクラスのどこかに置いてきてしまったようです。

女性(8)：いいですよ。それなら，新たに予約をして，レポートを持って再び来てもらうのがいいですね。

男性(9)：でも，締め切りが明日なんです。

女性(9)：大丈夫ですよ。今日の午後，私の予約が空いている最後の時間は2時40分からです。そこで私との面談の予約をとってはいかがですか。

男性(10)：そうします。予約をして，あとでもう一度来ます。

解説　問1　男性は誰と話しているか。

① 友人

② カウンセラー

③ 教授

④ ライティングの個人教師

　最初のやり取りから，女性はライティングサポートデスクの職員であることがわかるので，友人や教授ではないと考えられます。また，男性が自分のレポートを直してもらいたいと女性に願い出たところ，女性は，5番目の発話で we aren't supposed to correct your writing「私たちは書いたものを添削しないことになっているんです」と言っていることから，個人教師のような立場にはな

73

いとわかります。さらに、6番目の発話で、we can work together to improve your paper「あなたのレポートをよくするために協力することはできますよ」と言っているので、女性は困っている学生を手助けするカウンセリングを行っていると考えるのが妥当であると言えます。したがって、正解は ② です。④ の tutor は、a private teacher「個人教師」という意味で用いられます。

問2　女性の最後の予約可能な面談は何時に終了する予定か。

① 午後2時10分

② 午後2時40分

③ 午後3時10分

④ 午後3時40分

　女性は、3番目の発話で each session is only half an hour「1回の面談は30分しかない」と言い、9番目の発話で My last free appointment this afternoon starts at 2:40.「今日の午後、私の予約が空いている最後の時間は2時40分からです」と言っています。したがって最後の面談が終了する時刻は、2時40分の30分後ということになるので、正解は ③ です。

問3　この面談はなぜこんなに早く終わるのか。

① 男性に十分な時間がない。

② 女性に別の予約が入っている。

③ 女性が彼の書いたものを添削するのを拒んでいる。

④ 男性が自分の書いたレポートを持っていない。

　面談を始めようとした女性が男性に、レポートを持参しているかと尋ねたところ、男性は、8番目の発話で My essay is in my bag. Ah, oh no, where is it? I must have left it in one of my morning classes.「レポートはカバンの中にあります。あれ、おかしいな、どこいった？　午前中のクラスのどこかに置いてきてしまったようです」と答え、そのあと、新しい予約をとる話題に移っていきます。したがって、この面談が早く終わる理由は男性がレポートを持参していないことになるので、正解は ④ です。

語句　session 名「(面談や集まりなどの) 活動、期間」、literature 名「文学」、fix 動「〜を直す」、be supposed to do「…することになっている」、correct 動「〜を添削する」、professor 名「教授」、evidence 名「根拠、証拠」、book 動「〜を予約する」、appointment 名「面会 (の予約)」、deadline 名「締め切り」

ここが ポイント　時刻や数値を問う問題には簡単な計算が含まれる場合があります。会話内の時刻や数値はメモをとって計算に備えましょう。

3 **正解** 問1 ② 問2 ③ 問3 ③

〰〰〰〰〰〰〰〰〰〰〰〰〰〰〰〰〰〰〰〰〰〰〰〰〰〰〰〰〰〰〰〰〰〰〰〰

スクリプト

M(1)： Risa, got a minute?

W(1)： Sure, Justin. What's going on?

M(2)： Not much. I wanted to ask you about the new meal plan that the cafeteria is offering. Greg told me that you're on it now.

W(2)： Yes, I started it a month ago, when it was first offered.

M(3)： What do you think about it? Is it better than the one you were on before?

W(3)： Well, it depends on how often you eat.

M(4)： What do you mean?

W(4)： The new meal plan doesn't cover breakfast and weekends. That's why this option is about fifteen thousand yen cheaper every month. I realized that I was getting up too late to eat breakfast. I also often go home on the weekends to go to my part-time job and see my family.

M(5)： I see. The new plan definitely suits your lifestyle. I think I'll stick with the one I'm on, though. I rarely go home now, and I need to get up early for practice anyway. I can't skip breakfast or I'll be starving in my morning classes.

W(5)： Sounds like a smart choice.

和訳

男性(1)：リサ，今ちょっと時間ある？

女性(1)：ええ，ジャスティン。何かあった？

男性(2)：大したことじゃないんだ。カフェテリアが提供している新しい食事プランについて尋ねたくてね。グレッグが，今君がそれに入っていると言っていたから。

女性(2)：そうなの，1ヵ月前，初めてそのプランが出されたときから始めたの。

男性(3)：それについてどう思う？　以前君が入っていたものよりもいいの？

女性(3)：そうね，それは食べる頻度によるんじゃないかしら。

男性(4)：どういうこと？

女性(4)：新しい食事プランは朝食と週末を含まないのよ。だから，このプランでいくと毎月15,000円ほどは安くなるわ。私は起きるのが遅すぎて朝食を食べられていないことに気づいたの。それに週末はバイトに行くのと，家族に会うので実家に帰ることが多いのよ。

男性(5)：なるほど。新しいプランは確かに君の生活には合うんだね。でも，僕は今のプランを続けようと思うんだ。今のところめったに実家には帰らないし，いずれにせよ部活の練習で朝早く起きる必要がある。朝食は抜けないよ。抜いたら，午前の授業で腹ペコになっちゃう。

女性(5)：賢い選択なんじゃない。

解説 問1 男性は，女性が新しい食事プランを取り入れていることをどうして知っているのか。

① 彼の友人のほとんどがプランを変えた。

② 彼の友人が彼に教えた。

③ 彼女が彼にすでに話した。

④ 彼は彼女がそれに変更するのを見た。

男性は，2番目の発話で Greg told me that you're on it now.「グレッグが，今君がそれ（＝新しい食事プラン）に入っていると言っていたから」と言っているので，正解は ② です。

問2 女性の新しい食事プランについて正しいのは，次のうちどれか。

① 彼女はそれを1週間前に変えた。

② 彼女は今も週末に食事ができる。

③ 彼女は出費が抑えられている。

④ 彼女はより頻繁にカフェテリアを利用している。

女性は，4番目の発話で The new meal plan doesn't cover breakfast and weekends. That's why this option is about fifteen thousand yen cheaper every month.「新しい食事プランは朝食と週末を含まないのよ。だから，このプランでいくと毎月15,000円ほどは安くなるわ」と言っているので，正解は ③ です。

問3 男性が現在の食事プランを維持する理由として述べているものは，次のうちどれか。

① 彼は1日のどの時間でも食事ができる。

② そのプランは価格設定が手ごろだ。

③ そのプランには朝食が含まれる。

④ 彼のチームメイトがそのプランを取り入れている。

男性は，最後の発話で「僕は今のプランを続けようと思うんだ」と言っており，その理由として，I rarely go home now, and I need to get up early for practice anyway. I can't skip breakfast or I'll be starving in my morning classes.「今のところめったに実家には帰らないし，いずれにせよ部活の練習で朝早く起きる必要がある。朝食は抜けないよ。抜いたら，午前の授業で腹ペコになっちゃう」と言っているので，プランに朝食が含まれるという ③ が正解になります。

語 句 Got a minute?「少し時間ある？」(= Have you got a minute?)，*be* on ～「～に取り組んでいる」，definitely 副「確かに，間違いなく」，suit 動「～に合う，好都合だ」，stick with ～「～を続ける」，skip 動「～を（1 回）飛ばす，抜く」，starving 形「非常に空腹な」

ここが ▶ ポイント　2人の発話者が1つの話題についてそれぞれ異なる意見を述べる場合があります。本問では，「新しい食事プランに変える／変えない」，その理由やメリット・デメリットといったことが対話の内容になることを，紙面に書かれた質問から察することができます。このような場合，**それぞれの意見と理由を整理して聞き取る**ようにしましょう。

1 正 解

問1	F	問2	T	問3	F	問4	F	問5	T	問6	T

◇◇◇

スクリプト ※下線部は解答の根拠に当たる箇所です。

You might think that the traditional French ham and butter baguette sandwich would be the most popular fast food in France. But think again. 問1 A recent study shows that sales of American-style burgers have overtaken the sales of these sandwiches. According to a French restaurant marketing company, 問2 about 1.2 billion ham and butter baguette sandwiches were sold in France in 2017 while 1.4 billion burgers were sold during the same period. Sales of both baguette sandwiches and hamburgers are on the rise, the study says. It notes that 問3·4 baguette sandwiches saw a 1.3 percent growth in 2017, while burger sales recorded a 9 percent increase. Curiously, 問5 in France, the number of hamburgers sold by McDonald's has not varied for years. What has changed though is the growing number of restaurants putting burgers on their menu. In fact, 80 percent of restaurants surveyed in France included burgers on their menu in 2017. The rise of the American-style burger was noted in a story in *The New York Times* which reported that 問6 Restaurant Le Dalí and other famous restaurants in Paris added burgers to their menus for the first time 10 years ago.

和 訳 あなたは，フランスの伝統的なハムとバターのバゲットサンドがフランスで最も人気のあるファストフードだと思っているかもしれません。しかし考え直してください。問1 最近の調査によれば，アメリカ式のバーガーの売り上げが，これらのサンドイッチの売り上げを超えたということです。フランスのレストラン市場調査会社によると，問2 2017 年にフランスでハムとバターのバゲットサンドはおよそ 12 億個売れたのに対し，バーガーは同時期に 14 億個売れたそうです。この調査では，バゲットサンドイッチとハンバーガーはどちらも売り上げを伸ばしているとしています。問3·4 2017 年にバゲットサンドが 1.3 パーセント伸びたのに対し，バーガーの売り上げは 9 パーセントの増加を記録したことをこの調査は示しています。奇妙なことに，問5 フランスではマクドナルドで売られているハンバーガーの数は何年もの間変わっていません。しかし変わったのは，メニューにバーガーを加えたレストランがますます増えていることです。事実，2017 年，フランスで調査対象となったレストランのうち 8 割

においてメニューにバーガーが含まれていました。アメリカ式のバーガーの伸びは『ニューヨーク・タイムズ』の記事でも取り上げられており，問6 レストラン・ル・ダリやその他のパリの有名なレストランが初めてバーガーをメニューに加えたのは 10 年前のことであると報じられました。

解説 音声を聞く前に紙面の問いをざっと読んで，軽く内容を把握します。語句レベルでは「（ハムとバターの）バゲットサンド」，「バーガー」，「売り上げ」，「フランス」，「2017 年」，「マクドナルド」などを確認し，これらがどのような文脈で語られるか聞きながら確かめます。

問1 ハムとバターのバゲットサンドはフランスで最も人気のあるファストフードである。

　第 1・2 文に You might think that the traditional French ham and butter baguette sandwich would be the most popular fast food in France. But think again. とあり，「バゲットサンドがフランスで最も人気のあるファストフードではない」ことが示唆されています。そして実際，これに続く文で，sales of American-style burgers have overtaken the sales of these sandwiches と，バーガーの売り上げがバゲットサンドを追い抜いたことが述べられているので，正解は **F** です。

問2 2017 年，フランスの人々はハムとバターのバゲットサンドよりもバーガーをより多く買った。

　第 4 文 about 1.2 billion ham and butter baguette sandwiches were sold in France in 2017 while 1.4 billion burgers were sold during the same period 「2017 年にフランスでハムとバターのバゲットサンドはおよそ 12 億個売れたのに対し，バーガーは同時期に 14 億個売れた」より，正解は **T** です。これは直前の文の内容を，具体的なデータで示した文となっています。

問3 2017 年，フランスにおいてバゲットサンドの売り上げは 1.3 パーセント下がった。

　第 6 文の前半部 baguette sandwiches saw a 1.3 percent growth in 2017 より，正解は **F** です。問いの英文に 1.3％という数値が出ているので，その数値がどのような文脈で用いられているのかを聞き取ります。問いの 1.3 パーセント dropped 「下がった」に対し，音声では 1.3 パーセントの growth 「伸び」と言っています。

問4 2017 年，フランスのバーガーの売り上げはバゲットサンドの売り上げより落ちた。

　第 6 文 baguette sandwiches saw a 1.3 percent growth in 2017, while burger sales recorded a 9 percent increase より，正解は **F** です。話の流れを理解していれば，バーガーの売り上げがバゲットサンドの売り上げより落ちたことにはならないとわかるはずですし，この文で「1.3 パーセントの伸び」・「9 パーセントの増加」を正確に聞き取れれば，それを確かめることができます。

問5　近年, フランスのマクドナルドのバーガーの売り上げは増えていない。

第7文 in France, the number of hamburgers sold by McDonald's has not varied for years より, 正解は T です。has not varied は「変化がない」という意味なので, 「(売り上げが) 増えていない」と言い換えることができます。

問6　一部のフランスの有名レストランは 10 年前にハンバーガーをメニューに加えた。

最終文 Restaurant Le Dalí and other famous restaurants in Paris added burgers to their menus for the first time 10 years ago「レストラン・ル・ダリやその他のパリの有名なレストランが初めてバーガーをメニューに加えたのは 10 年前のことである」より, 正解は T です。

語句　baguette 图「バゲット, フランスパン」, overtake 動「～を追い抜く」, curiously 副「奇妙なことに」, vary 動「変わる」

ここが ポイント

・事前に問いの英文にざっと目を通します。**問いで用いられている語句が放送文ではどのような文脈で用いられているか聞きながら確認しましょう。**

・できる限り音声を聞きながら, 問いの英文の事実関係の正誤をチェックしていきましょう。

2 正解　問1 ④　問2 ①　問3 ②　問4 ③

スクリプト　※下線部は解答の根拠に当たる箇所です。

問1During World War II, when London was bombed, George VI and his queen won great public admiration by staying in London throughout the war. The present Queen has also been much respected, and her concern for the Commonwealth has strengthened the monarchy.

問2For many years, people expected the royal family to have high moral standards and to display all the ideals of family life, an attitude which developed in the time of Queen Victoria. Until recently, the public rarely saw the royal family except on formal occasions. They remained distant and dignified, and any family problems were kept private. 問3The younger royals, however, have lived more public lives and attracted enormous media interest. 問4Royal marriage problems and love affairs have become headline news. Alongside a hunger for yet more revelations, traditional respect for the royal family began to decline. The reported treatment of Diana, Princess of Wales, and Sarah, Duchess of York, especially after the breakdown of their marriages, brought criticism on the Queen and older members of the family. The family were again criticized for their apparent reluctance to share in the public's grief after the death of Princess Diana.

Questions:

1. Why did George VI and his queen win great public admiration during World War II?

2. What did people expect the royal family to have for many years?

3. How have the younger royals lived their lives?

4. What happened to traditional respect for the royal family after royal marriage problems became headline news?

和訳

問1第二次世界大戦中，ロンドンは爆撃を受けましたが，ジョージ6世と王妃は，戦争の間ずっとロンドンにとどまっていたとして大衆から大いに賞賛を受けました。現在の女王もたいへんに敬意を払われており，彼女が英連邦に対して気遣いを示すことで君主制は強化されています。問2長きにわたり，人々は王室が高い倫理基準を持ち，家庭生活の理想のすべてを体現することを期待していました。これはビクトリア女王の時代に現れた態度です。近年まで，公式行事以外で人々が王族の姿を見ることはめったにありませんでした。彼らは遠く威厳ある存在であり続け，家庭内のいかなる問題も表に出ることはありませんでした。問3しかし，若い世代の王族は公の目に触れる機会がより多い生活を送るようになり，メディアの関心を大いに引き付けています。問4王室の結婚問題や不倫騒動がトップニュースになっているのです。さらに内情を知りたいという強い思いに伴って，王室に対して伝統的にあった尊敬の念は薄れ始めました。ウェールズ公妃ダイアナやヨーク公爵夫人セーラの扱いが報じられると，特に彼らの結婚が破綻したあとは，女王や年配の王室の人々に非難が集まりました。王室は，ダイアナ妃の死後，大衆と悲しみを分かち合うことに気乗りがしないように見えたことで再び非難されました。

質問

1. ジョージ6世と土妃が第二次世界大戦中，大衆から大いに賞賛を受けたのはなぜか。

2. 人々は長年にわたって，王室に何を持つことを期待したか。

3. 若い世代の王族はどのような生活を送ってきているか。

4. 王室の結婚問題がトップニュースになったあと，王室に対して伝統的にあった尊敬の念に何が生じたか。

解説 選択肢の語句が出てくる文脈に気をつけながら聞き，質問が流れたら，順に1つずつ正解を判定していきましょう。この問題では音声は2回流れますが，1

回目にすべて解答を終えるつもりで解きたいところです。2回目は答えの確認程度ですませるのが理想です。

問1 ① 彼らがロンドンで結婚したから。

② 彼らがメディアの関心を引き付けたから。

③ 彼らが爆撃された都市から逃げたから。

④ 彼らが戦争中にロンドンにとどまったから。

第1段落第1文 During World War II, when London was bombed, George VI and his queen won great public admiration by staying in London throughout the war. より，正解は ④ です。

問2 ① 高い倫理基準。 ② 不完全な家庭生活。

③ メディアへの関心。 ④ 大衆に対する非難。

第2段落第1文 For many years, people expected the royal family to have high moral standards and to display all the ideals of family life より，正解は ① です。

問3 ① 家族の問題を表に出さずにいる。

② 公の目に触れる機会がより多い生活を送っている。

③ 家族の問題を持つことは全くない。

④ メディアの関心を全く引き付けない。

第2段落第4文 The younger royals, however, have lived more public lives より，正解は ② です。

問4 ① 徐々に高まり始めた。 ② 変わらなかった。

③ なくなり始めた。 ④ 完全に消滅した。

第2段落第5・6文 Royal marriage problems and love affairs have become headline news. Alongside a hunger for yet more revelations, traditional respect for the royal family began to decline. より，正解は ③ です。

語句 bomb 動「～を爆撃する」，admiration 名「賞賛」，the Commonwealth「英連邦」，strengthen 動「～を強める」，monarchy 名「君主制」，royal 形「王室の」名「王族」，dignified 形「威厳のある」，keep ～ private「～を公表しないでおく」，love affair「不倫，恋愛関係」，hunger for ～「～への渇望」，revelation 名「暴露」，criticism 名「非難，批判」，criticize ～ for ...「…のことで～を非難する」，apparent 形「見かけ上の」，reluctance 名「気乗りしないこと」，share in ～「～を共にする」，grief 名「悲しみ」

ここがポイント 質問が紙面に書かれていない場合は，選択肢を確認し，その中の語句がどんな文脈で使われるかに注意して聞きましょう。

82

3 　正解　　問1　②　　問2　④

〰〰〰

スクリプト　※下線部は解答の根拠に当たる箇所です。

The activity of a certain gene could determine how social you are and how well you bond with others. 　問1 The OXT gene is responsible for the production of oxytocin, a hormone linked with a large number of social behaviours in humans. 　It's often referred to as the "love hormone." In a recent study, researchers assessed more than 120 people, conducting genetic tests and assessments of social skills, brain structure and brain function. 　問2 They found that those with lower activity of the OXT gene had more difficulties in recognizing facial expressions and were more anxious about their relationships with loved ones. 　These individuals also had lower levels of brain activity in regions associated with social cognitive processing.

Questions:

1. What is oxytocin?

2. What is true about people with lower activity of the OXT gene?

和訳　ある遺伝子の活動が，あなたの社会性やあなたが他人とどのくらいうまく緊密な結びつきを築くかといったことを決定する可能性があります。　問1 OXT 遺伝子はオキシトシンという，人間の数多くの社会的行動に関連するホルモンを生成する大本となっています。それはしばしば「愛情ホルモン」と呼ばれています。最近の研究において，研究者は 120 人を超える人たちに対して，遺伝子検査と社会的スキルおよび脳の構造と機能に関する判定を行い，分析しました。　問2 OXT 遺伝子の活動が低い人たちは表情の読み取りにより難があり，愛する者との関係により多くの不安を持っていることがわかりました。これらの人々はまた，社会認知処理に関連する部位の脳の活動レベルがより低いこともわかりました。

質問

1. オキシトシンとは何か。

2. OXT 遺伝子の活動がより低い人々に関して正しいのは何か。

解説　問1　①　遺伝子。　　②　ホルモン。
　　　　　③　脳の部位。　　④　癌の一種。

　選択肢に用いられている語句を素早くチェックし，それぞれの語句がどのような文脈で用いられているのか聞き取ります。本問は，第 2 文に The OXT gene is responsible for the production of oxytocin, a hormone linked with a large number of social behaviours in humans.「OXT 遺伝子はオキシトシンという，

人間の数多くの社会的行動に関連するホルモンを生成する大本となっています」とあるので，② が正解となります。oxytocin, a hormone という表現によって，前者を後者が同格的に説明しています。④ は英文に全く出てこない内容なので，質問に関係なく消去することができます。

問2 ① 彼らは家族や友人との関係をそれほど不安に思っていない。

② 彼らはより知能が高い。

③ 彼らは表情を容易に読み取る。

④ 彼らは人付き合いにより苦労している。

第1文で述べられているように，この文章のトピックは「遺伝子が人間の社会性などを決定づける」というものですので，前半部を聞いて理解していれば，答えを特定できるでしょう。実際，第5文で They found that those with lower activity of the OXT gene had more difficulties in recognizing facial expressions and were more anxious about their relationships with loved ones.「表情の読み取りに難」・「親しい人との関係に不安」とあり，OXT 遺伝子の活動レベルが低い人たちは人付き合いの上でより苦労するという知見が得られたことが述べられますので，正解は ④ です。① や ③ のように，放送文中と反対の意味の表現が用いられている選択肢は勘違いを誘いやすいので，注意しましょう。② の「知能」は放送文で全く触れられていない内容です。

語句 certain 形「ある，特定の」, gene 名「遺伝子」, determine wh- 節「…であるかを決定する」, bond with ～「～と緊密に結びつく」, be responsible for ～「～の責任を担っている，～の原因である」, oxytocin 名「オキシトシン，脳下垂体後葉ホルモン」, hormone 名「ホルモン」, link *A* with *B*「A を B と結びつける」, refer to *A* as *B*「A を B と呼ぶ，称する」, assess 動「～を査定する，判定する」, conduct 動「～を行う」, genetic 形「遺伝子の」, assessment 名「査定，判定」, have difficulty in *doing*「…するのに苦労する」, recognize 動「～を認識する」, region 名「(脳の) 部位」, associate *A* with *B*「A を B と関連づける」, cognitive 形「認知の」, processing 名「処理」

ここが **ポイント** 初めの 1 ～ 2 文で，文章全体で語られるトピックや話者の問題意識を把握しましょう。

4 正解 問1 ④ 問2 ③

スクリプト ※下線部は解答の根拠に当たる箇所です。

問1 The estimated number of uninhabited houses in Japan is continuing to rise. The supply of newly built properties keeps growing despite the declining population, while the demolition of unused homes or efforts to list them on the market is making slow progress. There were 260,000 more vacant houses in Japan October 2018 than five years earlier. The number was put at a record 8 million, accounting for 13 percent of Japan's total housing stock. 問2 Unoccupied and badly maintained houses are safety hazards, because of their potential use in crimes and the danger that they could collapse during a natural disaster. A law was passed in 2015 that gave municipal authorities the power to tear down properties that pose safety problems, but the latest data indicate that the law has not had much effect so far.

Questions:

1. Which of the following is true about uninhabited houses in Japan?

2. Why are uninhabited houses potentially dangerous?

和訳 問1 日本の空き家の推定件数は上がり続けています。人口が減少しているにもかかわらず新築物件の供給数は増え続けていますが、使われていない家の解体や、それらを市場に出そうとする努力はあまり進んでいません。2018年10月の時点で、日本国内の空き家は5年前より26万件増えていました。その数は800万件という記録に上り、日本の住宅市場の全供給量のうちの13パーセントを占めます。問2 人の住んでいない、管理状態の悪い住宅は、犯罪に使われる可能性や、自然災害の際に倒壊する危険性があるので、安全上の問題となります。2015年、安全上の問題を引きおこす物件を解体する権限を地方自治体当局に与える法案が可決されましたが、最新のデータが示すところによれば、これまでのところその法律はあまり効果を発揮していません。

質問

1. 日本の空き家に関して正しいのは、次のうちどれか。

2. 空き家が危険なものになりうるのはなぜか。

解説 問1 ① それらのほとんどは解体されてきた。

② 人々はそれらを買いたがる。

③ その数は減少している。

2 短いモノローグ 解答・解説

85

④　その数は増加している。

第 1 文 The estimated number of uninhabited houses in Japan is continuing to rise. より，正解は ④ です。① は第 2 文の内容と矛盾します。② については触れられていませんが，空き家の数が増えているという事実から考えて，人々がそれらを買いたがるとは考えられません。

問 2　①　廃棄物の不法投棄の温床になりうるから。

　　　②　解体中に火事になるかもしれないから。

　　　③　台風や地震が来ると倒壊する恐れがあるから。

　　　④　野生動物がそれらに住みつくかもしれないから。

第 5 文 Unoccupied and badly maintained houses are safety hazards, because of ... the danger that they could collapse during a natural disaster. 「人の住んでいない，管理状態の悪い住宅は，…自然災害の際に倒壊する危険性があるので，安全上の問題となります」より，正解は ③ です。ここで「台風や地震」は自然災害の具体例として挙げられています。① の「廃棄物の不法投棄」，② の「火事」，④ の「野生動物が住みつく」はどれも放送文で触れられていないので，正解とはなりません。

[語句]　estimated 形「概算の，推定の」，uninhabited 形「人の住んでいない」，property 名「不動産物件」，demolition 名「解体，破壊」，list 〜 on the market「〜を市場での取引一覧に載せる」，account for 〜「〜 （割合など） を占める」，safety hazard「安全上の問題」，collapse 動「倒壊する」，municipal authority「地方自治体当局」，tear 〜 down / tear down 〜「〜を取り壊す，解体する」，so far「これまでのところ」

ここが ポイント　音声で聞こえてこない内容が選択肢にあっても，それが具体例や，まとめになっている場合には，正解となる可能性もあります。

3 長いダイアローグ

1	正解	問1	①	問2	①	問3	③	問4	③	問5	②
		問6	②	問7	①	問8	①	問9	③	問10	②

スクリプト ※下線部は解答の根拠に当たる箇所です。

(R: Richard　J: Jackie)

R(1): Not so long ago Jackie became a Portuguese citizen. So, Jackie, what did you need to do for that?

J(1): Lots of paperwork, that's for sure. But 問1 <u>you do need to um ... live some ... live in Portugal for six years, not have a criminal record and to pass a language test.</u>

R(2): And you need to hang ... hand over some cash as well.

J(2): Yeah, it was very expensive. At least 250 euros.

R(3): But for this week's podcastsinenglish.com 問2 <u>we're looking at how foreigners can become permanent residents or citizens of the UK.</u>

J(3): Well, 問2 <u>first of all you need to take, and pass of course, the Life in the UK Test.</u> Now this is in English of course, so you do need to have the right level of English to do it. Um ...

R(4): Yes. And it's based on a book, isn't it?

J(4): Yeah, now what's ... it's a handbook, Richard. What's that called?

R(5): 問3 <u>It's called *Life in the United Kingdom: A Guide for New Residents*. And this is available online.</u>

J(5): Yeah. Well, 問3 <u>actually you can practice online as well,</u> Richard, can't you? 問4 <u>The test consists of 24 questions.</u>

R(6): Multiple choice.

J(6): Yeah, multiple choice. And 問4 <u>you need to get at least 18 right to pass.</u>

R(7): And you get 45 minutes.

J(7): Yeah, 45 minutes, so what's that? Just under two minutes for each question.

R(8): And every question is based on the book.

J(8): Yes. OK. Now Richard and I have done this test a few times and um ... well perhaps not amazingly but I failed it quite a few times and you Richard ...?

R(9): 問5 I ... I ... did three tests. I passed two and failed one.

J(9): 問6 Now if you ... if you are doing this because you seriously want to become a resident of the UK, you can just retake the test, right ... you can hand over another fifty pounds. Um ... but it's interesting because the handbook, Richard ... there are five chapters, aren't there?

R(10): Yes, um ... 問7 "The values and principles of the UK", "What is the UK?" one titled: "A long and illustrious history", history questions um ..., "A modern, thriving society", and the final one is "The UK government, the law and your role" as a citizen.

J(10): Now I think I'm right, Richard. 問7 It's the third chapter, the history questions which let us down. I mean, let's give you some examples of the kind of questions they were asking from that chapter.

R(11): "What ..." sorry, "When did the Anglo-Saxon kingdoms establish in Britain?"

J(11): I mean we've got no idea, really.

R(12): Well, they're multiple choice ... the ... 問8 the multiple choices didn't give you much chance either. They were very close together.

J(12): Yes. But that's the same with all of them. "When were the first coins minted?"

R(13): And "The population of the British Empire".

J(13): I mean, you know, the ... 問9 the thing is, I think, there can be useful questions, things that people should know about the UK: the law, how we behave, things like that.

R(14): And yes and rather ... rather than useless questions which Brits don't even know themselves.

J(14): Well, we don't know and as a result of those history ones, we failed the test to become a British citizen.

R(15): So, Jackie, do you know of any other countries that have tests like this?

J(15): 問10 I think they do something similar in Spain and France.

R(16): 問10 But luckily for you, not in Portugal.

J(16)：No, I think I would have failed that one, certainly.

和訳 （R：リチャード　J：ジャッキー）

R(1)：最近，ジャッキーはポルトガル国民になったんですね。それで，ジャッキー，そのためにどんなことをする必要があったんですか。

J(1)：提出書類がたくさんありました，それは確かです。でも，_{問1}必要なのは，その…，いくらか住んでいる…，6年間ポルトガルに住んでいることと，犯罪歴がないこと，それに言語試験に合格することです。

R(2)：また，いくらかの現金を掲げる…，納めることも必要ですね。

J(2)：はい，とても高かったですよ。最低250ユーロです。

R(3)：さて，今週の『ポッドキャストインイングリッシュドットコム』では，_{問2}どのようにしたら外国人がイギリスの永住者や国民になることができるのかを見ていきます。

J(3)：ええ，_{問2}まず「イギリスでの生活についての一般常識テスト」を受けて，そしてもちろん受からなければなりません。そして，これはもちろん英語で行われますから，受かるのにふさわしい英語力を身につけている必要がありますね。えー…

R(4)：はい。そしてこれはある本に準拠しているんですね。

J(4)：そうです。で，何という…，それは教本ですね，リチャード。題名は何ですか。

R(5)：_{問3}『イギリスでの生活：新住民のための案内』というものです。そしてこれはネット上で手に入りますよ。

J(5)：はい。で，_{問3}実際ネット上で練習もできますよね，リチャード。_{問4}試験は24問からなります。

R(6)：選択式ですね。

J(6)：はい，選択式です。そして_{問4}合格するには最低18問正解する必要があります。

R(7)：それを45分で。

J(7)：ええ，45分ですよ，え，何ですって？　1問あたり2分弱しかないですね。

R(8)：そしてすべての問題がさきほどの本に準拠していますよ。

J(8)：そうです。オーケー。実はリチャードと私はこの試験を何回か受けまして，それで，あの，たぶん驚くことではありませんが，私はかなりの回数落ちました，そしてリチャード，あなたは…？

R(9)：_{問5}私はですね，私は3回試験を受けました。2回合格で，1回不合格です。

J(9)：_{問6}それでもしあなたが，もしあなたが真剣にイギリスの居住者になりたくてこの試験を受けているとしたら，再試験を受けられますよ，はい，また50ポンド払うことにはなりますが。ああ…，でもリチャード，この教本が5章からなっているとは興味深いですね。

R(10)：はい，ええと，_{問7}「イギリスの価値観と原則」，「イギリスとは何か」があります，

「長く輝かしい歴史」と題された章もあるな，歴史の質問か，うーん…，「繁栄する現代社会」，そして最後の章が「イギリスの政治と法律とあなたの（つまり国民としての）役割」です。

J (10)：リチャード，やはり私はたぶん間違っていないと思うのですが。_{問7}第3章です，歴史の質問のせいですよ，私たちを困らせたのは。じゃあ，その章から出されているタイプの質問の例をいくつかリスナーに出題しましょうか。

R (11)：「何が…」，すみません，「いつ，アングロサクソン王国はブリテンに成立したか」。

J (11)：いや，本当にわかりません。

R (12)：まあ，この試験は選択式ですが，せ，_{問8}選択肢があっても正解の可能性が上がったわけではないんですよね。どれもとても似通っていましたから。

J (12)：そのとおりです。でもそれに関してはどの質問もすべて同じですよ。「最初のコインはいつ鋳造されたか」。

R (13)：そして，「大英帝国の人口」。

J (13)：つまり，まあ，_{問9}大事なことは有益な質問が含まれうるということだと思うんです，人々がイギリスについて知るべきことです。例えば，法律や振る舞い方などです。

R (14)：ええ，はい，そうですね，イギリス人自身でさえ知らない無駄な質問というのではなくてね。

J (14)：まあ，わかりませんけど，歴史の質問の結果，私たちはイギリス国民になるための試験に落ちたんです。

R (15)：それで，ジャッキー，このような試験を課している国を他にどこか知っていますか。

J (15)：_{問10}スペインとフランスで似たようなものを実施していると思います。

R (16)：_{問10}でも，あなたにとってはラッキーでしたね，ポルトガルにはなくて。

J (16)：はい，きっと不合格になっていたと思いますよ。

解説 この放送文には現実の会話にしばしば見られる言いよどみや言い直しなどが含まれていて，聞き取りにくいかもしれませんが，質問を先に読み，聞き取るべき内容が何であるかを把握したうえで音声を聞くようにすれば，答えを選び出すことは難しいものではないはずです。話題の転換に注意し，会話の流れに遅れずついていくようにしましょう。

問1　ポルトガルの市民権を得るために，ジャッキーは（　　）必要があった。

① 言語試験に合格する

② 250ポンドを支払う

③ 6年間ポルトガルで働く

　最初の発話でリチャードにポルトガルの国民になるのに何が必要かと聞かれたジャッキーは，you do need to ... live in Portugal for six years, not have a criminal record and to pass a language test「必要なのは…6年間ポルトガル

に住んでいることと，犯罪歴がないこと，それに言語試験に合格することです」
と答えているので，正解は ① です。② は，ジャッキーが 2 番目の発話で「最
低 250 ユーロです」答えているので，正解にはなりません。「ポンド」ではな
く「ユーロ」と言っています。③ は，上で引用したジャッキーの言葉の中に
「6 年間ポルトガルに住む必要がある」とはありますが，「6 年間ポルトガルで
働く必要がある」とは言っていないので，誤りです。

問2　イギリスで（　　）ことを希望する人は「イギリスでの生活についての一般常識テス
　　　ト」を受けなければならない。

　　　　① 国民になる　　② 留学する　　③ 働く

　　リチャードが 3 番目の発話で we're looking at how foreigners can become
permanent residents or citizens of the UK「どのようにしたら外国人がイギリ
スの永住者や国民になることができるのかを見ていきます」と言うと，それを
受けてジャッキーが「まず『イギリスでの生活についての一般常識テスト』を
受けて，そしてもちろん受からなければなりません」と言っているので，正解
は ① です。これが対話全体の主題になっています。

問3　「イギリスでの生活についての一般常識テスト」の準備の方法として，リチャードと
　　　ジャッキーは（　　）に言及している。

　　　　① 書店で教本を買うこと

　　　　② 講座を受講すること

　　　　③ ウェブサイトに行くこと

　　リチャードは 4 番目の発言で「『イギリスでの生活についての一般常識テス
ト』は，ある教本に準拠している」と言い，それに続く発話で，this is available
online「これはネット上で手に入りますよ」と言っています。またジャッキー
も 5 番目の発話で「実際ネット上で練習もできますよね」と言っているので，
正解は ③ です。

問4　試験に合格するためには，最低（　　）しなければならない。

　　　　① 24 問中 16 問正解

　　　　② 20 問中 18 問正解

　　　　③ 24 問中 18 問正解

　　ジャッキーは 5 番目の発話で The test consists of 24 questions.「試験は 24
問からなります」と言い，続いての発話で you need to get at least 18 right to
pass「合格するには最低 18 問正解する必要があります」と言っているので，正
解は ③ です。数値の情報は質問で取り上げられることが多いので，注意する
ようにしてください。

問5　リチャードは試験に（　　）合格した。

①　1回　　②　2回　　③　3回

　ジャッキーが8番目の発話で，自分たちもこの試験を受けたと言っていて，ジャッキーは何度も落ちたと告白したあと，リチャードはどうかと尋ねました。リチャードはそれに対してI ... did three tests. I passed two and failed one.「私は3回試験を受けました。2回合格で，1回不合格です」と答えています。この発言より，リチャードが合格した回数は2回ということがわかるので，正解は②です。数値を含む問題は質問の仕方によって答えが変わるので注意が必要です。

問6　試験に不合格だった人は（　　）ことができる。
　　①　50ポンドの返金を受ける
　　②　お金を払って試験をもう一度受ける
　　③　無料で再試験を受ける

　ジャッキーは9番目の発話で，if you are doing this because you seriously want to become a resident of the UK, you can just retake the test, right ... you·can hand over another fifty pounds「もしあなたが真剣にイギリスの居住者になりたくてこの試験を受けているとしたら，再試験を受けられますよ，はい，また50ポンド払うことにはなりますが」と言っているので，正解は②です。

問7　リチャードとジャッキーが最も難しいと思う章は（　　）という題だ。
　　①　「長く輝かしい歴史」
　　②　「イギリスの政治とあなたの役割」
　　③　「イギリスの価値観と原則」

　リチャードが10番目の発話で教本の章の題名を紹介しています。その中に"A long and illustrious history"「長く輝かしい歴史」が含まれており，ジャッキーはそれを受けて，It's the third chapter, the history questions which let us down.「第3章です，歴史の質問のせいですよ，私たちを困らせたのは」と言っているので，正解は①です。let ～ down は「～を落胆させる，～を失敗に終わらせる」という意味です。

問8　一部の質問は（　　）ので難しい。
　　①　選択肢が似通っている
　　②　教本に載っていない
　　③　選択式でない

　リチャードは11番目の発話で，ジャッキーが答えられない難しい質問の例を紹介したあと，the multiple choices didn't give you much chance either. They were very close together「選択肢があっても正解の可能性が上がったわ

けではないんですよね。どれもとても似通っていましたから」と言っているので，正解は ① です。

問9　ジャッキーは，試験の質問はイギリスの（　　）に焦点を当てるべきだと考えている。

① 経済と政治　　② 歴史と社会　　③ 法律と慣習

　ジャッキーの 13 番目の発話 the thing is, I think, there can be useful questions, things that people should know about the UK: the law, how we behave, things like that「大事なことは有益な質問が含まれうる（＝歴史の質問よりも適切な質問が他にある）ということだと思うんです，人々がイギリスについて知るべきことです。例えば，法律や振る舞い方などです」より，正解は ③ です。how we behave「振る舞い方」を選択肢では custom「慣習」に言い換えています。

問10　「イギリスでの生活についての一般常識テスト」のような試験は（　　）では行われていない。

① フランス　　② ポルトガル　　③ スペイン

　リチャードが 15 番目の発話で「このような試験を課している国を他にどこか知っていますか」と聞くと，ジャッキーは「スペインとフランスで似たようなものを実施していると思います」と答えます。それに対してリチャードは，少し前にポルトガル国民になったというジャッキーに向かって，冗談めかして But luckily for you, not in Portugal.「でも，あなたにとってはラッキーでしたね，ポルトガルにはなくて」と言っているので，正解は ② です。

語句　paperwork 名「書類の作成」, criminal record「犯罪歴，前科」, hand ～ over / hand over ～「～を手渡す，納める」, permanent resident「永住者」, citizen 名「国民，市民」, handbook 名「手引書，教本」, consist of ～「～からなる」, multiple choice「（多肢）選択式の；選択肢」, not amazingly「驚くことではないが，当然のことだが」, quite a few ～「かなり多くの～」, illustrious 形「輝かしい，傑出した」, thriving 形「繁栄する」, let ～ down / let down ～「～を落胆させる，失敗させる」, kingdom 名「王国」, establish 動「成立する」, empire 名「帝国」, Brit 名「イギリス人」

ここが ポイント

・質問を頭に入れてから対話を聞き，話題を追いながら順に質問の答えを選択しましょう。

・数値情報は問われやすく，また問い方がさまざまにあるので注意しましょう。

正解

(解答例)

問1	A	The student did a "Mexican Hat Dance."
	B	a Canadian student / a student from Canada
	C	The student pretended to be a bullfighter with his friend, who wore a cow costume.
問2	X	He [Philip] doesn't have the courage to sing it in front of the whole university.
	Y	He [Philip] doesn't have his magic stuff with him in Japan and he really needs some of the objects for his magic to work.
	Z	That can be a bit messy (because the stage is too small for cooking) and it probably wouldn't work really well.
問3		生徒が教師に「やっていないことで罰せられるか」と尋ねたところ，教師は「そのようなことはしない」と答えたので，生徒は安心して，宿題をやってこなかったことを教師に告白したという冗談。教師は「生徒自身がかかわっていない悪事では罰しない」というつもりで言ったが，生徒は，本来自分でやらなければならない宿題をやっていないことを指して言っていた。

~~~~~~

スクリプト　※下線部は解答の根拠に当たる箇所です。

(J: Joji　P: Philip　A: Ayaka)

J(1): Hey, Philip, have you decided what kind of presentation you are going to do for the talent show on "Culture Night" for our ESS Club next month?

P(1): Yeah, well, I have a couple of ideas ... maybe you could help me decide which is best ...

A(1): Hi, guys ... what's up? What are you talking about?

J(2): Oh, I was just asking Philip what he plans to do for the talent show ...

A(2): Ahhh, yes ... the annual talent show! That is one of my favorite events. I love to see what all the foreign students' talents are.

P(2): Oh, no, is it that big of a deal? Now, I'm getting worried because I don't think I have any real talent.

A(3): Don't worry ... it is not so formal and mainly just fun. Last year,

問1 (A) a student from Mexico did a "Mexican Hat Dance" and 問1 (B) a student from Canada sang the Canadian national anthem. In fact, I remember one year, 問1 (C) a student from Spain pretended to be a bullfighter with his friend, who wore a cow costume. It was so funny. We laughed so hard.

J (3): Ayaka's right ... don't stress out about it too much. What do you like to do?

P (3): That's the problem ... I really don't have anything in particular that I do that is performance-based.

A (4): How about singing? I heard you singing in the student lounge a while back.

P (4): You heard that! I thought I was alone!

A (5): (laughing) Yeah, well, I was outside the room. I thought you sounded really good. Do you ever sing in public?

P (5): Not really. I did sing "Ave Maria" at my cousin's wedding when I was in junior high school, but ...

J (4): Come on, Philip, sing us a few notes. I want to hear it.

A (6): Me, too! Go on ...

J (5) / A (7): (together) PLEEEEASE!!!!!

P (6): Oh, all right ... I can't believe I'm doing this ... "Aaaaaveeee Maaarrriiiiia."

A (8): Wow, you can sing! Why not sing that?

P (7): Nah, 問2 (X) I don't have the courage to sing it in front of the whole university.

J (6): Well, what were the couple of ideas you mentioned before?

P (8): Uhhh, let's see ... I thought about doing a magic trick, but 問2 (Y) the problem is I don't have my magic stuff with me here in Japan and I really need some of the objects for it to work.

A (9): Ah, that's too bad ... magic is always fun to watch and people love it. What else were you thinking about?

P (9): 問2 (Z) I thought about preparing something to eat on stage ... you know ... the process of how to make a dish, but that can be a bit messy and it probably wouldn't work really well ...

J (7): You're right. 問2 (Z) The stage is too small. Any other ideas?

P (10): Umm, I could tell a couple of jokes ... what do you think of that?

A(10): I love it! I think the audience would enjoy that!

J(8): What kind of jokes ... can you give us a sample now?

P(11): Let's see ... let me think ... OK, "... Yeah, as a student, I'm so poor that when a thief broke into my room to search for money, I woke up and searched with him." Ba-da-dum!

A(11): I don't get it. Why is that funny?

P(12): Well, because the thief was looking for money in my room to steal, I searched with him because I need money because I'm a poor student ...

J(9): Maybe a different joke would be better ...

P(13): OK, one more. It's a knock, knock joke. When I say, "Knock, knock," you both say, "Who's there?" and then later, "Blah blah who?" OK, ready?

J(10)/A(12): (together) Ready!

P(14): "Knock, knock ..."

J(11)/A(13): "Who's there?"

P(15): Abie.

J(12)/A(14): Abie who?

P(16): A, B, C, D, E, F, G ...

J(13): Hmmm, that's a little better. I think the students would get it and laugh ...

P(17): Oh! How about this one? 問3 "The student asked the teacher: Would you punish me for something I didn't do? And the teacher replied: No, of course not! The student said: Good, because I haven't done my homework."

J(14)/A(15): (both laugh loudly)

P(18): OK ... I have decided ... I will tell jokes.

A(16): Great! I can't wait!

J(15): Me, too ... I think it will be fun!

和訳 （J：ジョウジ　P：フィリップ　A：アヤカ）

J(1)：やあ, フィリップ, 来月の僕ら ESS クラブの催し「カルチャーナイト」のタレントショーで, どんな出し物をするか決めた？

P(1)：うん, まあ, 2, 3の考えはあるんだ…, どれが一番いいか決めるのを君に手伝ってもらえるかもしれないなと思って…。

A(1)：こんにちは, お二人…, どうしたの, 何の話をしているの？

96

J（2）：やあ，フィリップにタレントショーで何をする予定か聞いていたところだよ。

A（2）：ああ，はい，年に１度のタレントショーね！　私のお気に入りの催しの１つよ。留学生たち全員の才能がどんなものか見るのが大好きなの。

P（2）：おい，待ってくれ，そんな大それた話なの？　心配になってきたな，僕には大した才能は何もないと思っているから。

A（3）：心配しないで…，そんなにかしこまったものではないし，ただ楽しむことが主な目的だから。去年は $_{問1(A)}$ メキシコ出身の学生が「メキシカン・ハット・ダンス」をやって，$_{問1(B)}$ カナダ出身の学生がカナダの国歌を歌ったわ。実際，ある年，$_{問1(C)}$ スペイン出身の学生が牛の格好をした友だちと組んで闘牛士のまねをしたのを覚えている。すごくおもしろくて，大笑いしたわ。

J（3）：アヤカの言うとおりだよ…，そんなに緊張することはないさ。何をやりたいの？

P（3）：それが問題なんだ…，僕は，特に能力を発揮するようなものでやれるものは何もないし。

A（4）：歌うのはどう？　しばらく前に学生ラウンジであなたが歌っているのを耳にしたのよ。

P（4）：聞いてたんだ！　自分ひとりだと思ってたのに！

A（5）：（笑って）聞いたわ，でも，部屋の外にいたのだけど。とてもいい声をしていると思った。人前で歌うことはある？

P（5）：そんなには。中学のときにいとこの結婚式で「アヴェ・マリア」を歌ったことはあるけど…。

J（4）：なあ，フィリップ，一節歌ってみてよ。聞いてみたいんだ。

A（6）：私も！　さあ…。

J（5）/ A（7）：（一緒に）お願いしまーす!!!!!

P（6）：ああ，わかったよ…，こんなことになるなんて信じられないな…，「アーーヴェーーマーリーーア」

A（8）：まあ，うまいじゃない！　それを歌ったら？

P（7）：いやいや，$_{問2(X)}$ 学生全体の前でこれを歌う勇気はないよ。

J（6）：そうだ，さっき君が２，３考えがあるって言っていたけど，それは何？

P（8）：ああ，ええと，手品をやろうかと考えていたんだけど，$_{問2(Y)}$ 困ったことに手品の道具を日本に持って来ていなくて，それを成功させるには，その道具のいくつかが本当に必要なんだよね。

A（9）：あら，それは残念…，手品はいつも見ていて楽しいし，みんな大好きよね。他にどんなことを考えていたの？

P（9）：$_{問2(Z)}$ ステージ上で何か食べるものを用意しようと思ったんだ，ほら，料理の作り方の途中過程をね，でもちょっと散らかることもあるし，たぶん，実際うまくいかな

いと思うんだ…。

J (7)：そうだよね。_{問2(2)} <u>ステージが狭すぎるよね</u>。他に何か考えは？

P (10)：うーん，ジョークを少し言うこともできると思うけど…，それについてはどう思う？

A (10)：私はいいと思う！　見ている人も楽しんでくれると思うわ！

J (8)：どんな感じのジョーク？　何か例を今出せるかい？

P (11)：どうだろう…，待ってくれよ…，オーケー，「…ええと，学生のころね，僕はとても
貧乏で，泥棒が僕の部屋に押し入ってお金を探しているとき，僕も起きて，彼と一
緒に探したんだ」，チャンチャン！

A (11)：わからない。どうしておもしろいの？

P (12)：だから，泥棒が僕の部屋で盗むためにお金を探していたところ，僕も彼と一緒にな
って探したということだよ，僕も貧乏学生でお金が欲しいからね…

J (9)：たぶん違うジョークのほうがいいかもね。

P (13)：オーケー，じゃあもう1つね。ノックノックジョークをいくよ。僕が「ノックノッ
ク」と言ったら，君ら二人は「どなたですか」と言って，それでその後で「どちら
の○○さん？」と言ってね，わかったかい，いくよ？

J (10)／A (12)：（一緒に）いいよ！

P (14)：「ノックノック…」

J (11)／A (13)：「どなたですか」

P (15)：「エイビーだよ」

J (12)／A (14)：「どちらのエイビーさん？」

P (16)：A, B, C, D, E, F, G …

J (13)：うーん，こっちのほうが少しはいいかな。学生は理解して笑ってくれると思うよ…

P (17)：ああ！　こういうのはどうだい？　_{問3}<u>生徒が先生に尋ねたんだ。『僕がやっていな
いことで僕を罰することはあるでしょうか』と。すると先生は『もちろん，罰する
ことはないね！』と答えた。生徒は言ったんだ。『よかった，宿題をやってないんで
す』」</u>

J (14)／A (15)：（二人とも大笑い）

P (18)：オーケー…，決めた…，ジョークを話すよ。

A (16)：いいわね！　楽しみだわ！

J (15)：僕もだよ…，楽しくなりそうだね！

解説　本問はすべて記述式です。表の空所補充では，項目名やすでに入っている情報
から，入るべき要素の予測を立てます。日本語でもよいので，手早くメモを取
りましょう。

問1　以下の学生たちは，過去に，毎年恒例の ESS の催しで何を披露したか。

学生	出し物
メキシコ人の学生	A
B	この学生は自分の国の国歌を歌った。
スペイン人の学生	C

　表の中の情報はすべてアヤカの3番目の発話内にあります。答えに必要な情報が1カ所に集中しているので，音声を聞いている間にできる限り素早くメモをとることが必要です。

A …a student from Mexico …「メキシコ出身の学生が『メキシカン・ハット・ダンス』をやった」より，正解は The student did a "Mexican Hat Dance." のようになります。

B …a student … national anthem「カナダ出身の学生がカナダの国歌を歌った」より，正解は a Canadian student / a student from Canada のようになります。

C …a student from Spain …「スペイン出身の学生が牛の格好をした友だちと組んで闘牛士のまねをした」より，正解は The student pretended to be a bullfighter with his friend, who wore a cow costume. のようになります。

問2　以下の考えにはいくぶん問題がある。その問題とは何か。

考え	問題
ステージで歌を歌う	X
手品	Y
ステージで料理をする	Z

　答えの該当箇所はフィリップの7～9番目の発話にあります。解答の記述が比較的長いので，要点をつかんで素早くメモをとり，あとで清書するようにしましょう。代名詞の変換や必要語句の補充は，主語や前後の内容に合わせて，適宜行いましょう。

X …7番目の発話 I don't have the courage … より，正解は He [Philip] doesn't have the courage to sing it in front of the whole university. のようになります。

Y …8番目の発話 I don't have my magic stuff … より，正解は He [Philip] doesn't have his magic stuff with him in Japan and he really needs some of the objects for his magic to work. のようになります。

Z …フィリップは9番目の発話で I thought about preparing something to eat on stage ... とステージ上で料理を作る案を出しますが，すぐに but that can be a bit messy ... と，問題点を述べています。それを受けてジョウジも The stage is too small. と指摘しているので，この点を解答に含めることもできます。したがって，正解は That can be a bit messy (because the stage is too small for cooking) and it probably wouldn't work really well. のようになります。

問3　「宿題」についての冗談は，フィリップの17番目の発話 "The student asked the teacher: Would you punish me for something I didn't do? And the teacher replied: No, of course not! The student said: Good, because I haven't done my homework." にあります。この冗談を，落ちの意味も含めて，日本語で説明します。正解は，次のようになります。

解答例：生徒が教師に「やっていないことで罰せられるか」と尋ねたところ，教師は「そのようなことはしない」と答えたので，生徒は安心して，宿題をやってこなかったことを教師に告白したという冗談。教師は「生徒自身がかかわっていない悪事では罰しない」というつもりで言ったが，生徒は，本来自分でやらなければならない宿題をやっていないことを指して言っていた。

語句　presentation 名「発表，お披露目」，talent show「タレントショー，演芸ショー」，What's up?「どうしたの？，元気？」，annual 形「1年に1度の」，national anthem「国歌」，pretend to *do*「…するふりをする」，bullfighter 名「闘牛士」，stress out「緊張する，不安になる」，in particular「特に」，performance-based 形「能力主義の」，note 名「旋律」，have the courage to *do*「…する勇気がある」，messy 形「散らかっている」，thief 名「泥棒」，break into 〜「〜に押し入る」，punish 〜 for ...「…のことで〜を罰する」

ここが ポイント

・記述式の問題もあらかじめ問われていることを確認してから，**必要な情報をこちらから求めていくような積極的な気持ちで聞く**ようにします。
・音声を聞きながら，解答に必要な情報はできる限り**手早くメモをとります**。英語で書き取れない場合は日本語でもかまいません。

3 **正解** (解答例)	問1		「ナミがどこにいるのか」という内容があれば正解として許容する。 (They are mainly discussing) Why Nami is not answering her phone and where she is. / Where Nami is and why she has not replied to the messages Mei sent to her phone.
	問2		人物と根拠の整合性があれば，以下のどの主旨の解答でもよい。 ・I think Mei is her best friend. (This is because) Mei is so worried about where Nami is that she has been texting and calling her all weekend. She almost called the police for that reason. ・I think Axel is Nami's best friend because he knows a lot about her, such as where and how many hours she works, what her hobby is, and what her uncle looks like. ・I think Barry is her best friend. He went to the nightclub with Nami and even borrowed her phone when his was dead. ・I think Nami's best friend is Kathy. Kathy is her roommate. Though Nami is afraid of using a laundromat, she is okay with sharing a washing machine with Kathy.
	問3	A	She is off today.
		B	She is hiking. / She is going on a long hike.
		C	She has a new washing machine. / She and her roommate have just bought a new washing machine.
		D	She was [has been] kidnapped by a stranger. / A (creepy-looking) guy kidnapped her.
		E	That is her uncle.
		F	She got into a car accident. / She was [has been] in a car accident.
		G	She doesn't drive.

スクリプト

（A: Axel　M: Mei　B: Barry）

A(1): Hi, Mei!

M(1): Huh? Oh. Hi, Axel. ...

A(2): Hey, what's wrong? 問2(メイ) <u>You look worried.</u>

M(2): Oh, it's probably nothing, but ... 問1・問2(メイ) <u>I've been trying to get ahold of Nami all weekend, and I can't. It's like she's disappeared off the face of the Earth or something. I've called again and again, but no answer.</u>

A(3): Did you leave a message?

M(3): Of course! Like, so many times! And I've texted her and texted her, but it looks like she hasn't even read the messages. It's so not like her!

A(4): Weird. 問2(アクセル) <u>Did you try calling the fitness club? I bet she's working there today. I know that she's been taking a lot more hours lately.</u>

M(4): I just called. 問3(A) <u>She's off today.</u>

A(5): Oh. Well, 問2(アクセル)・問3(B) <u>maybe she's on one of those long hikes she likes to take, and she just forgot to take her phone. She loves her hiking!</u>

M(5): Well, 問2(キャシー) <u>I just called her roommate, Kathy.</u> She says that Nami's hiking boots are still in the closet. So, that's not it. And the thing is, Nami doesn't go anywhere without her phone. It's like a part of her body.

A(6): Really? Well, Kathy must know where she is. I mean, she is her roommate.

M(6): You won't believe this. When I called, Kathy had just gotten back from a two-week vacation in Hawaii. So she has no idea where Nami is.

A(7): Hawaii ... sounds nice. ... Oh, I know! I bet she's at her parents' place! 問2(キャシー) <u>She doesn't have a washing machine, and you know how she doesn't like laundromats. Germs. ...</u>

M(7): Laundromats? ... Oh! You mean the place with coin-operated washing machines? Yes, I thought the same thing. But 問2(キャシー)・

問3(C) when I brought up that theory with Kathy, she told me that

they just bought a new washing machine. So, that can't be it. And

you know what?

A(8): What?

M(8): 問3(D) I was starting to think about how sometimes I see a creepy-

looking guy just sitting in his car outside her place. What if that

guy's a stalker? What if he finally went ahead and kidnapped her

or something?

A(9): Wait a minute. Does he have an eye patch?

M(9): Yes.

A(10): And a scar on his left cheek?

M(10): Yes!

A(11): And a long beard and a giant tattoo on his arm.

M(11): Yes, yes!

A(12): 問2(アクセル)・問3(E) That's her uncle!

M(12): What!?

A(13): 問2(アクセル) Yeah, they're really close. She and her uncle often go

fishing together. He was probably just waiting to pick her up.

M(13): He looks so scary!

A(14): He's actually a super nice guy. You should meet him! Hmmm.

問3(F) I hope she didn't get into a car accident or something.

M(14): Well, fortunately, 問3(G) that's not something we have to worry

about. ... She doesn't drive!

A(15): Yeah, but maybe she was hit by a bus or something!

M(15): Oh, that's true. Maybe she's been in an accident. That's got to be it!

A(16): Should we call the hospitals?

M(16): All the hospitals? And what about her parents? Do you know their

number?

A(17): Oh, my God, what are we going to do?

B(1): Hey guys!

A(18)/M(17): Aaah!

M(18): Barry! You scared the heck out of me!

A(19): Yeah, don't sneak up on us like that!

B(2): Sorry, guys. Say, have you seen Nami?

M(19): No. In fact, 問2(メイ) I've been trying to contact her all weekend!

B(3): Oh. Cuz I need to return her phone to her.

A(20)/M(20): What!?

B(4): Well, 問2(バリー) we were at a nightclub Friday night. And my phone went dead, so I borrowed her phone to make a call. When I tried to give it back to her, I couldn't find her. I guess she went home having forgotten that I had borrowed it.

M(21): 問2(メイ) I've been texting and calling all weekend! Why didn't you answer it?

B(5): Oh, I didn't notice the phone was ringing ... sorry.

M(22): Huh? Okay, whatever. Anyway, 問2(メイ) now I'm calling the police.

A(21): Hey, wait a minute. Isn't that her?

B(6): Oh, yeah! Hey, Nami! Over here!

A(22): Well, she looks as happy to see us as we are to see her.

M(23): Or she's just happy to see her phone!

和訳 (A：アクセル　M：メイ　B：バリー)

A(1)：やあ，メイ！

M(1)：え？　あ，こんにちは，アクセル。…

A(2)：ねえ，どうしたの？　問2(メイ) 心配そうな顔してるけど。

M(2)：うん，たぶん，大したことないと思うんだけど…，問1・問2(メイ) 週末ずっとナミに連絡を取ろうとしているんだけど，取れないの。地上から消えてしまったとか，なんかそんな感じなのよ。何度も電話しているけど，出てくれないし。

A(3)：留守電は残した？

M(3)：もちろん！　なんというか，すごくたくさん！　それにメッセージも何度も送ったわ，でもそれすら読んでないみたいで。彼女はそんなことしないのに！

A(4)：妙だね。問2(アクセル) フィットネスクラブには電話してみた？　きっと今日そこで働いているんだよ。最近はずっと多くの時間をとられているみたいだから。

M(4)：電話したところ。問3(A) 今日は休みだって。

A(5)：そうか。じゃあ，問2(アクセル)・問3(B) ひょっとすると，彼女が好きな長距離ハイキングにまた出かけていて，スマホを持って行くのを忘れてしまっただけかもね。彼女，本当にハイキングが好きだものな！

M(5)：それで，問2(キャシー) 彼女のルームメイトのキャシーにさっき電話をしたの。彼女が言うには，ナミの登山靴は今もクローゼットに入っているって。だから，その線はないわ。それにだいたいナミはスマホを持たずにどこにも出かけないわ。彼女の体の一部みたいなものなんだから。

104

A(6)：本当？　じゃあ，きっとキャシーはナミがどこにいるか知っているよ。だって，ルームメートなんだから。

M(6)：これは信じてもらえないと思うけど，私が電話したとき，キャシーはハワイでの2週間の休暇から戻ったところだったの。だから彼女はナミがどこにいるか知らないのよ。

A(7)：ハワイか…いいな。…あ，そうだ！　きっとご両親の所に行っているんだよ！　_{問2(キャシー)}彼女は洗濯機を持ってないし，ロードロマットは好きじゃないって知ってるだろう。ばい菌が，みたいなこと言って…

M(7)：ロードロマット？　…ああ！　コインランドリーのこと？　そう，私も同じことを考えた。でも_{問2(キャシー)・問3(C)}その説をキャシーに言ってみたら，彼女たちは新しい洗濯機を買ったばかりだと教えてくれた。だから，それもあり得ない。それと，あのね。

A(8)：何？

M(8)：_{問3(D)}彼女の住んでる場所の外に車が止まっていて，そこに気味の悪い感じの男性が乗っているのをときどき見かけることがあるなあって，それについて考え始めていたの。その男性がストーカーだったらどうしよう？　ついに事を進めて，彼女を誘拐か何かしてるなんてことがあったらどうする？

A(9)：ちょっと待ってくれ。その男性，眼帯をしていない？

M(9)：してるわ。

A(10)：それに左の頬に傷跡がある？

M(10)：ある！

A(11)：そして長いあごひげと腕に大きなタトゥーが入ってる。

M(11)：そう，そう！

A(12)：_{問2(アクセル)，問3(E)}それ，彼女のおじさんだよ！

M(12)：何ですって⁉

A(13)：_{問2(アクセル)}うん，二人はとても仲がいいんだ。彼女とおじさんはよく一緒に釣りに行っているよ。たぶん，おじさんはナミを迎えにいくために待っていただけだよ。

M(13)：外見がとても怖そうなのよ！

A(14)：実際はすごくいい人だよ。彼に会ったほうがいいよ！　うーん。_{問3(F)}自動車事故とかにあっていなければいいけどね。

M(14)：まあ，ありがたいことに，_{問3(G)}それは心配する必要がないわ。…彼女は車の運転をしないから！

A(15)：そうだね，でもひょっとしたらバスか何かにはねられたかもしれないじゃない！

M(15)：ああ，それはそうね。もしかしたら，事故にあっているのかも。きっとそうよ！

A(16)：病院に電話したほうがいいかな？

M (16)：病院全部ってこと？　そうしたらナミのご両親はどう？　電話番号は知ってる？

A (17)：なんてことだ，どうしよう。

B (1)：やあ，お二人！

A (18) / M (17)：わああ！

M (18)：バリー！　びっくりさせないでよ！

A (19)：そうだよ，そんなふうに忍び寄るなって！

B (2)：ごめん，ごめん。ねえ，ナミを見た？

M (19)：見てないの。実は _{問2 (メイ)} 週末ずっと彼女に連絡をとろうとしていたのよ！

B (3)：ああ。彼女にスマホを返す必要があってさ。

A (20) / M (20)：ええ!?

B (4)：いや，_{問2 (バリー)} 僕らは金曜の夜にナイトクラブにいたんだ。それで僕のスマホのバッテリーが切れたんで電話をするのに彼女のを借りたのね。それを返そうとしたら，彼女が見つからなくなっちゃって。たぶん，僕が借りたのを忘れて帰ってしまったんだね。

M (21)：_{問2 (メイ)} 週末ずっとメッセージを送って，電話をかけてたのよ！　どうして出てくれなかったの？

B (5)：ああ，電話が鳴っていたのに気づかなかった…ごめん。

M (22)：何よ。わかった，まあいいわ。とにかく，_{問2 (メイ)} さあ警察に電話をしてみましょう。

A (21)：おい，ちょっと待ってくれ。あれ，ナミじゃない？

B (6)：ああ，そうだ！　やあ，ナミ！　こっちだよ！

A (22)：やれやれ，僕らが彼女に会えてうれしいのと同じくらい，彼女も僕らを見てうれしそうだね。

M (23)：というか，彼女はただスマホが見つかってうれしいのよ！

解説　本問は書き取る内容が多く，素早くメモをとる技術も必要です。問いから「話題」「ナミの親友」「仮説と却下の理由」という聞き取るべき情報を把握し，「なんらかの理由でナミという人物がいなくなり，その理由を彼女の友人たちが話している」ことまで予測できるとよいでしょう。また，記述問題の場合，正解が1つに決まるとは限りません。問いの主旨を理解し，メモを元に自分なりに根拠を持った答えを作りましょう。

問1　彼らの会話の主題は何か。

　メイの2番目の発話とその後のやり取りからわかるように，話者はナミの居場所がわからず，なぜ電話をしてもメッセージを残してもナミが連絡をしてこないのかについて話し合っているので，会話の主題もこれをまとめたものになります。したがって，正解は（They are mainly discussing）Why Nami is not answering her phone and where she is. / Where Nami is and why she has not replied to the messages Mei sent to her phone. のようになります。

問 2　あなたは, ナミの一番の親友はどの人物だと思うか。会話から細部を聞き取り, それ
を用いてあなたの意見の根拠を書きなさい。

　この問いは, ナミの一番の親友が誰であるかを挙げ, その根拠を会話から抜
き出して記述する問題になっています。会話の中では誰がナミの一番の親友で
あるか明示されているわけではありません。したがって, 話者のメイ, アクセ
ル, バリー, そして会話の中で登場するキャシーの計 4 人が, ナミの親友であ
る可能性があります。誰を選んでもかまいませんが, その人物がナミの親友で
ある根拠を, 会話から抜き出してまとめなければなりません。

メイ………会話全般（特に, 2 番目, 19 番目, 21 番目の発話）から, 週末の間
ナミにずっと連絡をとろうとするなど, ナミの居場所を非常に心配
していることがわかります。22 番目の発話では警察にまで電話をか
けようとするほど心配しています。このことからメイがナミの一番
の親友であると考えることができます。したがって, 正解は I think
Mei is her best friend. (This is because) Mei is so worried about
where Nami is that she has been texting and calling her all
weekend. She almost called the police for that reason. のように
なります。

アクセル…4 番目の発話から, ナミの最近のアルバイトの状況などを知ってい
ます。また, 彼女の趣味やおじさんと仲がいいことなど, ナミのプ
ライベートについて詳しいと言えます（5 番目, 13 番目の発話な
ど）。このことからアクセルがナミの一番の親友であると考えるこ
とができます。したがって, 正解は I think Axel is Nami's best
friend because he knows a lot about her, such as where and how
many hours she works, what her hobby is, and what her uncle
looks like. のようになります。

バリー……遅れて登場したバリーは, 4 番目の発話からわかるように, ナミと
一緒にナイトクラブに行って, そこで彼女からスマートフォンまで
借りています。このことからバリーがナミの一番の親友であると考
えることができます。したがって, 正解は I think Barry is her best
friend. He went to the nightclub with Nami and even borrowed
her phone when his was dead. のようになります。

キャシー…会話の途中で話題に上ったキャシーは, メイの 5 番目の発話からわ
かるように, ナミのルームメートです。ナミは, アクセルの 7 番目
の発話からわかるように, 洗濯機を持っておらず, コインランドリ

ーも菌などを気にして使うのを嫌がっていたとのことですが，メイ
の7番目の発話によれば，ナミとキャシーは最近新しい洗濯機を購
入したということです。このことからナミはキャシーと洗濯機を共
有することは問題がないと考えていることになり，キャシーがナミ
の一番の親友であると考えることができます。したがって，正解は
I think Nami's best friend is Kathy. Kathy is her roommate.
Though Nami is afraid of using a laundromat, she is okay with
sharing a washing machine with Kathy. のようになります。

問3 ナミがいなくなったことを説明するのに話者たちが用いている仮説はどのようなも
のか。それらの仮説はなぜ却下されるのか。下の表の空所を埋めなさい。

	仮説	却下された理由
1	彼女は仕事をしている。	A
2	B	彼女の登山靴がクローゼットに今もある。
3	洗濯するために両親の家に行っている。	C
4	D	E
5	F	G

　ナミがどこにいるかについて，話者たちはいくつかの仮説を立てていますが，会話の中でそれらが次々と却下されていきます。この問いでは，それぞれの仮説と却下された理由について，表の空所を埋める形で答えることになります。表に書かれている情報をある程度頭に入れて，会話の展開を予測しながら聞くことが重要です。

A … 「ナミが仕事に行っている」という仮説は，メイの4番目の発話「今日は休み」で却下されています。したがって正解は She is off today. となります。

B … 「登山靴がクローゼットに今もある」という理由で却下された仮説は，アクセルの5番目の発話 maybe she's on one of those long hikes ... にあるとおり，「ナミがハイキングに行っている」というものです。したがって正解は She is hiking. / She is going on a long hike. のようになります。

C … 「洗濯するために両親の家に行っている」という仮説は，メイの7番目の発話 when I brought up that theory with Kathy, she told me that they just bought a new washing machine で否定されています。この that theory は洗濯のため両親の家に行っているという説を指します。したがって正解は She has a new washing machine. / She and her roommate have just bought a new washing machine. のようになります。

D … 「洗濯」の仮説が却下されたあと，メイは 8 番目の発話で，ナミの住居の前に怪しげな男性がいるのを見かけたという話をし，What if he finally went ahead and kidnapped her or something? と言って，不安がっています。したがって正解は She was [has been] kidnapped by a stranger. / A (creepy-looking) guy kidnapped her. のようになります。

E … 「見知らぬ人にストーカー被害にあい，誘拐された」という仮説は，アクセルが 12 番目の発話で，「（メイが怪しいという）その人はナミのおじさんだ」と言って否定しています。したがって正解は That is her uncle. となります。

F … 「誘拐」説が却下されたあと，アクセルは 14 番目の発話で I hope she didn't get into a car accident or something. と言って，「ナミが自動車事故にあったのではないか」と心配しています。したがって正解は She got into a car accident. / She was [has been] in a car accident. のようになります。

G … 自動車事故にあったのではないかと心配するアクセルにメイは，14 番目の発話で，「彼女は運転しないからそれは心配しなくていい」と言っています。したがって正解は She doesn't drive. となります。

[語 句] get ahold of 〜「〜に連絡を取る」，text 動「〜に携帯電話でメッセージを送る」，bet that *SV*「…と断言する」，laundromat 名「ローンドロマット（商標），コインランドリー」，creepy-looking 形「ぞっとするような，見た目が気味の悪い」，stalker 名「ストーカー」，kidnap 動「〜を誘拐する」，eye patch「眼帯」，scar 名「傷跡」，beard 名「あごひげ」，tattoo 名「タトゥー，入れ墨」，scary 形「恐ろしい，気味の悪い」，sneak up「忍び寄る」

ここが ポイント

・問いの内容を頭に入れ，**聞き取るべき情報を，こちらからつかみ取りにいくような気持ちで聞きましょう。**
・聞きながら必要な情報を素早くメモし，**メモをもとに答えを書き上げるところまで練習するようにしましょう。**

4 長いモノローグ

スクリプト ※下線部は解答の根拠に当たる箇所です。

[1]　I'm sure at some point you've all thought about what kind of job you want after graduation. But have you actually thought about how companies select their employees? You probably think that having the necessary skills and qualifications will be the key to your success. And you will be correct in thinking these two things will be very important. However, in addition to skills and qualifications, knowing about a company's recruitment procedure will also be crucial to improve your chances of success. Therefore, you need to be aware that a lot of major companies have started to use technology when deciding who they hire. 問1<u>They do this both to save time and because they think that using certain technologies can be an effective way of finding the candidates who will best meet their needs.</u> So today, I'll introduce three technologies that many multinational companies have adopted. I'll then move on to explain briefly one of the concerns that has arisen as a result of the spread of the use of these technologies.

[2]　One very common approach is to use special computer programs to check résumés. Companies use them to scan the résumés for keywords that match the potential employees' criteria. If a résumé does not contain these keywords, it will be discarded. Victoria McLean, founder of a career consultancy company, estimates that these computer programs reject 75% of résumés before a human even sees them. This can save companies a huge amount of time. Let's imagine that each résumé a company receives takes about five minutes to be reviewed by a member of a company's human resources department. That might be okay if the company only gets a hundred responses to a job ad. But what if a company receives tens or even hundreds of thousands of applications? For example, 問2<u>in 2016 Goldman Sachs, a multinational investment bank, received a quarter of a million job applications.</u> If humans had reviewed all these résumés it would have

110

taken hundreds of hours.

[3]   Another way that technological advances have modified the traditional recruitment procedure is through the use of video interview services.   Rather than talking to a person, in these interviews, candidates' responses to questions are recorded using the camera on their computer or mobile phone.   These recorded responses are then analyzed by an AI program.   Surprisingly, 問3 not only the content of the applicants' answers, but also less obvious aspects are evaluated such as minor changes in their sitting position, facial expression, and tone of voice.

[4]   Lastly and perhaps most interestingly, there's the use of computer games.   Advocates of this technique such as IBM and Marriott Hotels argue that games are a very efficient way to learn about an applicant's skills and traits.   One such game is called "Wasabi Waiter."   In this game, the applicant plays the role of the server in a sushi restaurant and has to decide what kind of food a customer wants based on their facial expressions.   The developers of this game claim that it allows companies to know how quickly and accurately applicants can react to the expressions.   More importantly, 問4 they claim that as the applicants become more involved in the game, they are more likely to show their true character.   For example, the developers claim that it can show how a person reacts to a task when it becomes more challenging.

[5]   Okay, let me finish by highlighting the concern that the use of technology in recruitment can discriminate against certain types of candidates.   Some argue that using AI to screen candidates can reduce the diversity of the people who are recruited.   This is because the technology has been trained to make its decision based on data collected from successful employees who currently work for the company.   As a result, 問5 candidates who are selected tend to possess similar characteristics to existing employees.

[6]   Another problem is that using computer games in the selection process may discriminate against older people who may not be so comfortable with them.   However, supporters of the use of technology in recruitment would probably argue that there has always been bias in the recruitment process and that it is easier to correct this bias in computers than in humans.   Clearly, this is a complex issue which is very much

related to the broader question of how much humans should hand over decision-making to technology. This is something that we will come back to again later in the course.

(732 words)

和 訳　[1]　皆さんは誰もが，どこかの時点で，卒業後どのような種類の仕事につきたいかについて考えたことがきっとあると思います。しかし，実際，企業がどのようにして従業員を選考しているか考えたことがありますか。おそらく，必要な技能と資格を持っていることが皆さんの成功のカギになると思っていることでしょう。そしてこの2つが非常に重要なものであると考えている点は間違いではないでしょう。しかし，技能と資格に加えて，企業の人材採用手順について知っていることも，成功の可能性を高めるには非常に重要なものとなるでしょう。したがって皆さんは，採用する人物を決める際に多くの大手企業がテクノロジーを利用し始めていることを認識する必要があります。問1企業がそうしているのは，時間を節約するためでもあり，ある種のテクノロジーを利用することが，彼らの求めているものに最もふさわしい志望者を見つけ出すのに有効な方法になりうると彼らが考えているからでもあります。そこで今日は，多くの多国籍企業が取り入れている3つのテクノロジーについて紹介します。その後続けて，こうしたテクノロジーの利用が広まった結果生じた懸念の1つを簡単に説明します。

[2]　よく見られる方法の1つは，履歴書を細かく調べるために特別なコンピュータープログラムを使用することです。企業は，従業員になる可能性のある人物を判断するための基準に合致するキーワードを，履歴書の中で探して調べるためにこれらを利用します。履歴書にこうしたキーワードが含まれていなければ，それは落とされることになります。職業コンサルタント会社を創設したビクトリア・マクリーン氏は，これらのコンピュータープログラムによって，人間が見てもいない段階で，75パーセントの履歴書がはじかれると推定しています。これによって企業は莫大な時間を節約することができます。企業が受け取った1通の履歴書を人事部の人が見るのに約5分かかると考えてみてください。その企業の求人広告に対して応募が100件しかないのであれば問題はないのかもしれません。しかし，1つの企業が何万，あるいは何十万もの志望者を受け付けることになったらどうでしょう。例えば，問22016年，多国籍の投資銀行であるゴールドマンサックスは25万人の入社志望者を受け付けました。もし人間がこれらすべての履歴書を吟味したとしたら，何百時間も要したことでしょう。

[3]　テクノロジーの発達が従来の人材採用手順を変えてきた別の方法は，ビデオ面接サービスの利用によるものです。これらの面接では，志望者と話をするのではなく，コンピューターや携帯電話に取り付けられたカメラを使って，質問に対する志望者の応答が記録されます。そして記録されたこれらの応答をAIプログラムが分析するのです。意外なことに，問3志望者の返答内容だけでなく，座った姿勢や表情や声の調子の微妙な変化など，それ程明瞭ではない面も評価されます。

[4]　最後に，そしておそらく最も興味深いものになりますが，コンピューターゲームの利用

をとりあげます。IBMやマリオットホテルなど，この技術の支持者は，ゲームは志望者の技能や特質について知るのに非常に有効な方法であると主張します。この種のゲームの1つに「ワサビウエイター」と呼ばれるものがあります。このゲームでは，志望者が寿司店の板前役になり，客の表情からその客が望んでいるネタの種類を決めなければなりません。ゲームの開発者は，このゲームによって企業は，志望者が相手の表情にいかに速く正確に反応できるかを知ることができると主張します。さらに重要なことに，_{問4}開発者は，志望者がゲームにのめりこんでいくにつれ，彼らの本当の性格が表に出てくる可能性が高くなると言います。例えば，開発者の主張によれば，このゲームは，課題の難易度が上がっていくときに人はどのようにそれに対処するかを示すことができるというのです。

[5] さてそれでは，人材採用におけるテクノロジーの利用が，ある種の志望者への差別につながりうるという懸念を強調して終わりにしたいと思います。志望者を選別するのにAIを利用すると，採用される人の多様性が損なわれることがあると主張する人がいます。というのも，テクノロジーは，現在その企業で働いている従業員の成功例から集めたデータに基づいて決定を下すよう設計されているからです。その結果，_{問5}選ばれる志望者は，今いる従業員と似たような特性を持つ傾向にあるわけです。

[6] もう1つの問題は，選考過程でコンピューターゲームを使うことは，ゲームにそれ程自信がないかもしれない年長の人を差別しかねないということです。しかし，人材採用にテクノロジーを利用することを支持する人たちはおそらく次のように主張するでしょう。人材採用過程での偏りはこれまでも常にあったし，人間が持つ偏りよりもコンピューターにおける偏りを正すほうが簡単であると。明らかにこれは，人間は意志決定をどの程度テクノロジーに譲り渡すべきなのかという，もっと大きな問題に密接に関係した複雑な問題なのです。このことはこの講座の後半で再び扱う予定です。

解説 実際の講義を聞くように，論理展開を追い，メモを取りながら聞くことを心がけてください。この講義では，「企業の人材採用過程におけるテクノロジーの利用」という主題が導入されたあと，「履歴書をチェックするコンピュータープログラム」，「ビデオ面接サービス」，「コンピューターゲームの利用」という3つの方法が説明され，最後にこれらの方法の懸念される点を挙げて終わります。講義の最初の方で，three technologies と one of the concerns を紹介すると説明しているので，概要はつかみやすいでしょう。問題を解くにあたっては質問を先に読み，聞き取るべき情報が何であるかを頭に入れておくようにしてください。選択肢の違いを素早く理解するだけの読み取り能力も必要です。

問1 人材採用過程においてテクノロジーを利用することが増えている理由として挙げられているのは次のうちのどれか。

① 志望者の時間を節約するため　　② 志望者の技能を伸ばすため

③ より適した志望者を雇用するため　　④ 志望者の数を減らすため

第1段落第7文の using certain technologies can be an effective way of finding the candidates who will best meet their needs「ある種のテクノロジーを利用することが，彼らの求めているものに最もふさわしい志望者を見つけ出すのに有効な方法になりうる」より，正解は ③ です。① は，同文に to save time とありますが，これは企業側の時間を節約するという意味なので正解とはなりません。② と ④ に関することは講義の中で話されていません。

問2　講義によると，ある多国籍投資銀行が 2016 年に受け付けた入社志望者の数は何人か。

　　① 10万人　　② 25万人　　③ 75万人　　④ 100万人

第2段落最後から2文目の in 2016 Goldman Sachs, a multinational investment bank, received a quarter of a million job applications「2016 年，多国籍の投資銀行であるゴールドマンサックスは 25 万人の入社志望者を受け付けました」より，正解は ② です。a quarter of a million「100 万の 4 分の 1 ＝ 25 万」を瞬時に理解する必要があります。数値は狙われやすいので，特に注意してください。

問3　講義によると，ビデオ面接の間 AI は何をするのか。

　　① 最も関連性の高いキーワードを志望者の履歴書の中から見つけ出す。

　　② 志望者がコンピューターに自分の応答を記録することを可能にする。

　　③ 志望者の非言語的コミュニケーションの要素を評価する。

　　④ 企業が応答内容に基づいて質問を修正することを可能にする。

第3段落最終文 not only the content of the applicants' answers, but also less obvious aspects are evaluated such as minor changes in their sitting position, facial expression, and tone of voice「志望者の返答内容だけでなく，座った姿勢や表情や声の調子の微妙な変化など，それ程明瞭ではない面も評価されます」より，正解は ③ です。言葉による情報伝達を verbal communication，言葉を用いず，身振りや表情，声などによって行われる情報伝達を non-verbal communication と言いますが，この箇所の「座った姿勢や表情や声の調子の微妙な変化」が non-verbal communication に当たります。このように同じ内容が別の表現で言い換えられた選択肢にも注意が必要です。① は，第2段落第2文で説明されている「履歴書をチェックする特別なコンピュータープログラム」の内容です。② と ④ に関することは講義の中で話されていません。

問4　コンピューターゲームが志望者の選考に役立つ道具になりうると企業が考える主な理由は次のうちのどれか。

　　① 志望者はゲームの役割演技を楽しむ。

　　② 志望者はゲームでより自然に振る舞う。

　　③ 志望者はゲームで表情を変える。

④　志望者はゲームでコンピューターの技能を示す。

　第4段落最後から2文目の as the applicants become more involved in the game, they are more likely to show their true character「志望者がゲームにのめりこんでいくにつれ，彼らの本当の性格が表に出てくる可能性が高くなる」より，正解は ② です。② にある behave naturally とは，「気取ることなく，自分らしく振る舞う」という意味なので，show their true character と同義と言えます。① は，第4段落第4文に plays the role「（板前の）役割を演ずる」という表現は出てきますが，それを楽しむことはゲームの主目的ではないので，不適です。③ も，同じく第4文の「表情に基づいて寿司のネタを判断する」という話の中で「表情」に触れていますが，表情を変えることがゲームの主目的ではないので，不適です。④ は，第4段落第2文に games are a very efficient way to learn about an applicant's skills and traits とありますが，ここでの skills は computer skills に限った話ではないので，これも講義の内容に一致しているとはいえません。

問5　講義によると，人材採用において AI を使うと，どうして職場の多様性を損ねることがあるのか。

　　① 非現実的な期待に基づいて志望者を評価することによって
　　② 意思決定過程において人間の考えが取り除かれることによって
　　③ 志望者の選考過程がより主観的になることによって
　　④ 現在の従業員と似た特質を持つ志望者を選ぶことによって

　第5段落最終文の candidates who are selected tend to possess similar characteristics to existing employees「選ばれる志望者は，今いる従業員と似たような特性を持つ傾向にある」より，正解は ④ です。② に似た表現が最終段落第3文にありますが，AI の利用が職場の多様性を損なう理由ではありません。① と ③ はいずれも講義の中で触れられていない内容です。

[語句] qualification 名「資格」，recruitment 名「人材採用」，procedure 名「手続き，手順」，effective 形「効果的な」，candidate 名「志望者，候補者」，multinational 形「多国籍の」，adopt 動「～を取り入れる」，résumé 名「履歴書」，scan 動「～を細かく調べる」，criteria < criterion 名「基準」，discard 動「～を捨てる，却下する」，consultancy 名「コンサルタント業」，estimate that SV「…と推定する」，review 動「～を吟味する」，human resources department「人事部」，application 名「志願，応募」，investment 名「投資」，a quarter of ～「～の4分の1」，modify 動「～を修正する」，analyze 動「～を分析する」，content 名「内容」，applicant 名「志望者，応募者」，evaluate 動「～を評価する」，advocate 名「提唱者」，efficient 形「有効な，能率的な」，trait 名「特質」，highlight 動「～を強調する」，discriminate against ～「～を差別する」，screen

動「〜を選別する」, diversity 名「多様性」, recruit 動「(人材) を採用する」, characteristic 名「特性」

ここが ポイント

・講義の最初で主題と概要をつかんで展開を予測します。実際の講義を聞くように, 論理を追い, メモをとりながら聞くようにしましょう。
・質問を先に読み, 聞き取るべき情報に集中できるようにしましょう。
・放送文と別の語句が使われた「言い換え表現」の選択肢に注意しましょう。

2 正解

| 問1 | ④ | 問2 | ④ | 問3 | ② | 問4 | ① | 問5 | ① |
| 問6 | ② | 問7 | ① | 問8 | ③ | 問9 | ③ | 問10 | ② |

スクリプト ※下線部は解答の根拠に当たる箇所です。

[1]　The Wright Brothers made the first human-powered flight in 1903, on the beaches of Kitty Hawk, North Carolina, but for most of the past 100 years, a city at the other end of the United States has been more closely associated with "flight." That's because 問1in 1916, Pacific Aero Products Company opened in Seattle — but just a year later, the name was changed to Boeing Airplane Company, and for the rest of the century, Boeing was the biggest name in aircraft manufacturing.

[2]　But William Boeing wasn't the first person in Seattle to reach for the sky. 問2That was Lyman Cornelius Smith, who had made his fortune manufacturing typewriters. In 1914, he built Smith Tower, the tallest building in the entire western United States.

[3]　Today, Smith Tower is made to seem small by the buildings to the north of it in downtown Seattle, but that doesn't mean there's no longer any reason to go up to the observation deck on the 35th floor. There are still good views: westward across Puget Sound to the Olympic Peninsula, southward to 4,392-meter high Mount Rainier, eastward to the Cascade Range and northward into a forest of newer, taller buildings. 問6It's a great place to relax with your favorite drink (there's a bar and café up there) and watch the sun sink below the horizon.

[4]　問3Smith Tower remained the tallest structure on the West Coast for

nearly 50 years, but then came the Space Needle, which is about 25 percent taller. 問4 Built for the 1962 World's Fair in less than one year (Smith Tower took three years to build), it's still the most famous structure in the city for its unique shape: a flying saucer set on a high, curved frame.

[5] Ride one of the elevators up to the observation floor, at 160 meters, and take in the views. Everything you can see from Smith Tower can be seen a little better from the Space Needle, a result of the fact that there's nothing remotely as tall anywhere near it. 問5 Jets from across North America and Asia fly past on their approach to Seattle-Tacoma International Airport, and you can even watch seaplanes taking off and landing on Lake Union, to the east.

[6] 問6 One floor down from the regular observation floor there's a fashionable new wine bar which revolves, doing a complete circuit every 47 minutes. Most of that lower level features a glass floor, so if you're afraid of heights it might be better to avoid a visit.

[7] 問7 In 1985, the city took another big step closer to the heavens with the opening of the Columbia Center, some 284 meters tall. Most of the building consists of private offices, but anybody can go up to the Starbucks on the 40th floor, and for an admission fee, you can ride to the Sky View Observatory on the 73rd floor. 問6 Here, too, food and drinks (both alcoholic and nonalcoholic) are available. The atmosphere can't compare to that at the Smith Tower, but the views are better. You can even look down at the Smith Tower, which seems tiny from this position.

[8] A slightly taller skyscraper was proposed in the early 2010s, but the necessary permits still haven't been granted and perhaps never will be. In the near future at least, the Columbia Center looks likely to keep its crown as the city's tallest building. But that doesn't mean that you can't get an even better view of Seattle, and your best option comes in the form of something that William Boeing pioneered: seaplanes.

[9] 問8 Many of Boeing's early planes were seaplanes, equipped with floats instead of wheels so that they could take off from any lake or slow-moving river, and his very first, the B&W seaplane, was assembled in a building at the edge of Lake Union. Today, that same Lake Union serves as the "runway" for Kenmore Air flights. Some of these flights transport passengers as far away as Vancouver and Victoria, British Columbia, but

many just take tourists up on a sightseeing loop around the city of Seattle.

[10]　For anybody used to traveling on Boeing and Airbus airliners, a seaplane flight comes full of surprises. 問9The flight crew consists solely of the pilot. There's no security check, no boarding pass and no meal service. For in-flight entertainment, 問9you and the other nine passengers just look out the windows while the narration through your headphones tells you what you're seeing. 問10All in all, if you're in the market for somewhere to visit that has a lot to see, you might just find that Seattle is the right place for you!

(763 words)

和訳 [1]　1903年，ノースカロライナ州キティホークの浜辺でライト兄弟が初の人力飛行を行いましたが，過去100年間の大半の期間は，アメリカの反対側に位置するある都市が「飛行」とより密接に関係してきました。というのも，問11916年にパシフィック・エアロ・プロダクツ・カンパニーがシアトルで創業したからです。ただし，たった1年後にその名前はボーイング航空機株式会社に変更され，その後20世紀末まで，ボーイング社は航空機の製造において最も有名でした。

[2]　しかし，ウィリアム・ボーイングはシアトルで空を目指した最初の人物ではありませんでした。問2それはライマン・コーネリアス・スミスで，彼はタイプライターの製造で財産を築いていました。1914年に彼はスミスタワーを建設し，それはアメリカ西部全体の中で最も高いビルとなりました。

[3]　現在，シアトルの中心部では，スミスタワーの北側に建設されたビル群によってスミスタワーは小さく見えてしまっていますが，それは35階の展望デッキに上がる理由がもはやなくなったことを意味しません。そこにはいまもすばらしい眺望があるのです。西側にはピュージェット湾があり，その先にはオリンピック半島，南側は高さ4,392メートルのレーニア山，東側はカスケード山脈，北側はさらに高層の新しいビル群が見渡せます。問6そこは，好きな飲み物を持ってくつろぎ（デッキにはバーとカフェがあります），太陽が水平線に沈むのを眺めることのできるすばらしい場所なのです。

[4]　問3スミスタワーは50年近くにわたって西海岸で最も高い建築物でしたが，その後，およそ25パーセント高いスペースニードルが建設されました。問4それは1962年の万国博覧会のために1年足らずで建設され（スミスタワーは建設に3年かかりました），いまでも，高く湾曲した骨組みに取り付けられた空飛ぶ円盤に似たそのユニークな形状によって，シアトルで最も有名な建築物となっています。

[5]　地上160メートルに設置された展望フロアーまでエレベーターに乗って上がり，眺望を堪能してください。近くにこれ程高い建物が全くないという事実により，スミスタワーから見えるものはすべてスペースニードルから若干よく見ることができます。問5北米じゅうとアジアからくるジェット機がシアトル・タコマ国際空港に向かって飛んでいき，東側にある

ユニオン湖で水上飛行機が発着するのを見ることさえできます。

[6] 問6通常の展望フロアーから1階降りたフロアーに，周回するおしゃれな新しいワインバーがあり，47分ごとに1周しています。下のフロアーはそのほとんどがガラスの床になっているのが特徴なので，高所恐怖症の人はそこに行くのは避けたほうがよいでしょう。

[7] 問7<u>1985年，シアトル市は天に近づくためのさらなる大きな一歩を踏み出しました。</u>高さおよそ284メートルのコロンビアセンターが開業したのです。ビルの大半は民間のオフィスからなりますが，40階にあるスターバックスには誰でも行くことができ，入場料を払えば，73階にあるスカイビュー展望台に上ることもできます。問6<u>ここでも，食べ物と飲み物（アルコール類とソフトドリンク類の両方）が売られています。</u>雰囲気はスミスタワーに及びませんが，眺望はこちらのほうがすばらしいです。スミスタワーを見下ろすことさえできますが，ここからはごく小さく見えます。

[8] 2010年代初頭にこれよりわずかに高い超高層ビルが提案されましたが，必要となる許諾がいまだおりていません。おそらくこれからもおりることはないでしょう。少なくともこれからしばらくはコロンビアセンターが，シアトルで最も高い建物であるという称号を持ち続ける可能性が高いように思われます。しかしこのことは，シアトルにおいてこれよりさらにすばらしい眺望を見ることはできないということを意味しません。最良の選択はウィリアム・ボーイングが切り開いた形によって表れています。水上飛行機です。

[9] 問8<u>ボーイングの初期の飛行機の多くは水上飛行機で，湖や流れの緩やかな川であればどこからでも飛び立つことができるよう車輪の代わりに浮舟を装備していましたし，</u>ボーイングの最初のB＆W水上機は，ユニオン湖岸の作業場で組み立てられました。現在，同じユニオン湖がケンモアエアーのフライトの「滑走路」としての役割を果たしています。これらのフライトの中には，遠くブリティッシュコロンビア州のバンクーバーやビクトリアにまで旅客を運ぶものもありますが，多くはシアトルの町を周遊する遊覧飛行のために観光客を乗せているだけのものです。

[10] ボーイング社やエアバス社の空の旅に慣れている人は，水上飛行機で飛ぶとかなり驚きます。問9<u>搭乗員はパイロットただ1人です。</u>保安検査も，搭乗券も，食事サービスもありません。飛行中の楽しみといえば，問9<u>あなたと他の9人の乗客</u>はただ窓から外を眺め，ヘッドフォンから流れる音声案内が今あなたが見ているものを説明してくれるというだけです。問10<u>だいたいのところを考え合わせると，あなたがどこか訪れたくて，見るべきものがたくさんある場所を探しているのであれば，シアトルこそがあなたにとって最適な場所であると気づくことになるかもしれませんよ！</u>

解説 本問の放送文は学術的な講義ではありませんが，1つの主題を持った説明文にはちがいありません。年や数値，固有名詞が多く，トピックの移り変わりも速いテンポで展開するので，話についていくためにも，問われていることを頭に入れておき，展開を予測しながら聞き取るようにしたいものです。

問1 ボーイング航空機株式会社がこの名前で業務を開始したのは何年のことか。

① 1903年　② 1914年　③ 1916年　④ 1917年

第1段落第2文の in 1916, Pacific Aero Products Company opened in Seattle — but just a year later, the name was changed to Boeing Airplane Company で説明されているとおり，ボーイング社の前身である「パシフィック・エアロ・プロダクツ・カンパニー」が創立されたのが1916年で，「ボーイング航空機株式会社」に名前が変わったのがその1年後ですから，正解は④の1917年です。数値や年は質問されやすい項目です。

問2 スミスタワーの建設者は（　　）を製造することで財産を築いた。

① 航空機　② 針　③ 水上飛行機　④ タイプライター

第2段落第2・3文の That was Lyman Cornelius Smith, who had made his fortune manufacturing typewriters. In 1914, he built Smith Tower「それはライマン・コーネリアス・スミスで，彼はタイプライターの製造で財産を築いていました。1914年に彼はスミスタワーを建設し」より，正解は④です。

問3 スペースニードルはスミスタワーよりどれくらい高いか。

① 15%　② 25%　③ 35%　④ 50%

第4段落第1文 Smith Tower remained the tallest structure on the West Coast for nearly 50 years, but then came the Space Needle, which is about 25 percent taller.「スミスタワーは50年近くにわたって西海岸で最も高い建築物でしたが，その後，およそ25パーセント高いスペースニードルが建設されました」より，正解は②です。数値を正確に聞き取りましょう。

問4 スペースニードルが完成するのにどれだけの期間を要したか。

① 1年未満　② 1年　③ 3年　④ 3年以上

第4段落第2文 Built for the 1962 World's Fair in less than one year (Smith Tower took three years to build)「それは1962年の万国博覧会のために1年足らずで建設され（スミスタワーは建設に3年かかりました）」より，正解は①です。分詞構文 Built の意味上の主語は文脈上 Space Needle であることは明らかです。

問5 スペースニードルから見ることのできるものは次のうちどれか。

① 飛びゆくジェット機　② 空飛ぶ円盤

③ レーニア湖　④ ボーイングタワー

第5段落第2文に「スミスタワーから見えるものはすべてスペースニードルからも見える」とあり，それに続けて，Jets from across North America and Asia fly past on their approach to Seattle-Tacoma International Airport「北米じゅうとアジアからくるジェット機がシアトル・タコマ国際空港に向かって

飛んでいき」と説明しているので，スペースニードルから見えるものの1つは
「ジェット機」であるとわかります。したがって，正解は ① です。② の「空飛
ぶ円盤」はスペースニードルの形状を説明するために第4段落最終文に出てき
ているにすぎません。スミスタワーから見えるものについては第3段落で説明
されており，その中に Mount Rainier「レーニア山」は出てきますが，③ の
「レーニア湖」は出てきません。④ の「ボーイングタワー」という建物も説明
に出てきていません。

問6　スペースニードル，スミスタワー，コロンビアセンターの3つの場所すべてで売られ
　　　ているものは何か。

　　　　① 航空機のチケット　　② 食べ物と飲み物　　③ 宝飾品　　④ 不動産

　スミスタワーについては第3段落最終文 It's a great place to relax with
your favorite drink (there's a bar and café up there)，スペースニードルにつ
いては第6段落第1文 One floor down from the regular observation floor
there's a fashionable new wine bar which revolves，コロンビアセンターにつ
いては第7段落第3文 Here, too, food and drinks (both alcoholic and
nonalcoholic) are available. にあるとおり，これら3つの場所すべてで売られ
ているものは「食べ物と飲み物」なので，② が正解となります。

問7　話者によると，最も高いのは次のうちどれか。
　　　　① コロンビアセンター　　　② シアトル・タコマ国際空港
　　　　③ スミスタワー　　　　　　④ スペースニードル

　放送文によると，シアトルの高層建築としてはまずスミスタワーが建設さ
れ，その後その高さを超えるスペースニードルが建設され，その後，第7段落
第1文 In 1985, the city took another big step closer to the heavens with the
opening of the Columbia Center, some 284 meters tall.「1985年，シアトル市
は天に近づくためのさらなる大きな一歩を踏み出しました。高さおよそ284メ
ートルのコロンビアセンターが開業したのです」にあるとおり，さらに高いコ
ロンビアセンターが建設されたので，正解は ① になります。シアトル・タコ
マ国際空港に関しては高さについての言及がありません。

問8　水上飛行機は（　　　　）。
　　　　① 水中を進むことができる
　　　　② 海外に飛んでいくだけの燃料の容量がある
　　　　③ 車輪の代わりに浮舟を持っている
　　　　④ たいてい，ユニオン湖の隣にあるB＆Wの建物に停泊している

　第9段落第1文の Many of Boeing's early planes were seaplanes, equipped
with floats instead of wheels so that they could take off from any lake or

slow-moving river「ボーイングの初期の飛行機の多くは水上飛行機で，湖や流れの緩やかな川であればどこからでも飛び立つことができるよう車輪の代わりに浮舟を装備していました」より，正解は ③ です。

問9　ケンモアエアーの水上飛行機でのフライトが満席の場合，パイロットを含めて何人が搭乗していると考えられるか。

　　　　① 9人　　② 10人　　③ 11人　　④ 12人

　ケンモアエアーの水上飛行機の人員については，まず，第10段落第2文で搭乗員はパイロット1名のみだと言い，そのあとの第4文で you and the other nine passengers「あなたと他の9人の乗客」と言っています。したがって，パイロット1人，乗客10人となるので，正解は ③ の11人です。

問10　この文章の目的は何か。

　　　① シアトルの観光客の遊びはすべて，水上飛行機が中心であることを説明すること

　　　② シアトルは魅力的な観光地であることを示すこと

　　　③ シアトルのレストランで飲食するよう読者を説得すること

　　　④ シアトルは訪れる価値のない所であると主張すること

　最終段落最終文 All in all, if you're in the market for somewhere to visit that has a lot to see, you might just find that Seattle is the right place for you! にあるとおり，話は全体を通じて，シアトルが訪れるのにすばらしい場所であることを説明した内容です。したがって，正解は ② です。

[語句] *be* associated with 〜「〜と関連がある」，manufacturing 名「製造業」，manufacture 動「〜を製造する」，observation deck「展望デッキ」，a forest of 〜「林立する〜」，structure 名「建造物」，World's Fair「万国博覧会」，flying saucer「空飛ぶ円盤」，remotely 副「(否定文で) ほんのわずかも〜ない」(= slightly)，jet 名「ジェット機」，approach 名「(着陸のための) 進入」，seaplane 名「水上飛行機」，revolve 動「回転する」，circuit 名「一周すること」，feature 動「〜を特徴とする，呼び物とする」，consist of 〜「〜からなっている」，admission fee「入場料金」，observatory 名「展望台」，skyscraper 名「超高層ビル」，permit 名「承認，許可証」，grant 動「〜を承諾する」，crown 名「最高位」，pioneer 動「〜を開拓する」，(*be*) equipped with 〜「〜を装備して (いる)」，float 名「浮舟，フロート」，assemble 動「〜を組み立てる」，edge 名「端，岸」，runway 名「滑走路」，transport 動「〜を運ぶ，輸送する」loop 名「周遊」，(*be*) used to *doing*「…することに慣れて (いる)」，flight crew「飛行機の搭乗員」，all in all「概して見れば」，in the market for 〜「〜を探し求めて，買い求めて」

ここがポイント　数値は問われることが多いので，音声情報から数値情報をすぐに取り出せるように，何度も音読をして慣れるまで練習しましょう。

スクリプト ※下線部は解答の根拠に当たる箇所です。

[1]　Farmers and plant breeders are in a race against time. According to Lee Hickey, an Australian plant scientist, "We face a grand challenge in terms of feeding the world. We're going to have about 10 billion people on the planet by 2050," he says, "so we'll need 60 to 80 percent more food to feed everybody."

[2]　Breeders develop new kinds of crops — more productive, disease-resistant — but it's a slow process that can take a decade or more using traditional techniques. So, to quicken the pace, Dr. Hickey's team in Australia has been working on "speed breeding," which allows them to harvest seeds and start the next generation of crops sooner. Their technique was inspired by NASA research on how to grow food on space stations. 問1 They trick crops into flowering early by shining blue and red LED lights 22 hours a day and keeping temperatures between 17 and 22 degrees Celsius. They can grow up to six generations of wheat in a year, whereas traditional methods would yield only one or two.

[3]　Researchers first started growing plants under artificial light about 150 years ago. At that time, the light was produced by what are called carbon arc lamps. Since then, 問1 advances in LED technology have vastly improved the precision with which scientists can adjust light settings to suit individual crop species.

[4]　Researchers have also adopted new genetic techniques that speed up the generation of desirable characteristics in plants. Historically, humans have relied on a combination of natural variation followed by artificial selection to achieve these gains. Now, breeders use gene-editing tools to alter DNA with great speed and accuracy. 問2 In 2004, scientists working in Europe identified a variation on a single gene that made a type of barley resistant to a serious disease. Ten years later, researchers in China edited the same gene in wheat, one of the world's most important crops, making it resistant as well.

[5]　問3 Gene-editing tools have been used to protect rice against disease, to

give corn and soybeans resistance to certain chemicals, and to save oranges from a type of bacteria that has destroyed crops in Asia and the Americas. In South Korea, scientists are using these tools to rescue an endangered variety of bananas from a devastating soil disease.

[6]　With cheaper, more powerful technology, opportunities are opening up to improve crops around the world.　問4 Dr. Hickey's team plans to use these discoveries to help farmers in India, Zimbabwe and Mali over the next couple of years, since he wants the discoveries to benefit developing countries, too.

[7]　問5 According to Hickey, we will need to combine speed breeding and gene editing with all the other tools we have if we are to meet the food security challenges of the future.　"One technology alone," he says, "is not going to solve our problems."

[8]　However, while basic speed breeding is generally accepted, many are reluctant to embrace gene-editing technology.　They worry about unexpected long-term consequences.　The benefits of this revolutionary technology, they feel, must be weighed against its potential dangers.

(501 words)

和訳　[1]　農業に従事する人も植物育種家も時間と競争をしています。オーストラリアの植物学者リー・ヒッキーによると、「私たちは世界中の人々に食料をいきわたらせるという壮大な難題に直面しています。2050 年までに、地球上にはおよそ 100 億人の人々が暮らすことになるため、全員を食べさせるためには、食料を 6 割から 8 割増やす必要があるでしょう」というのです。

[2]　育種家は、生産性がより高く、病気に耐性のある新たな種類の作物を開発していますが、それはなかなか進まず、従来の手法を使っていては 10 年かあるいはそれ以上かかることもあるのです。そこで、オーストラリアのヒッキー博士のチームは、開発のペースを上げるため、より早く種を収穫し次世代の作付けを始めることを可能にする「促成栽培」に取り組んできました。彼らの技術は、宇宙ステーション内で作物を栽培する方法に取り組んだ NASA の研究に触発されました。問1 彼らは、作物に青と赤の LED 照明を 1 日 22 時間照らし、温度を摂氏 17 度から 22 度に保つことで、作物の開花を早めるよう仕向けるのです。小麦は従来の方法では 1 年に 1，2 回しか収穫されませんが、この方法なら 1 年で最高 6 世代まで栽培することができます。

[3]　研究者たちが人工照明を使った植物栽培を初めて行ったのは 150 年ほど前のことでした。当時は、炭素アーク灯と呼ばれるもので明かりを作り出していました。それ以降、問1 LED 技術の進歩によって、科学者が個々の作物種に適した照明設定の調節を可能にする精度が大

きく改善されてきました。

[4] 研究者は，植物に望ましい特質を持たせることを加速する新たな遺伝子技術も取り入れてきました。歴史的に人間は，こうした結果を得るのに，自然変異とそれに続く人為的選択の組み合わせに頼ってきました。今では，植物育種家は遺伝子編集ツールを使って，かなりの速度と精度で DNA を組み換えています。_{問2}2004 年，ヨーロッパで研究している科学者が，ある種類の大麦に重い病気への耐性を持たせる単一遺伝子の変異を突き止めました。10 年後，中国の研究者が，世界で最も重要な作物の 1 つである小麦の同じ遺伝子を編集して，同様に耐性を持たせました。

[5] _{問3}遺伝子編集ツールは，稲が病気にかかるのを防ぐため，トウモロコシと大豆に特定の化学物質に対する耐性を与えるため，またアジアと南北アメリカで作物を破壊してきたバクテリアからオレンジを守るために，使われてきました。韓国では，科学者が，絶滅が危惧されるバナナ種を壊滅的な土壌の病気から救うためにこれらのツールを使っています。

[6] より安価で，より強力な技術によって，世界中の作物を改善する機会が広がりつつあります。_{問4}ヒッキー博士はこれらの発見が発展途上国にも恩恵をもたらすよう望んでいるので，彼のチームはこの先 2，3 年にわたり，インドやジンバブエやマリの農家を助けるためにこれらの発見を利用する計画を立ています。

[7] _{問5}ヒッキー博士によれば，私たちが将来の食料確保の難題に対処するつもりならば，促成栽培および遺伝子編集と，私たちが手にしている他のすべてのツールとを組み合わせる必要があるとのことです。「1 つの技術だけでは，私たちの問題が解決に向かうことはないでしょう」と彼は言います。

[8] しかし，基本的な促成栽培は一般に受け入れられてはいるものの，多くの人は遺伝子編集技術を受け入れるのにちゅうちょしています。彼らは長期にわたる予期せぬ影響を心配しているのです。この画期的な技術の恩恵とその潜在的危険性をはかりにかけなければならないと感じています。

解説 この講義は，人口増加が進む世界でいかに食料を確保するかという問題を主題とし，その解決策として「促成栽培」と「遺伝子編集」の 2 つを取り上げて説明しています。促成栽培技術の説明では LED 照明の利用という具体的手法について言及し，遺伝子編集技術の説明では，研究が行われている地域や作物名などに言及しています。最後に将来の食料確保における展望と課題が述べられています。質問を先読みし，講義の展開をとらえつつ，細部に目を配ることができるようにしましょう。

問1 促成栽培の最近の進歩を可能にしたのはどの科学的発展か。

① より優れた宇宙飛行技術。

② LED 技術の発展。

③ 気象制御技術の改善。

④ 作物収穫のより効率的な方法。

⑤ 炭素アーク灯の発明。

　第2段落第4文に，ヒッキー博士のチームが取り組んでいる促成栽培はLED照明によって行われているとあり，第3段落第3文で advances in LED technology have vastly improved the precision with which scientists can adjust light settings to suit individual crop species「LED技術の進歩によって，科学者が個々の作物種に適した照明設定の調節を可能にする精度が大きく改善されてきました」と説明されているので，正解は②です。①は，第2段落第3文に関連しますが，ヒッキー博士のチームはNASAの研究に触発されたのであって，「優れた宇宙飛行技術」が促成栽培を可能にしたわけではないので，不適です。③と④は講義で触れられていない内容です。⑤は第3段落第2文に関連しますが，炭素アーク灯は150年前に使われていた照明技術なので，最近の進歩とは無関係です。

問2　中国の科学者が，世界で極めて重要な作物の1つに病気への耐性を与えることにおいて飛躍的成功に至ったのはいつのことか。

　　　① 2002年　　② 2004年　　③ 2008年　　④ 2012年　　⑤ 2014年

　第4段落第4・5文の In 2004, ... resistant to a serious disease. Ten years later, researchers in China edited the same gene in wheat, one of the world's most important crops, making it resistant as well. より，中国の科学者は2004年の10年後に飛躍的成功に至ったので，⑤が正解です。

問3　下に挙げられている作物のうち，遺伝子編集がいかにして植物を病気から守ってきたかを例示するために使われていないものは，どれか。

　　　① バナナ　　② 大麦　　③ 稲　　④ 大豆　　⑤ 小麦

　第5段落第1文 Gene-editing tools have been used to protect rice against disease, to give corn and soybeans resistance to certain chemicals より，トウモロコシと大豆に関しては，病気ではなく特定の化学物質に対して耐性を与えるために遺伝子編集ツールが使われてきたことがわかるので，正解は④です。この部分より，③の稲は病気から守るために遺伝子編集ツールが使われていることがわかります。また，第4段落第4・5文より，②の大麦と⑤の小麦も同様のことが言えます。第5段落最終文より，①のバナナも同様です。

問4　研究プロジェクトが現在行われている場所として言及されていないのは次のうちどれか。

　　　① オーストラリア　　② 中国　　③ ヨーロッパ　　④ インド　　⑤ 韓国

　第6段落第2文の Dr. Hickey's team plans to use these discoveries to help farmers in India, Zimbabwe and Mali over the next couple of years より，イ

ンドはこれから助ける地域として挙げられているので，現在研究プロジェクト
が行われている場所としては言及されていません。したがって，正解は ④ で
す。① のオーストラリアは第2段落第2文，② の中国と ③ のヨーロッパは第
4段落第4・5文，⑤ の韓国は第5段落最終文で，それぞれ現在研究が進めら
れている地域として言及されています。

問5 ヒッキー博士によると，食料確保という将来の難題に対処するのに必要となるのは
（　　）である。

① 促成栽培の継続的な進歩
② 人口増加を制御する努力
③ 遺伝子編集における新たな飛躍的発展
④ 利用可能なあらゆる技術の応用
⑤ 新たなツールの開発

　第7段落第1文 According to Hickey, we will need to combine speed
breeding and gene editing with all the other tools we have if we are to meet
the food security challenges of the future.「ヒッキー博士によれば，私たちが
将来の食料確保の難題に対処するつもりならば，促成栽培および遺伝子編集
と，私たちが手にしている他のすべてのツールとを組み合わせる必要があると
のことです」より，正解は ④ です。

語句 breeder 名「育種家，品種改良する人」，grand 形「壮大な」，in terms of 〜「〜の観点
から」，feed 動「〜に食料を与える」，resistant 形「抵抗力がある，耐性のある」，speed
breeding「促成栽培」，harvest 動「〜を収穫する」，generation 名「世代，生み出すこ
と」，inspire 動「〜を触発する，奮起させる」，trick 〜 into *doing*「〜をだまして…さ
せる」，LED 名「発光ダイオード」（＝ light-emitting diode），artificial 形「人工的な」，
carbon arc lamp「炭素アーク灯」，precision with which *SV*「…する際の精度」，
combination of 〜 followed by ...「〜とそれに続く…との組み合わせ」，variation 名
「変異」，gene-editing 形「遺伝子編集の」，identify 動「〜を特定する」，resistance
名「抵抗力，耐性」，endangered variety「絶滅危惧種」，devastating 形「甚大な被害
をもたらす」，combine 〜 with ...「〜を…と組み合わせる」，food security「食料確保，
食料安全保障」，*be* reluctant to *do*「…することに乗り気でない」，embrace 動「〜を受
け入れる」，consequence 名「影響，結果」，weigh 〜 against ...「〜を…と比較考察す
る」

ここが ポイント　質問を先に読み，講義の展開を予測しながら，質問の答えに当
たる情報を聞き出すようなつもりで聞きましょう。

5 複合問題

1

Part 1

正解

① designed	② renowned	③ size	④ permanent
⑤ critics	⑥ manipulating	⑦ fascinated	⑧ enormous
⑨ brings	⑩ responsible		

スクリプト （J: Jenkins　K: Kapoor）

J(1): Hello. I'm Jake Jenkins. A sculpture called *The Orbit* is Britain's largest piece of public art. It was ① designed by one of the country's most ② renowned artists. *The Orbit*, which can be seen in London's Olympic Park, is twice the ③ size of New York's Statue of Liberty and it stands at 115 meters in height. Made of approximately 2,000 tons of steel, it also includes the world's tallest and longest tunnel slide. It was built as a ④ permanent reminder of the 2012 Olympic and Paralympic games, and was completed in May 2012. Since then, it has raised eyebrows of fans and ⑤ critics alike. And this is just one example of what Anish Kapoor considers art. Known for ⑥ manipulating form and perspective, the Mumbai-born British artist has ⑦ fascinated the public with his bean-shaped sculpture in Chicago's Millennium Park, turned New York's Rockefeller Center upside down with his 10 meter *Sky Mirror*, and astonished art fans with his ⑧ enormous installation of *Giant*, in London. This week, on our show, we meet Anish Kapoor in Seoul, as he ⑨ brings his eye-catching pieces to the East. Anish Kapoor, welcome to the show.

K: Hello. Thank you for inviting me.

J(2): You are one of the most famous sculptors in the world, and many believe that you are ⑩ responsible for changing the way that people view sculpture. How do you think you've done this? (227 words)

和訳　（J：ジェンキンズ　K：カプーア）

J (1)：こんにちは。私はジェイク・ジェンキンズです。《オービット》と呼ばれる彫刻はイギリス最大のパブリックアート作品です。それはイギリスで最も有名な芸術家の１人によって設計されました。ロンドンオリンピック公園にある《オービット》は，ニューヨークにある自由の女神像の２倍の大きさで，高さが115メートルあります。それはおよそ2,000トンの鋼鉄からできており，世界一高く長い，チューブ型の滑り台も併設されています。2012年のオリンピック・パラリンピック大会を恒久的に記念するものとして建設され，2012年５月に完成しました。それ以来，愛好する人と批判的な人を共に驚かせ，あきれさせてきました。そしてこれはアニッシュ・カプーア氏が何を芸術とみなしているかについての一例にすぎません。フォルムとパースペクティブを操ることで知られる，このムンバイ生まれのイギリス人芸術家は，シカゴのミレニアムパークで豆の形をした彫刻作品によって大衆を魅了し，10メートルの《スカイミラー》でニューヨークのロックフェラーセンターを上下さかさまにして見せ，ロンドンでは《ジャイアント》の大インスタレーションによって芸術愛好家を驚かせたのです。今週，私たちの番組は，その人目を引く作品を東洋にもたらしているアニッシュ・カプーア氏を，ソウルでお迎えします。アニッシュ・カプーアさん，当番組へようこそ。

K：こんにちは。お招きいただきありがとうございます。

J (2)：あなたは世界で最も有名な彫刻家の１人であり，多くの人は，あなたが人々の彫刻の見方を変えた大本になっていると信じています。どのようにしてあなたはこのことをなしてきたとお思いですか。

（注：ムンバイ市は1995年までボンベイと呼ばれていた。現在，ムンバイとボンベイはインドの同一の都市を指す。）

解説

① design「～を設計する」の過去分詞 designed が入ります。語末の ed を落とさないようにしましょう。語末の子音，特に [d], [t] は弱く発音されたり，消えたりするので注意が必要です。

② 「有名な」という意味の renowned が入ります。語末の ed を忘れないでください。renown だと名詞になってしまいます。「有名な」にあたる形容詞は famous, well-known, celebrated, distinguished, famed など多数あります。

③ 名詞 size が入ります。次の前置詞 of と結合して「サイゾ（ヴ）」のように聞こえるので注意してください。size は「大きさ」ですが，ここでは彫刻の高さを指しています。ちなみに「自由の女神像（Statue of Liberty）」は本体のみの高さは約46メートルで，台座を含めると約93メートルあります。

④ 「恒久的な，永久の」という意味の形容詞 permanent が入ります。第１音節の発音とつづりに注意してください。[pəː(r)] と発音し，つづりは per です。

par とつづらないようにしましょう。

⑤　名詞 critic の複数形 critics が入ります。「批評家，評論家」という意味と「批判者，あらさがしをする人」という意味がありますが，ここでは fan「愛好家」と対で用いられているので，後者の意味となります。

⑥　「～を（巧みに）操る」という意味の他動詞 manipulate の動名詞 manipulating が入ります。語末の ing は弱いので，原形と勘違いしないよう，文法にも注意してください。また，つづり方に戸惑っていると，⑦ がすぐに発音されてあわてることになります。素早く書くことも重要です。

⑦　他動詞 fascinate「～を魅了する」の過去分詞 fascinated が入ります。現在完了であることを考慮し，語末の d を忘れないように注意しましょう。

⑧　「非常に大きい」という意味の形容詞 enormous が入ります。「非常に大きな」の意味の形容詞も huge, vast, gigantic, giant, massive, extensive など多数あります。ちなみにこの enormous installation の installation は美術用語で，和訳でも「インスタレーション」とカタカナにしています。「設置，据え付け」の原義から派生し，展示空間全体を美術作品とする場合に用います。

⑨　「～をもたらす」という意味の他動詞 bring に，いわゆる三単現（主語が三人称単数で時制が現在）の s がついた brings が入ります。語末の s は聞き取るというよりも文法上忘れてはならないものです。

⑩　形容詞 responsible が入ります。*be* responsible for ～ は「～に対して責任を負っている，～の原因を招いている」という意味の基本熟語です。

語句　sculpture 名「彫刻（作品）」, public art「パブリックアート（公共空間を飾る芸術作品）」, renowned 形「有名な」, Statue of Liberty「自由の女神像」, approximately 副「およそ，ほぼ」, steel 名「鋼鉄」, permanent 形「恒久的な」, reminder 名「思い出させるもの」, complete 動「～を完成させる」, raise eyebrows「眉を上げる（＝人を驚かせる，人のひんしゅくを買う）」, critic 名「批判者」, *A* and *B* alike「A も B も（同様に）」, manipulate 動「～を（巧みに）操る」, perspective 名「パースペクティブ，遠近（画）法」, fascinate 動「～を魅了する」, bean-shaped 形「豆の形をした」, upside down「さかさまに」, astonish 動「～を驚かす」, enormous 形「非常に大きい」, installation 名「インスタレーション，据え付け」, eye-catching 形「人目を引く」, sculptor 名「彫刻家」, *be* responsible for ～「～に対して責任を負っている，～の原因になっている」, view 動「～を見る」

ここが ポイント

ディクテーションの問題は，音声情報だけでなく，**意味や文法・語法の知識も活用しましょう。速く書き取る練習をすることも重要です。**

Part 2

正解 (解答例)	問 1	He thinks his sculpture helps people to perceive the everyday world in which they live from a different point of view or perspective.
	問 2	He thought he would become a professional, like an engineer.
	問 3	He felt for the first time he was doing what he really wanted to do.
	問 4	He feels he is deeply connected with things Indian and he is very proud of his Indian background and roots. But he also feels like a foreigner in India.
	問 5	Because he felt for the first time that the audience was understanding and enjoying the story about the world that he was telling with his sculptures.

 ※下線部は解答の根拠に当たる箇所です。

(K: Kapoor J: Jenkins)

K (1): You say I have changed the way people view sculpture, but I don't know that I have, but, you know, we live, of course, in a world of objects. And we often have an image of ourselves and our whole life and environment which includes the objects we interact with. Sculpture can question or kind of pose problems that make us think again about daily objects, and by doing that it also makes us think again about our lives and environment.

J (1): Well, some people would say your work is very hard to explain — difficult to categorize. How would you describe your work?

K (2): I expect it is hard to categorize. 問1 What I think my sculpture is doing is helping people to perceive the everyday world in which they live from a different point of view or perspective. I want my sculpture to make people see everyday things like office buildings, cars, bridges etc. in a way they have never thought of before. Art is very good at changing the way people see and think about the world around them, you know. Not just sculpture, but all forms of visual art, like painting, photography, and dance, can make us see the world around us in a way which is new and novel, and surprising.

J(2): Anish, your background is quite fascinating. You were born and raised in India. Your father was a sailor with the Indian Navy. Your mother was originally from Iraq. Tell me about your childhood and were you creative as a child?

K(3): Yes, I was born in Bombay and grew up in a place called Dehra Dun, which is in the north of India. My childhood was pretty ordinary, really. Like all good Indian boys, 問2 I grew up thinking I was going to be a professional. You know, an engineer or something like that. Something professional in any case. And when I became an adult, in my late teens, I decided I was going to be an artist. My father was horrified. He told me I would never make enough money to survive and buy a house if I became an artist. But I sort of knew that it was what I had to do. And I never — once I knew it — I never thought about it again, and I never changed my mind.

J(3): You moved to London and started art school. And I believe that you said you felt utterly free. What did you feel free from?

K(4): You know, if only it was that straightforward. But anyway, 問3 I think I felt for the first time, I was doing what I really wanted to do. That there was a sense of discovery. A sense of adventure. And I think that's what's lived with me over these last 35 years, or whatever it is, that I've been professional as an artist. The sense that making a work is a kind of discovery. I feel the studio where I make my sculptures is more like a laboratory than it is like a factory or a place of manufacture. I spend my time inventing and discovering things that I think nobody has ever seen before.

J(4): You have lived in London since 1973. When you go back to India, does it feel like you're going home? Do you still have that connection? Or is the U.K. now very much home?

K(5): Well, I've lived in the U.K. for, you know, about 40 years. And 問4 I'm deeply connected with things Indian and I'm very proud of my Indian background and roots and so on. But in a way, I guess I feel like a foreigner in the U.K. and also a foreigner in India. So, it's become a permanent condition. I feel like a foreigner wherever I go now.

J (5): Anish, in 1990, you represented Britain at the Venice Festival. And you say it was a moment that changed your life. How did it change your life?

K (6): Well, you know, what you do as an artist, especially as a young artist, is tell a new story. As an artist you don't really just make things. What you're doing is telling a story about the things you create, whether it's a painting or a sculpture — whatever it is. You are telling a story about the world that you want the audience to understand and enjoy. And I experienced that in a very real way in the Venice Festival, when I represented Britain. _{問5}I felt for the first time that the audience was understanding and enjoying the story about the world that I was telling with my sculptures. It was a moment I will never forget.

(769 words)

和訳　(K：カプーア　J：ジェンキンズ)

K (1): あなたは私が人々の彫刻への見方を変えたとおっしゃいましたが, 変えたという認識はありません。しかし, 何と言いますか, 私たちは当然のことながら, 物の世界に生きています。そして私たちはしばしば, 自分自身と自分の生活と環境全体のイメージを持っており, そのイメージには私たちが相互に影響し合う物が含まれているのです。彫刻は疑問を投げかけたり, 日常のさまざまな物について私たちに改めて考えさせる問題点を提示したりするようなことができます。また, そうすることは, 私たちの生活と環境を改めて考えさせることにもなるのです。

J (1): ええ, 一部の人は, あなたの作品は説明するのがとても難しい, 分類しづらいと言いますね。あなたはご自分の作品をどのように説明しますか。

K (2): 分類しづらいと思います。_{問1}私の彫刻がしていると私が思っていることは, 人々が自分の暮らしている日常世界を, 異なる視点や観点から認識することを手助けすることです。私は, 自分の彫刻によって, 人々が今まで考えたこともないような仕方で, オフィスビルや自動車, 橋などの日常の事物を見るよう仕向けたいのです。芸術は, 周囲の世界についての人々の見方や考え方を変えることを非常に得意としていますよね。彫刻だけでなく, 絵画や写真や舞踊など, あらゆる形態の視覚芸術は, 新しく, 奇抜で, 驚くべき仕方で, 周囲の世界を私たちに見せることができるのです。

J (2): アニッシュさん, あなたの経歴はとても興味深いですね。あなたはインドで生まれ, 育ちました。お父様はインド海軍の水兵でした。お母様はもともとイラクのご出身です。あなたの子供時代のことを教えてください。子供のころから創造的だったのです

か。

K（3）：はい，私はボンベイで生まれ，インドの北部にあるデラドゥーンという所で育ちました。私の子供時代は本当のところ，いたって普通でした。優秀なインドの少年たちが皆そうであるように，_{問2}何かの専門家になろうと思いながら大人になっていきました。まあ，エンジニアとかそういうようなものです。とにかく専門的な何かです。そして 10 代の終わりで成人して，芸術家になると決めました。私の父はショックを受けていました。父は，私が芸術家になったら，日々生活をしながら家を買うのに十分なお金を稼ぐことはないだろうと言いました。しかしそれが私のするべきことだとなぜかわかっていたんです。いったんそれがわかってしまうと，考え直すことは決してしませんでしたね。決心は変わりませんでした。

J（3）：あなたはロンドンに引っ越し，美術学校に通い始めました。あなたは完全なる自由を感じていると言ったと思います。どんなことから自由になったと感じたのですか。

K（4）：まあ，それがそれほどすっきりしたものであればいいなとは思うのですがね。しかしとにかく，_{問3}自分が本当にしたいことをしていると初めて感じたと思います。発見の感覚，冒険の感覚があると感じましたね。そしてそれこそが過去 35 年間私と共にあり続けているもの，あるいはそれが何であれ，私が芸術家という形でずっと専門家であり続けてきたということだと思います。作品を作るというのはある種の発見であるという感覚です。私が彫刻を作っているアトリエは，工房や製作所というよりも，研究室のようなものです。私は，これまで誰も見たことがないと思うものを発明し，発見することに自分の時間を費やしています。

J（4）：あなたは 1973 年からロンドンに住んでいます。インドに戻るときは，故郷に帰るような気持ちになるのですか。まだ，そのようなつながりを持っていますか。それとも今ではイギリスが故郷そのものと感じますか。

K（5）：そうですね，私はイギリスに，かれこれ，40 年ほど住んでいます。それでいて，_{問4}インド的なものに深く結びついていますし，私のインドでの生い立ちや出自などに大いに誇りを持っています。しかしある意味で，イギリスでも自分を外国人と感じ，インドでも自分を外国人と感じているように思います。ですから，常にそのような状態になりましたね。今ではどこに行っても自分を外国人のように感じています。

J（5）：アニッシュさん，あなたは 1990 年のベネチア・ビエンナーレに，イギリス代表として参加されました。そして，そのときに人生が変わったとおっしゃっていますね。それはあなたの人生をどのように変えたのでしょうか。

K（6）：まあ，そうですね，芸術家，特に若い芸術家として行うのは，新しい物語を語ることです。芸術家は実際，ただものを作るだけではないのです。芸術家がしていることというのは，絵画であれ彫刻であれ何であれ，自分たちが創造する物についての物語を語るということです。見ている人に理解し，楽しんでもらいたい世界についての物語

を語っているのです。そして私はベネチア・ビエンナーレにイギリス代表として参加したとき，非常にリアルにそれを経験しました。_{問5}私は，私が彫刻によって語った世界についての物語を，それを見ている人が理解し，楽しんでいると初めて感じました。それは二度と忘れることのない瞬間でした。

解説 事前に，問いに合うように答えの出だし部分を書いておきましょう。おおよそ次のようになります。

問1：He thinks his sculpture helps people
問2：He thought he would become
問3：He felt ／問4：He feels ／問5：Because

次に質問内容を頭に入れ，音声に耳を傾けて，問いの答えにかかわる部分が聞こえてきたら要点を素早くメモします。2回目では答えの不足を補ったり，確認をしたりするようにします。書き取る分量が多いので，解答に苦労する場合もあると思います。実質的にセンテンスレベルのディクテーション（書き取り）問題だと思ったほうがよいでしょう。

問1 アニッシュ・カプーアは自分の彫刻が人々にどのように役立っていると思っているか。

カプーアの2番目の発話の第2文 What I think my sculpture is doing is helping people to perceive the everyday world in which they live from a different point of view or perspective.「私の彫刻がしていると私が思っていることは，人々が自分の暮らしている日常世界を，異なる視点や観点から認識することを手助けすることです」より，正解は，He thinks his sculpture helps people to perceive the everyday world in which they live from a different point of view or perspective. のようになります。

問2 アニッシュ・カプーアは子供のころ何になるだろうと思っていたか。

カプーアの3番目の発話の第3・4文 I grew up thinking I was going to be a professional. You know, an engineer or something like that.「何かの専門家になろうと思いながら大人になっていきました。まあ，エンジニアとかそういうようなものです」より，正解は，He thought he would become a professional, like an engineer. のようになります。

問3 アニッシュ・カプーアはロンドンに引っ越して美術学校に通い始めたときどのように感じていたか。

カプーアの4番目の発話の第2文 I think I felt for the first time, I was doing what I really wanted to do「自分が本当にしたいことをしていると初めて感じたと思います」より，正解は He felt for the first time he was doing what he really wanted to do. のようになります。

問4 アニッシュ・カプーアは現在インドについてどのように感じているか。

カプーアの5番目の発話の第2・3文 I'm deeply connected with things Indian and I'm very proud of my Indian background and roots and so on. But in a way, I guess I feel like a foreigner in the U.K. and also a foreigner in India.「私はインド的なものに深く結びついていますし，私のインドでの生い立ちや出自などに大いに誇りを持っています。しかしある意味で，イギリスでも自分を外国人と感じ，インドでも自分を外国人と感じているように思います」より，He feels he is deeply connected with things Indian and he is very proud of his Indian background and roots. But he also feels like a foreigner in India. のようになります。

問5 ヴェニス・フェスティバル（ベネチア・ビエンナーレ）が，アニッシュ・カプーアが決して忘れることのない時であったのはなぜか。

カプーアの6番目の発話の最後から2番目の文 I felt for the first time that the audience was understanding and enjoying the story about the world that I was telling with my sculptures.「私は，私が彫刻によって語った世界についての物語を，それを見ている人が理解し，楽しんでいると初めて感じました」より，Because he felt for the first time that the audience was understanding and enjoying the story about the world that he was telling with his sculptures. のようになります。

語句　interact with ～「～と相互に影響し合う」, kind of「いくぶん，多少」(= sort of), pose 動「(問題など) を提起する」, categorize 動「～を分類する」, describe 動「～を (言葉で) 説明する，記述する」, perceive 動「～を感じ取る」, view 名「視点，観点」, perspective 名「観点，見地」, visual art「(絵画・彫刻などの) 視覚芸術」, Indian Navy「インド海軍」, ordinary 形「普通の」, professional 名 形「(技術職などの) 専門家 (の)」, horrified 形「ぞっとする，ショックを受ける」, change one's mind「気が変わる」, utterly 副「全く，完全に」, straightforward 形「明白な，単刀直入の」, studio 名「作業場，アトリエ」, laboratory 名「研究室，実験室」, manufacture 名「製造」, represent 動「～を代表する」

ここがポイント

・質問に答えを対応させて，聞き取った語句を適切な答え方に整えましょう。その際，**時制や代名詞の転換**などにも注意しましょう。
・記述問題の多くは実質的にディクテーションの問題です。該当箇所を素早く書き取る練習を積みましょう。

Part 3

◇◇

スクリプト ※下線部は解答の根拠に当たる箇所です。

（J: Jenkins　K: Kapoor）

J(1): What made you decide that you wanted to use mirrors in your sculpture? For the benefit of our audience I should add that I am referring to perhaps your most famous work, *Sky Mirror*, an artwork that you have duplicated and have had installed in three locations, including the Rockefeller Center in New York City.

K(1): 問1<u>I'm really interested in the way art relates to the spaces around the art</u>, and the artwork you are referring to, *Sky Mirror*, the sculpture itself, because it mirrors the ever-changing sky, fully interacts with space it reflects. For those of your audience who have not seen *Sky Mirror*, it's a circular mirror placed outside and pointed skyward. The effect is that it seems to pull the sky, upside down, toward the ground. I initially made one for the Nottingham Playhouse in the U.K. This first one was 6 meters in diameter. 問2<u>Later I made a larger version that is about 10 meters in diameter. This is the one installed at the Rockefeller Center.</u> Because this work points upward to capture this very tall building and the sky beyond, it gives the viewer another perspective of the famous New York skyline.

J(2): One of your best-known sculptures is named *Giant*, which you finished in 2002. It was shown at the Tate Modern Art Museum in London, and was seen by roughly 1.8 million people according to the museum records office. 問3<u>This made it one of the most visited works of sculpture in the world.</u>

K(2): The great hall at the entrance of the Tate Modern Art Museum, is, you know, one of the biggest museum spaces that there is for indoor sculpture. I decided to use the whole of the space. Up until then, other artists only used about one third of this space. That's big enough, but I am a little crazy about size. I really believe in large-scale projects, and I think that expanding into enormous spaces with art is interesting.

J(3): Because I'm sure that does scare off a lot of artists, using such a large space. For our listeners who have not seen *Giant*, this was truly an enormous piece of work that is difficult to describe in words. You used a combination of plastic and steel that seemed to stretch throughout the hall. The work was 150 meters long and 10 storeys high. 問4 In overhead pictures of the work, the people walking through seem antlike under this work.

K(3): Well, you know, the theory is that as sculpture gets bigger, it gets less meaningful. I'm not sure that's really true. So I think that large-scale works can have a wonderful effect. With the work, *Giant*, at the Tate, I wanted to make a work that people could actually walk into and experience from within the art. I also wanted the sculpture itself to seem bigger than the very large hall where it was installed. Some of your listeners may not be familiar with my work, so I should explain that *Giant* was inspired by an old Greek story. It's a story about how the God Apollo became jealous of someone who could play the flute better than Apollo could, so Apollo stretched the person out. This story is the subject of a famous painting by the Italian painter, Titian. It's an awful story but the idea of stretching a person, cruel though it may be, evokes the idea of large-scale suffering. However, 問5 the point is that we feel sorry for the man who was punished, so I think that the artwork also evokes sympathy on a large scale.

J(4): How does a new idea for a project like this start out?

K(4): Well, when you make large sculptures like *Giant* and others, there are no rehearsals. You know, you can make a model but a smaller model doesn't tell you very much. Not really. 問6 You never can tell what will happen when you expand your model into a large sculpture. The first time I see it finished is the first time the public sees it.

J(5): So tell us about the process. I mean, it starts as drawings and then you make small models?

K (5): Often there are drawings, yes. 問7 <u>Drawings or models but quite</u> <u>often no drawings, no models.</u> Sometimes you just have to make something. Anything.

J (6): Just play with whatever materials are in the studio?

K (6): Yes, yes exactly. I think that is often the process. 問7 <u>I can't</u> <u>actually do it all myself.</u> So I work with a team. We work together to make things.

J (7): Anish, your work, *Cloud Gate*, which is the name of one of your truly stunning and enormous sculptures, is located in Chicago, U.S.A. 問9 <u>It is now known as "The Bean" because it is shaped like a</u> <u>bean.</u> Is this an example of a large project that had an outcome <u>that you did not intend?</u> From your title it seems that it was intended to represent a cloud but now, for many, it represents a large bean.

K (7): Yes, and I have nothing but good things to say about the people of Chicago. They truly love their city. 問8 <u>They asked me to make</u> *Cloud Gate*, <u>and in front of a group of Chicago's leaders I made a</u> <u>little drawing and said, "This is what I want to do."</u> They approved <u>it.</u> So it is given another name, well, that is what happens with big art and sculpture. You start with one concept and sometimes something else ends up happening. And the artist at one point has no more control over how people will interpret the art. There is a kind of magic in this.

J (8): 問9 <u>Another unintended outcome was that they had a budget of 9</u> <u>million American dollars, and the price to finish expanded, like one</u> <u>of your sculptures, to an enormous 23 million dollars.</u>

K (8): Yes, that was unintended, but the good people of Chicago understood and supported us. I am told now that it is so much part of the city that people could never imagine it not being there, and also it has drawn enormous money as a tourist attraction.

J (9): I should add that I think every single person who has seen "The Bean" absolutely falls in love with it. It is truly loved by the city. I understand it is cleaned every day.

K (9): That's correct. 問10 <u>It is cleaned every day because there are</u> <u>thousands of people who visit it and touch it every day.</u> (1,065 words)

（J：ジェンキンズ　K：カプーア）

J（1）：あなたが彫刻に鏡を使いたいと決めたのはなぜでしたか。リスナーの便宜のために付け加えるべきだと思いますが，私が今言及しているのは，あなたのおそらく最も有名な作品である《スカイミラー》のことで，同じものがニューヨーク市のロックフェラーセンターなど3か所に設置されている芸術作品です。

K（1）：問1 私は芸術作品がその周囲の空間とどのように関係するかということに非常に興味があり，あなたが今おっしゃった作品《スカイミラー》は彫刻そのものが，たえず変わりゆく空を映し出すがゆえに，それが映し出している空間と完全に作用しあっています。《スカイミラー》をご覧になったことがないリスナーのために申しますと，それは屋外に設置された円形の鏡で，空に向けられています。その効果は，それが空を地面に向かってさかさまに引き込んでいるように見えるというものです。一番初めは，イギリスのノッティンガムにあるプレイハウス劇場のために制作しました。この最初の作品は直径が6メートルでした。問2 後に，直径が約10メートルの大型バージョンを作りました。これがロックフェラーセンターに設置されているものです。この作品はこの高層ビルとその向こうにある空をとらえるために上に向けて置かれているので，見ている人にニューヨークの有名なスカイラインに対する別の遠近図を与えます。

J（2）：最もよく知られているあなたの彫刻作品の1つは，2002年に完成した《ジャイアント》と呼ばれている作品です。それはロンドンのテートモダン美術館に展示され，美術館記録室によると，およそ180万人がそれを見たということです。問3 これによって，世界で最も多くの訪問者があった彫刻作品の1つになりました。

K（2）：テートモダン美術館のエントランスにある大ホールは，まあ，室内彫刻のために現存する最も大きな美術館スペースの1つですね。私はそのスペース全体を使うことにしたのです。それまで他の芸術家たちは，このスペースの3分の1ほどしか使っていませんでした。それは十分大きいのですが，私はサイズに関しては少し無茶なところがありましたね。私は大規模プロジェクトの価値を心から信じていまして，芸術によって広大な空間に展開していくことがおもしろいと考えているのです。

J（3）：というのも，そのことが，つまりそのような巨大スペースを使うことが，多くの芸術家をしり込みさせているのも確かなことですよね。《ジャイアント》をご覧になったことのない方のために言うと，これは言葉で説明するのが難しい，本当に大きい作品でした。あなたはプラスチックと鋼鉄を組み合わせて使い，それはホール中に広がるように見えました。この作品は長さが150メートル，高さは10階建ての建物に相当しました。問4 この作品を上から撮った写真では，歩き回っている人々がこの作品の下にいるアリのように見えますね。

K（3）：ええ，そうですね，彫刻作品は大きくなっていくにつれ，意味を失っていくという考

えがあります。それが本当に正しいとはどうも思えません。とにかく私は大規模作品がすばらしい効果を持つこともあると思っているのです。テートの《ジャイアント》という作品で，人々が実際にその中に入っていき，内部から体験できる作品を作りたいと思いました。また，彫刻作品それ自体が，それが設置されている巨大ホールよりも大きく見えるものにしたいとも思いました。私の作品になじみがないリスナーもいるかもしれないので，《ジャイアント》が古いギリシャの物語に触発されたものだということは説明しておいたほうがいいですね。これは，アポロンという神が自分よりも上手に木管楽器を演奏することのできる人に嫉妬し，この人間を拷問にかけるという話です。この物語は，イタリアの画家ティツィアーノによる有名な絵画の題材になっています。それは恐ろしい話で，人を拷問するという考えが残酷ではあるものの，大きな苦しみという考えを喚起します。しかし問5重要なことは，私たちは罰せられた人を哀れに思うということであり，この作品も大きな規模で同情を喚起すると考えます。

J (4)：このようなプロジェクトに至る新たな考えはどのように始まるのでしょうか。

K (4)：まず，《ジャイアント》などの大きな彫刻を作るときに，試作品はありません。まあ，模型を作ることはできますが，小さめの模型からわかることはあまりありませんね。実際ないのです。問6その模型を大きな彫刻に拡大するときに何が起こるのかわかりません。私がその完成した姿を初めて見るのは，一般の人々が初めてそれを見るときです。

J (5)：では，プロセスをお話しくださいませんか。つまり，デッサンから始まり，続いて小さな模型を作るということですね。

K (5)：そうですね，デッサンを描くことが多いですね。問7デッサンか模型を作りますが，デッサンも模型もなし，ということもよくあります。ときにはただ何かを作らなければならないのです。どんなものであれ。

J (6)：アトリエにある素材ならどんな素材でも使うということですか。

K (6)：そうです，まさにそのとおりです。それがプロセスであることが多いと思います。問7実際，すべてを1人で行うことはできません。ですから，チームを組んで取り組みます。協力してさまざまな物を作るのです。

J (7)：アニッシュさん，あなたの本当に驚くべき巨大彫刻の1つ，《クラウドゲート》という名の作品が，アメリカのシカゴにあります。問9それは豆のような形をしていることから今では「ザ・ビーン」として知られています。これは意図しない結果を生み出した巨大プロジェクトの一例でしょうか。あなたの付けたタイトルからすると雲を表現するおつもりであったように思われますが，今では多くの人にとってそれは巨大な豆を表しています。

K (7)：ええ，シカゴの人たちについて言いたいことはよいことばかりです。彼らは本当に彼

らの町を愛しています。_{問8}彼らから《クラウドゲート》を作るよう依頼があったとき, 私はシカゴのリーダーの一団の前で, 軽くデッサンを描いて, それで「これが私のやりたいことです」と言ったのです。彼らはそれを認めてくれました。それで, その作品には別の名前もつけられていますが, まあ, 巨大芸術や巨大彫刻にはそういうことが起こりますよ。あるコンセプトからスタートし, 最終的には何か別のものが生じることがあるのです。そして, 芸術家はある時点から, 人々が作品をどのように解釈するかについてもはやコントロールできません。ここにある種の魔法が存在します。

J (8)：_{問9}他の予期せぬ結果としては, 900万ドルの予算だったものが, あなたの彫刻の1つのように, 完成させるのにかかる金額が 2,300万ドルという莫大（ばくだい）な額に膨らむということがありました。

K (8)：はい, それは予期せぬことでしたが, シカゴの善良な人々は私たちのことを理解し, 支えてくれました。今私の耳に入るのは, それが実にシカゴの一部となっているので, 人々はそれがそこにないことを想像することなどできないだろうし, 観光の呼び物として, 大金を引き寄せてくれてもいるということです。

J (9)：「ザ・ビーン」を見た人はひとり残らずそれに心から魅了されるだろうということを, 付け加えておくべきですね。それは間違いなくシカゴ市民に愛されています。毎日きれいにされていると聞いています。

K (9)：そのとおりです。_{問10}そこを訪れて, 触れる人が毎日何千人もいるので, 日々それはきれいにされているのです。

解説 事前に質問文をよく読み, 問われていることを把握します。時間が許す限り, 選択肢同士の違いも確認しましょう。また, 固有名詞を押さえることで, トピックの把握がしやすくなります。設問は概ね音声で流れる順番どおりに設定されているので, できる限り, 音声を聞きながら答えを出していきましょう。

問1 カプーアが作品に鏡を使うことに決めたのはなぜか。

① 見ている人に, 円環から映し出されている自分自身の姿を見てほしいと思った。

② 見ている人に, 宇宙に引き込まれていく感覚を与えたいと思った。

③ 芸術作品がその周囲の空間とどのようにかかわるのかに興味がある。

④ 彫刻が周囲の空間からそれ自体をどのようにして切り離すのかに興味がある。

　カプーアは最初の発話の第1文で I'm really interested in the way art relates to the spaces around the art「私は芸術作品がその周囲の空間とどのように関係するかということに非常に興味がある」と言い, 続けて, 《スカイミラー》がその鏡によって, たえず変わりゆく空の様子を映し出し, 作品と空間とが作用しあっている点について説明しています。したがって正解は ③ です。

問2 カプーアは最初の《スカイミラー》を制作した後, もう1つ《スカイミラー》を制作

したが，それは（　　　）た。

　① 直径が6メートルで，ノッティンガムに設置され

　② 直径が6メートルで，ロックフェラーセンターに設置され

　③ 直径が10メートルで，ロックフェラーセンターに設置され

　④ 直径が10メートルで，ニューヨークのスカイラインの上に設置され

　カプーアは最初の発話の第4・5文で，直径6メートルの最初の《スカイミラー》をノッティンガムに設置したと言った後，続く第6・7文で Later I made a larger version that is about 10 meters in diameter. This is the one installed at the Rockefeller Center.「後に，直径が約10メートルの大型バージョンを作りました。これがロックフェラーセンターに設置されているものです」と説明しているので，正解は ③ です。④ については，カプーアが第8文で，ロックフェラーセンターに置かれた《スカイミラー》が，「見ている人にニューヨークの有名なスカイラインに対する別の遠近図を与える」と説明してはいますが，「スカイラインの上に設置された」とは言っていないので，不適です。

問3　カプーアの作品《ジャイアント》はその大きさと並んで，どんなことで知られているか。

　① 世界で最も多くの訪問者を集めた彫刻作品の1つであること。

　② テートモダン美術館の大ホールのほぼ3分の1を占めていること。

　③ 人々がこの巨大芸術作品を見ると，気がおかしくなってしまうこと。

　④ テートモダン美術館がその大ホールの面積を拡張するのを手助けしたこと。

　ジェンキンズは2番目の発話の第1・2文で，《ジャイアント》に触れて，およそ180万人がこの作品を見たと言い，続けて This made it one of the most visited works of sculpture in the world.「これによって，世界で最も多くの訪問者があった彫刻作品の1つになりました」と説明しているので，正解は ① です。

問4　インタビューアーのジェンキンズは《ジャイアント》の大きさについて何と言っているか。

　① それは拡大された巨大なアリのように見える。

　② それは150メートルを超える高さがある。

　③ それは人々をアリのように見せる。

　④ それはあまりに大きいので意味を持たない。

　ジェンキンズは，3番目の発話で，《ジャイアント》が長さ150メートル，高さがビル10階建てに相当することを説明したあとで，In overhead pictures of the work, the people walking through seem antlike under this work.「この作

品を上から撮った写真では，歩き回っている人々がこの作品の下にいるアリのように見えますね」と言っているので，正解は ③ です。④ は，カプーアが3番目の発話で紹介した説です。ジェンキンズ自身はこのことに触れていません。

問5 《ジャイアント》の基本テーマは人間の苦しみだが，カプーアはこの彫刻が（　　　）と感じている。

　　① 人間の深い同情心をも喚起する

　　② あまりに大きいので，意味を持たない

　　③ いまもアポロンの神に敬意を表している

　　④ ティツィアーノの絵画ほどは残酷でない

　カプーアは3番目の発話で，《ジャイアント》がギリシャ神話から触発されたものであり，人間の大きな苦しみを喚起すると説明しています。そして同発話の最終文で the point is that we feel sorry for the man who was punished, so I think that the artwork also evokes sympathy on a large scale「重要なことは，私たちは罰せられた人を哀れに思うということであり，この作品も大きな規模で同情を喚起すると考えます」と言っているので，正解は ① です。② は，第1文に「彫刻作品は大きくなっていくにつれ，意味を失っていくという考えがあります」とありますが，その直後でこの説に懐疑的であることを述べているので，不適です。③ については触れられていません。④ は，ティツィアーノ作品への言及はあるものの，残酷さを比較してはいないので，不適です。

問6 新しい巨大彫刻の制作を始めるときにカプーアが直面する可能性のある問題の1つは何か。

　　① その彫刻のでき上がりがどのようなものになるか知るすべがない。

　　② 巨大芸術作品の模型のほうが完成した彫刻よりも優れていることがしばしばある。

　　③ 芸術家が見るよりも先に，一般の人々がその彫刻を見る。

　　④ 一般の人々は模型を見ることがないので，拡大された作品を理解することはできないかもしれない。

　カプーアは4番目の発話の第1文で，試作品を作ることはないと言っています。また，模型を作ることはできるが，模型からわかることはほとんどないとしたうえで，You never can tell what will happen when you expand your model into a large sculpture.「その模型を大きな彫刻に拡大するときに何が起こるのかわかりません」と言っています。したがって，正解は ① です。② と ④ については述べられていません。③ は，同発話の最終文 The first time I see it finished is the first time the public sees it. に関連しますが，一般の人が

芸術家よりも先に作品を見るとは言っていないので，不適です。

問7　新たなプロジェクトを始めるために，カプーアは（　　　）作業する。

① 巨大彫刻の小型模型を使って，1人で

② 巨大彫刻の完成形を方向づけるデッサンによって，チームで

③ たいていは自分のアトリエにある素材を用いて，1人で

④ ときにはどんなものでもよいので，ただ何かを作りつつ，チームで

　カプーアは5番目の発話で，新しいプロジェクトに取り組むときのプロセスを問われて，Drawings or models but quite often no drawings, no models. Sometimes you just have to make something. Anything. 「デッサンか模型を作りますが，デッサンも模型もなし，ということもよくあります。ときにはただ何かを作らなければならないのです。どんなものであれ」と説明しています。また，次の発話で，カプーアは I can't actually do it all myself. So I work with a team. We work together to make things. と言っており，制作作業はチームで行われることがわかるので，正解は ④ です。② は，デッサンが「完成形を方向づける」とは述べられていないので，不適です。

問8　《クラウドゲート》は（　　　）巨大彫刻だ。

① カプーアとシカゴの人々は満足しているが，シカゴ市のリーダーたちは満足していない

② シカゴ市のリーダーたちがちょっとしたデッサンを見ただけですぐに承認した

③ カプーアがその完成品を見届けた後「ザ・ビーン」に改名した

④ 人々がそれについてどのように解釈するかカプーアが完全にコントロールしたので，彼が満足している

　カプーアは7番目の発話の第3・4文で They asked me to make *Cloud Gate*, and in front of a group of Chicago's leaders I made a little drawing and said, "This is what I want to do." They approved it. 「彼らから《クラウドゲート》を作るよう依頼があったとき，私はシカゴのリーダーの一団の前で，軽くデッサンを描いて，それで『これが私のやりたいことです』と言ったのです。彼らはそれを認めてくれました」と言っているので，正解は ② です。③ は，カプーアがこの直後の文で，it is given another name と言って，「ザ・ビーン」という名が人々によって与えられたものだと示唆しているので，不適です。④ は，この後の文で，「芸術家はある時点からは人々の作品の解釈の仕方をコントロールすることができない」と言っているので，不適です。

問9　《クラウドゲート》の2つの意図せぬ結果とは何だったか。

① 人々がそれを「ザ・ビーン」と呼び始め，計画よりもずっとお金がかかった。

② 人々がそれを「ザ・ビーン」と呼び始め，計画よりも安くすむ結果になった。

③ 計画よりもややお金がかかったが，観光客を呼び込む巨大アトラクションとなった。

④ 公式に「ザ・ビーン」に名前が変えられ，シカゴ市民よりも観光客のほうがそれを気に入っている。

ジェンキンズは7番目の発話の第2・3文で It is now known as "The Bean" because it is shaped like a bean. Is this an example of a large project that had an outcome that you did not intend? と尋ねており，カプーアはそれを否定していないので，1つ目の意図せぬ結果は，人々が《クラウドゲート》を「ザ・ビーン」と呼び始めたことになります。もう1つは，ジェンキンズが8番目の発話で Another unintended outcome was that they had a budget of 9 million American dollars, and the price to finish expanded, like one of your sculptures, to an enormous 23 million dollars. と言って，カプーアもそれを認めているように，《クラウドゲート》の完成に予定の2倍以上の金額がかかってしまったことです。以上より，正解は ① です。③ については，「観光客を呼び込む巨大アトラクションとなった」の部分はカプーアの8番目の発話に関連しますが，意図せぬ結果であるとは言っていませんし，2倍以上の金額がかかったので「やや」というのも不適です。④ は前半の「公式に名前が変えられ」という部分が事実と異なり，後半の「シカゴ市民よりも観光客のほうがそれを気に入っている」という部分も言及がないので，不適です。

問10 《クラウドゲート》について，このインタビューからどのようなことが推論されるか。

① 観光客よりもシカゴ市民に愛されている美しい彫刻だ。

② 3,300万ドルを超えるお金がかかった美しい彫刻だ。

③ お金がかかった芸術作品でありながらも，人々はそれに触れることを許されている。

④ お金のかからなかった芸術作品だが，それは愛され，日々大事にされている。

問9でも見たように，《クラウドゲート》は計画よりも多額のお金を要した高価な作品ですが，カプーアの最後の発話の第2文 there are thousands of people who visit it and touch it every day にあるように，手で触れることが許されている作品であると考えられます。したがって，正解は ③ です。① は，観光客とシカゴ市民のどちらがより《クラウドゲート》を愛しているかについての言及がないので，不適です。② は，ジェンキンズの8番目の発話にあるとおり，実際にかかった金額は2,300万ドルなので，不適です。数値は正確に聞き取りましょう。④ は，この作品は予算の2倍以上を要した高価な作品だったので，inexpensive という部分が誤りとなります。

語句 for the benefit of 〜「〜の（便宜の）ために」, refer to 〜「〜に言及する」, duplicate 動「〜を複製する」, ever-changing 形「千変万化の」, interact with 〜「〜と相互に作用する」, circular 形「円形の」, skyward 副「空の方に」, upside down「さかさまに」, initially 副「最初に」, diameter 名「直径」, skyline 名「スカイライン, 地平線」, roughly 副「およそ」, according to 〜「（情報源）によると」, scare 〜 off / scare off 〜「〜をしり込みさせる, 追い払う」, storey 名「（建物の）階（米語では story）」, antlike 形「アリのような」, stretch 〜 out / stretch out 〜「〜を無理に伸ばす, 拷問にかける」, cruel 形「残酷な」, evoke 動「〜を喚起する, 呼び覚ます」, sympathy 名「同情心」, rehearsal 名「リハーサル, 下稽古」, expand 〜 into ...「〜を…に拡大する」, outcome 名「結果, 完成」, represent 動「〜を表す, 象徴する」, nothing but 〜「〜しか, 〜以外は何も」, approve 動「〜を承認する」, end up *doing*「結局…する」, interpret 動「〜を解釈する」, unintended 形「意図しない」, budget 名「予算」

ここが ポイント

・先に質問を読み, 問われていることを把握しましょう。**選択肢同士の違いや固有名詞など, カギになると思われる表現には印をつけておくことが重要です。**

・設問はほぼ, 音声の順序どおりに設定されています。音声の長さに圧倒されることなく, 100 語程度の長さの英文を聞く問題が 10 問連続で流れてくると考え, 落ち着いて取り組むようにしましょう。

2

Part 1

正解　問1　⑤　問2　③　問3　④　問4　②　問5　②

スクリプト　※下線部は解答の根拠に当たる箇所です。

（V: Vedantam, Host　G: Gopnik）

V(1): This is *Hidden Brain*, and I'm your host, Shankar Vedantam. This week our guest is well-known psychologist Alison Gopnik. Her most recent book, *The Gardener and the Carpenter*, is about the different ways parents approach raising kids. Dr. Gopnik, welcome to the show.

G(1): Glad to be here.

V(2): Your book is built around comparisons: parents behaving like gardeners, parents behaving like carpenters. Explain that for us.

G(2): Well, 問1④ if you look at the dominant culture of parenting in the developed world now, it's a lot like being a carpenter. 問1① The idea is that you're working with fixed materials that can be shaped or rearranged, and 問1②③ if you have the right skills and follow the right instructions, then you'll be able to shape your child into a particular kind of adult. That approach is very different from what you get if you think of parenting as more like being a gardener. For one thing, a gardener never knows exactly what is going to happen because 問1⑤ the gardener is working with partners — Mother Nature, the plants, as active factors — not with fixed objects. So gardeners try to create a rich, supportive environment in which a lot of different things can happen. 問5 Personally, I'm convinced that taking care of human beings is much more like being a gardener than like being a carpenter. It's much more about providing a nurturing space in which both predictable and unpredictable things can happen than about constructing a particular kind of desirable adult.

V(3): 問5 Hearing you describe it, the gardening model seems so natural, so, well, "organic." How did we turn into a society of carpenters?

G(3): Good question. For most of human history, the whole village has been involved in caring for children — brothers, sisters, uncles, aunts, cousins, everybody. And that meant that, by the time we had our own children, we had had lots of experience caring for children. 問2, 問3①② During the 20th century, though, families got smaller and more mobile, couples had children at a later age, and, for the first time, many people starting families didn't have much experience caring for children but did have lots of experience going to school and working. So 問3③ I think it was natural for people to think, OK, this will be like going to school and working. 問3⑤ If I can just find the right manual or the right formula, I'll do the job well and produce a good product.

V(4): You also point out that, compared to most other animals, humans have a very long childhood.

G(4): That's right. We need a lot more time before we are ready to function on our own. So why are we different? _{問4}One idea is that a long childhood gives you this protected period where you can figure out how to adapt to new conditions. And that's what makes it possible for humans to live in so many different environments.

V(5): _{問5}It seems to me that the gardening model is a perfect match for those conditions, the lengthy human childhood.

G(5): That's exactly right. Imagine you could do the carpentering thing, you know, plan it all out, here is how I want my child to turn out, here is how I'm going to make that happen. You would have lost the whole point of childhood, which is to cultivate new ideas, new ways of being in the world, new ways of understanding the environment.

V(6): Fascinating. We'll continue our discussion after a brief break.

(564 words)

和訳 （V：ヴェダンタム，司会者　G：ゴプニック）

V(1)：『ヒドゥン・ブレイン』のお時間です。私は司会を務めるシャンカール・ヴェダンタムです。今週のゲストは著名な心理学者であるアリソン・ゴプニックさんです。彼女の最新の著書『庭師と大工』は，親が子育てに取り組むうえでのさまざまな方法を扱ったものです。ゴプニック博士，当番組へようこそ。

G(1)：お呼びいただき光栄です。

V(2)：今回の著作は比喩によって組み立てられていますね。庭師のように振る舞う親や大工のように振る舞う親というように。そのことを説明していただけますか。

G(2)：はい，_{問1④}今，先進国社会で子育てに関する支配的な文化を見ますと，それは大工であることにかなり近いんですね。_{問1①}この考えは，形を変えたり，整え直したりすることのできる決まった材料を使って作業していて，_{問1②③}適切な技能を持ち，適切な手引きに従うならば，自分の子供をある特定の種類の大人に作り上げることができるだろうという考えなのです。このアプローチは，子育てをどちらかというと庭師であることに近いものと考えている場合に得られるものとは，非常に異なるものです。まず，庭師はこれから何が起こるのか正確には知りえません。なぜなら_{問1⑤}庭師は，決まった物体でなく，活動を伴う要素として母なる自然，つまり植物というパートナーと共に作業するからです。ですから庭師は，多種多様なことが起こりうる，豊かで成長の支えとなるような環境を作り出そうとするのです。_{問5}私個人としては，人の世話をすることは大工であることよりも庭師であることのほうにずっと近いと確信しています。それは，ある特定の好ましい大人を作り上げることに関するものというより，むしろはるかに，予測可能なことと予測不可能なことがどちらも起こりうる養育

149

空間を提供することに関するものなのです。

V(3)：_{問5}あなたの説明を聞いておりますと，庭師モデルはとても自然，つまりとても，そうですね，「有機的」に思えます。どうして，私たちは大工の社会になってしまったのですか。

G(3)：よい質問です。人間の歴史の大半において，村全体が子育てにかかわってきました。兄弟姉妹，おじ，おば，いとこ，すべての人です。そしてそれは，私たちが自分の子供を持つまでに子供を世話する経験を十分に積んでいたことを意味しました。_{問2, 問3①②}しかし20世紀の間に，家族はより小さく，より流動的になり，夫婦はより遅い年齢で子供を持つようになりました。そして歴史上初めて，家族を持ち始める人の多くが，子供を世話する経験はあまりないけれども，学校に行って働きに出る経験は十分に持っているということになったのです。ですから，_{問3③}人々が，そうだ，これは学校に行き，働くことに似たものだと，考えるのも当然だったと思います。_{問3⑤}もし適切な手引きや適切な公式を見つけることができさえしたら，自分はその仕事を上手にするだろうし，優れた製品を作るだろうと。

V(4)：あなたは，人間は，他の大半の動物と比べると，幼少期が非常に長いということも指摘なさっていますね。

G(4)：そのとおりです。私たちは自立する準備ができるのにずっと長い時間を要します。では，なぜ私たちは違っているのでしょう？　_{問4}1つの考え方としては，長い幼少期によって保護された時期が与えられ，その間に新しい状況に対応する方法を身につけることができるというものです。そしてそのことによって，人間は非常に多様な環境で生きていくことが可能となるのです。

V(5)：_{問5}庭師モデルは，そうした状況，つまり人間の長い幼少期に，完全に適合するように私には思えます。

G(5)：全くそのとおりです。あなたが大工仕事をこなすことができると想像してみてください。つまり，子供にはこんなふうになってほしい，それをこんな形で実現するつもりだ，など，すべての計画を立てることができるところを。そうすると，あなたは，新しい考えや世界での新たな在り方，また環境を理解する新たな方法，こうしたことを育むことになる幼少期の重要性をすべて失ったことでしょう。

V(6)：とても興味深いですね。少し休憩をいただき，その後お話を続けます。

解説　これまでと同様に，質問を先に読み，聞き取るべき内容を頭に入れ，展開を予測します。選択肢を確認し，それぞれの違いを把握しておきます。特に問1や問3のように「本文で言及されていないものを選ぶ」問題では，選択肢の内容を理解したうえで，音声を聞きながら消去法を利用して答える必要があります。本問のように比較的長い選択肢が5つあり，しかも放送文の内容を言い換えたものが多い問題で正答率を上げるには，英語の音声を聞き取る「聴解力」

だけでなく，選択肢を素早く正確に読んで意味を把握する「読解力／速読力」も重要な要素となります。

問1 子育てを大工に見立てた考えに<u>合わないもの</u>は，次の記述のうちどれか。

① 子育ては基本材料をある特定の形に作り変えることに似ていると考える。

② 子育ての最終目標に関する明確な考えを含む。

③ 子育てを上手に行う特定の計画に従うことに関係する。

④ 今日の先進国社会において子育てに関する支配的モデルである。

⑤ 親と他の活動主体とが協力することが必要だ。

　子育てを大工に見立てた考えは，ゴプニックの2番目の発話の第1・2文で説明されています。①は The idea is that you're working with fixed materials that can be shaped or rearranged で，②と③は if you have the right skills and follow the right instructions, then you'll be able to shape your child into a particular kind of adult で，④は if you look at the dominant culture of parenting in the developed world now, it's a lot like being a carpenter で述べられています。⑤は，同発話の第4文 the gardener is working with partners — Mother Nature, the plants, as active factors — not with fixed objects「庭師は，決まった物体でなく，活動を伴う要素として母なる自然，つまり植物というパートナーと共に作業する」でたとえられていることに近い内容で，これは子育てを庭師に見立てた考えになります。したがって，正解は⑤です。

問2 先進国社会において子育ての支配的モデルを作るうえでより重要であったのは，次の人間社会の変化のうちどれか。

① 産業経済の発展。

② 高等教育の出現。

③ 自分の子供を持つ前に子供の世話をする経験の減少。

④ 大きな拡大家族の増加。

⑤ 狩猟採集から定住農耕社会への移行。

　問1において確認したように，先進国社会における子育ての支配的モデルとは「大工モデル」（＝基本素材を手引きに沿って作り，完成品に仕上げること）です。なぜ先進国社会において「大工モデル」が優勢になったかというと，ゴプニックの3番目の発話によれば，かつて村全体で誰もが参加していた子育てのあり方が20世紀に変化したからです。ゴプニックは，同発話の第4文で During the 20th century, though, families got smaller and more mobile, couples had children at a later age, and, for the first time, many people starting families didn't have much experience caring for children but did have lots of experience going to school and working. と述べ，「20世紀になる

と，家族が小さくなり，自分の子供を持つまで子供を世話する経験を持つことがなくなった」と説明しています。以上のことから，正解は ③ です。①，②，⑤ については述べられていません。④ は上述の内容と正反対の内容です。

問3　インタビューで言及されていないのは次の記述のうちどれか。

① 現代社会において，人々はしばしば，先に子供を世話する経験を持つことなく家族を持ち始める。

② 子育ては 20 世紀に変化し始めた。

③ 子育ては学校に行ったり仕事をしたりすることと似ているとみなされてきた。

④ 子育ては，先に仕事で成功していればよりスムーズに進むだろう。

⑤ 子供を上手に育てるために適切な手引書を求める親もいる。

　問2で確認したように，ゴプニックは，3 番目の発話の第 4 文で，「子育ては20 世紀に変化し始めた」点と「自分の子供を持つまで子育てを経験することがあまりない」点について述べているので，① と ② は言及されていることになります。③ は続く第 5 文 I think it was natural for people to think, OK, this will be like going to school and working で，⑤ は第 6 文 If I can just find the right manual or the right formula, I'll do the job well and produce a good product. で言及されています。④ に関することは述べられていないので，正解は ④ です。

問4　人間が特に長い幼少期を持っている理由としてゴプニックが言及しているのは次のうちどれか。

① 人間が言語を習得できるようにするため。

② 人間がより柔軟で順応できるようにするため。

③ 人間がより大きな脳を持てるようにするため。

④ 人間がより充実した人生を経験できるようにするため。

⑤ 人間が周囲の環境を保護できるようにするため。

　ゴプニックは，4 番目の発話の第 4 文で，人間の幼少期が他の動物よりも長い理由の 1 つとして a long childhood gives you this protected period where you can figure out how to adapt to new conditions 「長い幼少期によって保護された時期が与えられ，その間に新しい状況に対応する方法を身につけることができる」と述べています。これは，人間が長い幼少期を経ることで新しい環境に適応できる柔軟性と順応性を身につけることを意味しているので，② が正解となります。①，③，④，⑤ の内容はインタビューの中で言及されていません。

問5　この会話に基づくと，ゴプニックと司会者のヴェダンタムの考えを最もよく表しているのは次の記述のうちどれか。

① ゴプニックとヴェダンタムはどちらも大工モデルのほうを好んでいる。

② ゴプニックとヴェダンタムはどちらも庭師モデルのほうを好んでいる。

③ ゴプニックとヴェダンタムは両方のモデルに評価すべきところを多く見出している。

④ ゴプニックは大工モデルのほうを好んでいるが，ヴェダンタムは庭師モデルのほうを好んでいる。

⑤ ゴプニックは庭師モデルのほうを好んでいるが，ヴェダンタムは大工モデルのほうを好んでいる。

　ゴプニックは，2番目の発話の第6文で Personally, I'm convinced that taking care of human beings is much more like being a gardener than like being a carpenter.「私個人としては，人の世話をすることは大工であることよりも庭師であることのほうにずっと近いと確信しています」と言って，庭師モデルのほうを好んでいることを表明しています。ヴェダンタムは3番目の発話の第1文で Hearing you describe it, the gardening model seems so natural, so, well, "organic."「あなたの説明を聞いておりますと，庭師モデルはとても自然，つまりとても，そうですね，『有機的』に思えます」と言い，庭師モデルに理解を示しています。またヴェダンタムは5番目の発話で It seems to me that the gardening model is a perfect match for those conditions, the lengthy human childhood.「庭師モデルは，そうした状況，つまり人間の長い幼少期に，完全に適合するように私には思えます」と言っており，ここからもヴェダンタムが庭師モデルを好んでいることがわかります。以上より，どちらも庭師モデルのほうを好んでいることになるので，② が正解です。

語句　psychologist 名「心理学者」，gardener 名「庭師」，carpenter 名「大工」，approach 動「(問題など) に取り組む」名「方法，取り組み方」，raise 動「(子供) を育てる」，comparison 名「たとえ，比喩」，dominant 形「支配的な，優勢な」，parenting 名「子育て，育児」，fixed 形「決まった，固定した」，material 名「素材，材料」，shape 動「～を形作る」，rearrange 動「～を整え直す」，instruction 名「指示，手引き」，active factor「活動している因子，活性因子」，supportive 形「支えとなる」，be convinced that SV「…と確信している」，nurturing 形「養育の」，predictable 形「予測可能な」，unpredictable 形「予測不可能な」，construct 動「～を構築する」，desirable 形「好ましい，望ましい」，organic 形「有機体の，生物の」，be involved in ～「～にかかわっている」，mobile 形「流動的な」，formula 名「公式，基本原則」，point out that SV「…と指摘する」，compared to ～「～と比べて」，childhood 名「幼少期，子供時代」，turn out (to be) ～「(結果的に) ～になる」，cultivate 動「(才能，考え) を育む，養う」，fascinating 形「すばらしい，とても興味深い」

・「本文で言及されていないものを選ぶ」問題では，選択肢の内容を理解し，音声を聞きながら合致するものを消去していきましょう。
・英語の音声を聞き取る「聴解力」だけでなく，選択肢を素早く正確に読み取る「読解力／速読力」も身につけましょう。

Part 2

正解 問1 ③ 問2 ① 問3 ① 問4 ② 問5 ⑤

スクリプト ※下線部は解答の根拠に当たる箇所です。

(V: Vedantam　G: Gopnik　W: Webb)

V(1): Welcome back to *Hidden Brain*. I'm your host, Shankar Vedantam, and we're discussing parenting with Dr. Alison Gopnik. We're also joined by Maurice Webb, head of a school for gifted children. Firstly, Dr. Gopnik, you've written that today's adolescents are in a very different situation from those in the past. Remind us of what you've observed.

G(1): You know, in some ways, they're doing much better than at any other time in modern history. 問1<u>They're achieving more, but that's partly because they're less likely to take risks.</u> But that goes with a lot of anxiety — high levels of anxiety and fear. And I think, you know, that is kind of what you would predict from the carpenter story.

V(2): How do you mean?

G(2): Well, in the carpenter story, you're so concerned that the child comes out "correctly" that you're not giving the child the freedom to take risks and explore and be autonomous. And it's not risk-taking unless there is some chance that it could really go wrong, and I think that's another aspect of the current parenting culture that's problematic.

V(3): 問2<u>So, Dr. Gopnik, your argument is that by creating an environment where children can freely learn and explore, you raise</u>

children who perhaps are going to be better able to deal with what the world throws at them. But Dr. Webb, I wonder if things look different from your perspective?

W(1): Well, I think our world rewards people who can do very specific things and do them very well. Like in the Olympics, for example. People who are winning gold medals in ice skating in the Olympics, you know, those are usually kids who started lessons when they were three. 問3 And even though you might say, you know, let the child figure out what he or she might want to do, if a child discovers that she really wants to be an ice skater when she's fourteen, it's probably too late at that point to really be very good at it. That's the problem.

V(4): Right, and so I'm wondering if there could be reasonable differences here in what people might be aiming for as parents?

W(2): I suspect that there is. The question is, are we aiming for children who are well-adjusted, or for children who are successful? And I wish there wasn't a tension between those two things, but, unfortunately, I think there is.

G(3): There's no question that most parents have a sense of being in a very competitive universe. 問4 I mean, parents see their teenagers staying up until 2 o'clock every night studying to get that little extra advantage that's going to get them into the best college. That's crazy. I'm genuinely sympathetic, but there is something wrong here.

W(3): I agree, and I wish that success didn't require those extremes. But 問5 perhaps it isn't parenting that needs to change; instead, it's how society rewards and punishes success in school. A small advantage in a test shouldn't make the enormous difference to anyone's life that it currently does. Competition based on fairness and equality is valuable, but life shouldn't actually be like a contest, where there is either success or failure, and most people fail. But that's what we have to prepare children for and I think the real issue is there, not with the models of parenting themselves.

V(5): Unfortunately, we're out of time and will have to end our discussion on that note. Thank you both for talking with us today.　(570 words)

和訳 （Ｖ：ヴェダンタム　Ｇ：ゴプニック　Ｗ：ウェブ）

Ｖ(1)：再び，『ヒドゥン・ブレイン』にようこそ。私は司会のシャンカール・ヴェダンタムです。私たちはアリソン・ゴプニック博士と子育てについて話し合っています。ここで，才能ある子供たちのための学校の校長を務めておられますモーリス・ウェブさんにも加わっていただきます。最初にゴプニック博士，あなたは，現代の青少年は昔の青少年と置かれている状況がかなり違うとお書きになっていますね。あなたの述べられたことをここでもう一度お話しいただけますか。

Ｇ(1)：そうですね，ある意味で，彼らは近現代史における他のどの時代よりも，ずっと高い水準にいます。_{問1}彼らはより多くのことを成し遂げていますが，それは１つには，危険を冒さない傾向にあるからです。しかし，それには多くの不安が伴います。それも高いレベルの不安と恐怖です。そして，何と言いますか，それは大工理論から予測されるようなものだろうと思うのです。

Ｖ(2)：それはどういうことですか。

Ｇ(2)：つまり，大工理論では，親たちは，子供が「正しく」育つことを気にしすぎて，子供に危険を冒して探求し自律的でいる自由を与えていないのです。そして実際に物事がうまく運びえない可能性がない限り危険を冒していることになりませんし，それが，現在の子育て文化の，問題ある別の側面だと思います。

Ｖ(3)：_{問2}ということは，ゴプニック博士，あなたの主張は，子供たちが自由に学び探求できる環境を創出することで，世界から投げかけられるものに対して，よりよく対処できるようになるであろう子供を育てるのだ，ということですね。しかしウェブ博士，あなたの見方とはいろいろと異なっているようなのですが。

Ｗ(1)：ええ，私たちの世界は，極めて限られた物事を行い，それらをとても上手にできる人々に報酬を与えていると思います。例えば，オリンピックで見られるようにですね。オリンピックのアイススケートで金メダルを取っているような人は，まあ普通は，３歳のときにレッスンを始めた子供たちなわけです。_{問3}そして，自分がやりたいかもしれないことを子供に見つけさせてやりなさいと，まあ，あなたは言うかもしれませんが，たとえ，子供が14歳になってからアイススケートの選手に本気でなりたいと思ったとしても，その時点ではそれに十分に習熟するにはおそらく遅すぎるでしょう。それが問題なわけです。

Ｖ(4)：はい，ですから，人が親として目指しているかもしれないものに関して，この点でそれなりの相違があり得るのではないかと思うのです。

Ｗ(2)：私はあると思っています。問題は，私たちは子供が社会に適応することを目指しているのか，子供が成功することを目指しているのか，ということです。そしてこの２つの間に対立がなければいいと思うのですが，残念ながら，対立はあると思います。

Ｇ(3)：大半の親が非常に競争的な世界で生きている自覚を持っていることは疑いありませ

ん。_{問4} つまり親は，自分の 10 代の子供が，その差が最高の大学に入れてくれるであろう少し秀でた優位を得るために，毎晩午前 2 時まで起きて勉強しているのを見ているのです。これは異常なことです。私は心から同情しますが，これには間違ったところがありますよ。

W (3)： 同意しますし，成功というものがそのような極端な状態を必要とするものでないことを願うばかりです。しかし，_{問5} ひょっとすると，変化が必要なのは子育てのあり方ではなく，むしろ，学校での達成に対する，社会による報酬や罰の与え方のほうではないでしょうか。テストでのちょっとした優位が，誰であれ人の一生を，今そうしているような形で，大きく左右するべきではありません。公正と平等に基づいた競争は価値のあるものですが，人生は実際，成功者と敗者がいてしかもほとんどが敗者であるコンテストのようなものであるべきではないのです。しかし，それこそが，私たちが子供たちに準備させなければならないことであり，真の問題はそこにあると思うのです。子育てのモデルそのものにではなく。

V (5)： 残念ながらお時間が来てしまいまして，そろそろ議論を打ち切らなければなりません。お二人とも，本日はお話しいただきありがとうございました。

解説 話者が 1 人増え，テーマに関して意見の対立が生まれています。Part 1 におけるゴプニック博士の主張を踏まえつつ，2 人の論点を明確にとらえることが重要です。設問を読み，どの話者の意見を問われているか，またどのような対立軸を基盤にしているか，把握してください。正解の選択肢は放送文の内容を言い換えているものが多いので，論旨を正確に聞き取ると同時に，消去法を活用して，選択肢を素早く絞り込みましょう。

問1　ゴプニックによると，大工モデルの子育てをすることで起こりうる結果とは何か。

① 子供たちは危険を冒すことによってより多くのことを成し遂げる。

② 子供たちは不確かなことによりよく対処できるようになる。

③ 子供たちは用心深くなる可能性が高まる。

④ 子供たちはのちの人生でバランスの取れた人になる。

⑤ 子供たちはより大きな自由から恩恵を得る。

　ゴプニックは最初の発話の第 2 文で They're achieving more, but that's partly because they're less likely to take risks.「彼らはより多くのことを成し遂げていますが，それは 1 つには，危険を冒さない傾向にあるからです」と言い，子供たちが危険を冒さず，より用心深くなっていることを示唆しているので，正解は ③ です。① はこの文と矛盾するので不適です。また，ゴプニックの最初の発話の第 3 文や 2 番目の発話によると，大工モデルで育てられた子供は常に不安を抱えており，自ら探求する自由も自律的でいる自由も与えられていないので，不確かなことに対処することも，バランスの取れた人生を送るこ

とも，自由から恩恵を得ることもできないと考えられます。したがって，②，④，⑤はどれも不適です。

問2　ヴェダンタムによると，ゴプニックは何を主張しているか。

 ① 子供たちは危険を冒すことで貴重な教訓を学ぶ。

 ② 子供たちは幼いときから特定の技能を伸ばす必要がある。

 ③ 親は子供たちのための特別な目標を持つ必要がある。

 ④ 大工モデルは子供たちの自由の意識を増加させるように作られている。

 ⑤ 現在の子育て文化がうまくいくためにはほんの少ししか調整する必要はない。

　ヴェダンタムは，問1で見たゴプニックの考え（今の親は子供に危険を冒し探求し自律的になる自由を与えていない）を踏まえて，3番目の発話の第1文で，your argument is that by creating an environment where children can freely learn and explore, you raise children who perhaps are going to be better able to deal with what the world throws at them「あなたの主張は，子供たちが自由に学び探求できる環境を創出することで，世界から投げかけられるものに対して，よりよく対処できるようになるであろう子供を育てるのだ，ということですね」とゴプニックの考えをまとめています。つまり，ヴェダンタムはゴプニックの主張を「子供たちに危険を冒す環境を与え，それによって学びを得られるようにする」とまとめたことになるので，正解は ① です。②は，ウェブが最初の発話で語っていることなので，不適です。また，ゴプニックは子育ての大工モデルに批判的な意見を持っています。大工モデルでは，親が子供に対して明確な成長目標を定めており，子供に自由である意識を植え付けるようには作られていないと言えます。したがって，③ と ④ は不適です。⑤は，ゴプニックの支持する庭師モデルは現在支配的な大工モデルとは大きく異なり，「ほんの少しの調整」ではすまないと考えられるので，不適です。

問3　ゴプニックの主張に対してウェブはどのような異議を唱えているか。

 ① 子供たちに多くの自由を与えることは，将来の機会を制限することになりうる。

 ② 不安から解消されようとするなら，組み立てられた人生が必要となる。

 ③ 成功しようとするなら，1つのことに絞る前に多くのことを試す必要がある。

 ④ オリンピック選手になるためには，14歳以前にレッスンを受け始めなければならない。

 ⑤ 人生での成功の基盤は子供の生得的能力である。

　ウェブは最初の発話の第1〜3文で，現代社会はある特定の技能に秀でた人が有利になるような社会であると述べ，具体例として，オリンピックで活躍するような人は幼いときにその競技を始めているということを挙げています。さらに続く第4文でウェブは even though you might say, you know, let the child figure out what he or she might want to do, if a child discovers that she really wants to be an ice skater when she's fourteen, it's probably too late at that point to really be very good at it「自分がやりたいかもしれないことを子供に見つけさせてやりなさいと，まあ，あなたは言うかもしれませんが，たとえ，子供が14歳になってからアイススケートの選手に本気でなりたいと思ったとしても，その時点ではそれに十分に習熟するにはおそらく遅すぎるでしょう」と言っています。これは「オリンピック選手を育成するには幼いころから始めるべきだ」と主張しているのではなく，「自由を与えすぎると将来特定の何かを達成するには遅すぎることもある」ということを伝えるための具体例であることに注意してください。したがって，正解は ① であり，④ ではありません。②，③，⑤ については，ウェブは述べていない内容なので，不適です。

問4 ウェブが説明している問題についてゴプニックはどう思っているか。

① 子供たちは親を信頼するよう促されるべきだ。

② 子供たちは成功するためにそこまで一生懸命に頑張ることを期待されるべきでない。

③ 競争的な文化にいる親は自分の子供たちに大きな要求をするべきだ。

④ 親は子供たちの成功を助けるよう，彼らにできる限りあらゆる優位を与えるべきだ。

⑤ 私たちはこのような状況にいる親に同情するべきだ。

ウェブが説明している問題とは，ウェブの2番目の発話にある The question is, are we aiming for children who are well-adjusted, or for children who are successful? And I wish there wasn't a tension between those two things, but, unfortunately, I think there is. 「問題は，私たちは子供が社会に適応することを目指しているのか，子供が成功することを目指しているのか，ということです。そしてこの2つの間に対立がなければいいと思うのですが，残念ながら，対立はあると思います」を指しています。これに対して，ゴプニックは，3番目の発話の第1文で，「大半の親は競争的な世界で生きている自覚がある」としたうえで，続く第2・3文で I mean, parents see their teenagers staying up until 2 o'clock every night studying to get that little extra advantage that's going to get them into the best college. That's crazy. 「つまり親は，自分の10代の子供が，その差が最高の大学に入れてくれるであろう少し秀でた優位を得るために，毎晩午前2時まで起きて勉強しているのを見ているのです。これは異常なことです」と言っています。これは「子供たちが成功するために頑張りすぎる現在の状況は異常だ」と言っていることになるので，正解は ②

159

です。① は述べられていない内容です。③ は上述のゴプニックの発言と矛盾する内容です。④ は，上述の箇所に「子供が優位を得るために頑張りすぎる」とはありますが，「親が子供に優位を与える」とは言っていないので，不適です。⑤ は，ゴプニックの同発話最終文に関連しますが「親に同情すべきだ」とは言っていないので，不適です。

問5　ウェブはこの議論から最終的にどのような結論を導いているか。

① 人生は不公平な競争のようなものだ。

② 子育てモデルの大半は子供に人生に対する準備を十分にさせるものではない。

③ 自分の子供が人生で成功するにはどのように手助けすればよいのか理解している親は十分にはいない。

④ 子育ては非常に報われない活動である可能性がある。

⑤ 真の問題は社会にある。

　ウェブは3番目の発話の第2文で perhaps it isn't parenting that needs to change; instead, it's how society rewards and punishes success in school「ひょっとすると，変化が必要なのは子育てのあり方ではなく，むしろ，学校での達成に対する，社会による報酬や罰の与え方のほうではないでしょうか」と言っているので，正解は ⑤ です。① は同発話の第4文に関連しますが，ウェブは「公正と平等に基づいた競争は価値あるものだ」と言っていますが，現代の人々の人生が不公平な競争のようになっていると結論づけてはいないので，不適です。② は，同発話の最終文でウェブは「真の問題は子育てモデルそのものにはない」と言っているので，不適です。③ と ④ に関する発言は，ウェブの議論には見られません。

語句　gifted 形「天賦の才を持った」，adolescent 名「青年，若者」，predict 動「〜を予測する」，autonomous 形「自律的な，自主的な」，tension 名「緊張（関係），（二者の）対立」，genuinely 副「真に，本当に」，sympathetic 形「同情的な」，extreme 名「極端さ」，out of time「時間切れで」，on that note「（話の打ち切りを示して）それでは，そろそろ」

ここが ポイント　正解の選択肢は本文の内容を言い換えている場合が多いので，論旨を正確にとらえると同時に，間違いの選択肢を見抜いて消去する「消去法」を活用して，効率よく正解に至りましょう。

音読・ディクテーショントレーニング

復習のしかた

● **音読**
　トレーニング用音声の発音をまねて，スクリプトを声に出して読みましょう。
● **シャドーイング**
　トレーニング用音声を聞きながら，すぐあとに続いて繰り返しましょう。
● **ディクテーション**
　スクリプトを見ないでトレーニング用音声を聞き，英文を書き取りましょう。

 和訳 ▶ p.13 　　　　　　　　　　　◀))26

W(1): Chris, can I talk to you for a minute? I'm so nervous about studying abroad. I'm worried I won't be able to communicate with anyone.
M(1): You worry too much, Hana. You speak English well.
W(2): Yeah, but some Americans speak so fast. I don't know if I'll be able to understand them.
M(2): But you can understand me, can't you?
W(3): Yeah, but you speak very clearly. I don't think everyone is as easy to understand as you.
M(3): Well, I'm having lunch with a couple of friends from New York tomorrow. Why don't you join us? You can practice with us.
W(4): Really? Thanks, Chris. That will make me feel better.
M(4): Sure. Meet us in the cafeteria at lunch time.
W(5): I'll be there. Thank you.

1 和訳 ▶ p.70 　　　　　　　　　　　◀))27

M(1): Hi, Reiko.
W(1): Oh, hi, Taka. I didn't know you took this bus from the station to campus.
M(2): No, I usually ride my bicycle from here. The bus is too expensive. But it's raining so hard today.

W(2): Oh, I never ride my bike. The campus is too far from the station. I normally get the bus.

M(3): But it only takes 20 minutes by bike. And when you have to wait for the bus, it takes ages.

W(3): Well, yeah, the buses are pretty infrequent. But the worst thing is when it's too crowded to get on.

M(4): What do you do then?

W(4): I try to share a taxi so I won't be late for class.

M(5): I think you should get a bike. It would be much cheaper in the long run.

W(5): Oh, that sounds like too much exercise to me. Maybe the best thing would be a dorm room on campus.

2 和訳▶p.72　　　　　　　　◀))28

M(1): Hello? Is this the Writing Center?

W(1): Yes. Hi, have a seat.

M(2): My name is Yoshi.

W(2): Nice to meet you, Yoshi. Welcome to the Writing Support Desk. I'm Wendy. Is this your first time here?

M(3): Yes. I feel very nervous.

W(3): Well, it's great that you've come. Okay, each session is only half an hour, so we need to decide how we're going to use the time. Can you tell me what you'd like to work on today?

M(4): Yeah. It's my English literature paper.

W(4): I see.

M(5): Can you fix it for me?

W(5): Well, we aren't supposed to correct your writing.

M(6): Oh no, I'm going to fail.

W(6): But we can work together to improve your paper. Can you tell me what problems you are having with it?

M(7): Well, my professor said I needed more evidence to support my ideas. But I'm more worried about my grammar mistakes.

W(7): Okay. So evidence and grammar. Do you have your work with you?

M(8): Yes. My essay is in my bag. Ah, oh no, where is it? I must have left it in one of my morning classes.

W(8): Okay. In that case, it would be better if you booked another appointment and came back with your essay.

M(9): But the deadline's tomorrow.

W(9): It's all right. My last free appointment this afternoon starts at 2:40. Why don't you make another appointment with me then?

M(10): Okay. I'll make an appointment and come back later.

---

3 和訳▶p.75   ◀))29

M(1): Risa, got a minute?

W(1): Sure, Justin. What's going on?

M(2): Not much. I wanted to ask you about the new meal plan that the cafeteria is offering. Greg told me that you're on it now.

W(2): Yes, I started it a month ago, when it was first offered.

M(3): What do you think about it? Is it better than the one you were on before?

W(3): Well, it depends on how often you eat.

M(4): What do you mean?

W(4): The new meal plan doesn't cover breakfast and weekends. That's why this option is about fifteen thousand yen cheaper every month. I realized that I was getting up too late to eat breakfast. I also often go home on the weekends to go to my part-time job and see my family.

M(5): I see. The new plan definitely suits your lifestyle. I think I'll stick with the one I'm on, though. I rarely go home now, and I need to get up early for practice anyway. I can't skip breakfast or I'll be starving in my morning classes.

W(5): Sounds like a smart choice.

 和訳▶p.19   ◀))30

The Bode Museum in Germany is known for its collection of rare coins. But on

March 27, 2017, the collection's largest coin was stolen. Known as the "Big Maple Leaf," it weighs 100 kilograms and is 53 centimeters wide. The face value of the coin is $1 million, but experts say it may be worth up to $4 million because its gold is so pure. It had been kept behind bulletproof glass since it was loaned to the museum in 2010. Berlin police believe the thieves climbed in through a window, broke the case and took the coin in just 25 minutes. People question how the thieves got such a large and heavy coin out of the museum. One person guessed that the thieves must all be weightlifters.

| 1 | 和訳 ▶p.78

◀))31

You might think that the traditional French ham and butter baguette sandwich would be the most popular fast food in France. But think again. A recent study shows that sales of American-style burgers have overtaken the sales of these sandwiches. According to a French restaurant marketing company, about 1.2 billion ham and butter baguette sandwiches were sold in France in 2017 while 1.4 billion burgers were sold during the same period. Sales of both baguette sandwiches and hamburgers are on the rise, the study says. It notes that baguette sandwiches saw a 1.3 percent growth in 2017, while burger sales recorded a 9 percent increase. Curiously, in France, the number of hamburgers sold by McDonald's has not varied for years. What has changed though is the growing number of restaurants putting burgers on their menu. In fact, 80 percent of restaurants surveyed in France included burgers on their menu in 2017. The rise of the American-style burger was noted in a story in *The New York Times* which reported that Restaurant Le Dalí and other famous restaurants in Paris added burgers to their menus for the first time 10 years ago.

| 2 | 和訳 ▶p.81

◀))32

During World War II, when London was bombed, George VI and his queen won great public admiration by staying in London throughout the war. The present Queen has also been much respected, and her concern for the Commonwealth has strengthened the monarchy.

For many years, people expected the royal family to have high moral standards and to display all the ideals of family life, an attitude which developed in the time of Queen Victoria. Until recently, the public rarely saw the royal family except on formal occasions. They remained distant and dignified, and any family problems were kept private. The younger royals, however, have lived more public lives and attracted enormous media interest. Royal marriage problems and love affairs have become headline news. Alongside a hunger for yet more revelations, traditional respect for the royal family began to decline. The reported treatment of Diana, Princess of Wales, and Sarah, Duchess of York, especially after the breakdown of their marriages, brought criticism on the Queen and older members of the family. The family were again criticized for their apparent reluctance to share in the public's grief after the death of Princess Diana.

 3 和訳 ▶ p.83　　　　　　　　　　　　◀)) 33

The activity of a certain gene could determine how social you are and how well you bond with others. The OXT gene is responsible for the production of oxytocin, a hormone linked with a large number of social behaviours in humans. It's often referred to as the "love hormone." In a recent study, researchers assessed more than 120 people, conducting genetic tests and assessments of social skills, brain structure and brain function. They found that those with lower activity of the OXT gene had more difficulties in recognizing facial expressions and were more anxious about their relationships with loved ones. These individuals also had lower levels of brain activity in regions associated with social cognitive processing.

 4 和訳 ▶ p.85　　　　　　　　　　　　◀)) 34

The estimated number of uninhabited houses in Japan is continuing to rise. The supply of newly built properties keeps growing despite the declining population, while the demolition of unused homes or efforts to list them on the market is making slow progress. There were 260,000 more vacant houses in Japan October 2018 than five years earlier. The number was put at a record 8 million, accounting for 13 percent of Japan's total housing stock. Unoccupied and badly maintained houses are safety hazards, because of their potential use in crimes and the danger that they could collapse during a natural disaster. A law was passed in 2015 that gave municipal authorities the power to tear down properties that pose safety problems, but the latest data indicate that the law has not had much effect so far.

 和訳 ▶p.28   ◀)) 35

(**A**: Interviewer   **B**: Interviewee)

A(1): Good morning and welcome to the "Japan Life" podcast. Today I'm speaking with John Shaw. John is a young writer and currently lives right here in Tokyo. John, welcome to the podcast.

B(1): Glad to be here. Thanks for having me.

A(2): So, tell me, how long have you been living in Japan?

B(2): Well, I came to Japan just over two years ago. I lived in Osaka for about a year before relocating to Tokyo.

A(3): OK. So, what brought you to Japan?

B(3): It's kind of a long story, but I guess it all started when I first visited Japan when I was seven years old. You see, my parents are travel writers and they used to drag me along with them on their trips all over the world. By the time I turned eight, I had been to over ten countries.

A(4): Did you like traveling that much as a child?

B(4): Well, I didn't always enjoy those trips because I couldn't really appreciate the new places I was visiting. I remember finding some places quite boring, but my trip to Japan was different.

A(5): How so?

B(5): Well, I grew up in a pretty rural area of the US where people get around almost entirely by car. I had seen trains on TV and in movies, but I had never actually ridden on one. So, when I came to Japan, I rode a train for the first time in my life. And according to my parents, I absolutely loved it. I wasn't interested in doing anything other than riding on the trains during my trip here.

A(6): It must have been hard for you when it was time to go back home.

B (6): Maybe it was, but my parents bought me a toy train from a shop in Kyoto before we left Japan. It instantly became my favorite toy and one of my prized childhood possessions.

A (7): That's great. So, did your interest in trains continue once you were back home?

B (7): For a little while, yes, but over time I found new hobbies and interests. And in high school I realized I had a skill and a passion for writing.

A (8): Just like your parents.

B (8): Yeah, the apple didn't fall very far from the tree, I guess. In university I studied creative writing and decided to make writing my career. So, one day, after graduation, I was having some trouble trying to come up with an idea for my next project. As I was sitting at my computer in my bedroom I looked up and noticed my old toy train that I got in Japan sitting on a shelf, and it hit me. My next book will be based in Japan and involve trains, and I should go to Japan to write this book.

A (9): Had you considered coming to Japan again before this moment?

B (9): Not at all. The idea came to me totally out of the blue. And I moved here within two months from that day.

A (10): Wow! That's pretty fast for such a big decision.

B (10): Yeah, it was, but I'm glad I did it.

A (11): So, have you been traveling a lot on the trains here?

B (11): Of course! I've spent a lot of time riding the trains in and around Osaka and Tokyo, of course, and I've taken the bullet train across most of the country to cities like Nagoya, Kyoto, and Hiroshima. And I'd really like to go to Kagoshima. I've heard it's really beautiful there.

A (12): And how is your writing process going?

B (12): Great! I've just finished my final manuscript.

A (13): So, can you tell me what the book is about?

B (13): It's a suspense novel about a young man who while visiting Japan on vacation gets into a pretty unusual situation while riding a train late at night in Osaka.

A (14): That sounds interesting.

B (14): I've really enjoyed writing it, and I'm already working on the next book in the series. I've also learned something about myself during my time here.

A (15): What's that?

B(15): I can actually write better while riding on a train. Back home I always did my writing alone in my bedroom or in a café, but I've been writing on my laptop while riding the trains here and it's great. I'm more creative. I'm more focused. And I can come up with better ideas for characters and stories.

A(16): That's great. So, the train is now your writing space!

B(16): Exactly. It can be difficult at times, like if the train is crowded, but that's not the biggest challenge I've encountered with my new writing technique.

A(17): What challenge is that?

B(17): Using the train as your office isn't cheap!

A(18): John, what a story. Thank you for sharing it on the podcast. Best of luck with your book and have fun riding all those trains!

B(18): Thanks for having me.

---

1 和訳 ▶ p.89　　　　　　　　　　　　◀)) 36

（R: Richard　J: Jackie）

R(1): Not so long ago Jackie became a Portuguese citizen. So, Jackie, what did you need to do for that?

J(1): Lots of paperwork, that's for sure. But you do need to um ... live some ... live in Portugal for six years, not have a criminal record and to pass a language test.

R(2): And you need to hang ... hand over some cash as well.

J(2): Yeah, it was very expensive. At least 250 euros.

R(3): But for this week's podcastsinenglish.com we're looking at how foreigners can become permanent residents or citizens of the UK.

J(3): Well, first of all you need to take, and pass of course, the Life in the UK Test. Now this is in English of course, so you do need to have the right level of English to do it. Um ...

R(4): Yes. And it's based on a book, isn't it?

J(4): Yeah, now what's ... it's a handbook, Richard. What's that called?

R(5): It's called *Life in the United Kingdom: A Guide for New Residents*. And this is available online.

J(5): Yeah. Well, actually you can practice online as well, Richard, can't you?

The test consists of 24 questions.

R(6): Multiple choice.

J(6): Yeah, multiple choice. And you need to get at least 18 right to pass.

R(7): And you get 45 minutes.

J(7): Yeah, 45 minutes, so what's that? Just under two minutes for each question.

R(8): And every question is based on the book.

J(8): Yes. OK. Now Richard and I have done this test a few times and um ... well perhaps not amazingly but I failed it quite a few times and you Richard ...?

R(9): I ... I ... did three tests. I passed two and failed one.

J(9): Now if you ... if you are doing this because you seriously want to become a resident of the UK, you can just retake the test, right ... you can hand over another fifty pounds. Um ... but it's interesting because the handbook, Richard ... there are five chapters, aren't there?

R(10): Yes, um ... "The values and principles of the UK", "What is the UK?" one titled: "A long and illustrious history", history questions um ..., "A modern, thriving society", and the final one is "The UK government, the law and your role" as a citizen.

J(10): Now I think I'm right, Richard. It's the third chapter, the history questions which let us down. I mean, let's give you some examples of the kind of questions they were asking from that chapter.

R(11): "What ..." sorry, "When did the Anglo-Saxon kingdoms establish in Britain?"

J(11): I mean we've got no idea, really.

R(12): Well, they're multiple choice ... the ... the multiple choices didn't give you much chance either. They were very close together.

J(12): Yes. But that's the same with all of them. "When were the first coins minted?"

R(13): And "The population of the British Empire".

J(13): I mean, you know, the ... the thing is, I think, there can be useful questions, things that people should know about the UK: the law, how we behave, things like that.

R(14): And yes and rather ... rather than useless questions which Brits don't even know themselves.

J(14): Well, we don't know and as a result of those history ones, we failed the test to become a British citizen.

R(15): So, Jackie, do you know of any other countries that have tests like this?

J(15): I think they do something similar in Spain and France.

R(16): But luckily for you, not in Portugal.

J(16): No, I think I would have failed that one, certainly.

2 和訳 ▶p.96 ◀))37

(J: Joji P: Philip A: Ayaka)

J(1): Hey, Philip, have you decided what kind of presentation you are going to do for the talent show on "Culture Night" for our ESS Club next month?

P(1): Yeah, well, I have a couple of ideas ... maybe you could help me decide which is best ...

A(1): Hi, guys ... what's up? What are you talking about?

J(2): Oh, I was just asking Philip what he plans to do for the talent show ...

A(2): Ahhh, yes ... the annual talent show! That is one of my favorite events. I love to see what all the foreign students' talents are.

P(2): Oh, no, is it that big of a deal? Now, I'm getting worried because I don't think I have any real talent.

A(3): Don't worry ... it is not so formal and mainly just fun. Last year, a student from Mexico did a "Mexican Hat Dance" and a student from Canada sang the Canadian national anthem. In fact, I remember one year, a student from Spain pretended to be a bullfighter with his friend, who wore a cow costume. It was so funny. We laughed so hard.

J(3): Ayaka's right ... don't stress out about it too much. What do you like to do?

P(3): That's the problem ... I really don't have anything in particular that I do that is performance-based.

A(4): How about singing? I heard you singing in the student lounge a while back.

P(4): You heard that! I thought I was alone!

A(5): (laughing) Yeah, well, I was outside the room. I thought you sounded really good. Do you ever sing in public?

P(5): Not really. I did sing "Ave Maria" at my cousin's wedding when I was in junior high school, but ...

J(4): Come on, Philip, sing us a few notes. I want to hear it.

A(6): Me, too! Go on ...

J(5)/A(7): (together) PLEEEEASE!!!!!

P(6): Oh, all right ... I can't believe I'm doing this ... "Aaaaaveeee Maaarrriiiiia."

A(8): Wow, you can sing! Why not sing that?

P(7): Nah, I don't have the courage to sing it in front of the whole university.

J(6): Well, what were the couple of ideas you mentioned before?

P(8): Uhhh, let's see ... I thought about doing a magic trick, but the problem is I don't have my magic stuff with me here in Japan and I really need some of the objects for it to work.

A(9): Ah, that's too bad ... magic is always fun to watch and people love it. What else were you thinking about?

P(9): I thought about preparing something to eat on stage ... you know ... the process of how to make a dish, but that can be a bit messy and it probably wouldn't work really well ...

J(7): You're right. The stage is too small. Any other ideas?

P(10): Umm, I could tell a couple of jokes ... what do you think of that?

A(10): I love it! I think the audience would enjoy that!

J(8): What kind of jokes ... can you give us a sample now?

P(11): Let's see ... let me think ... OK, "... Yeah, as a student, I'm so poor that when a thief broke into my room to search for money, I woke up and searched with him." Ba-da-dum!

A(11): I don't get it. Why is that funny?

P(12): Well, because the thief was looking for money in my room to steal, I searched with him because I need money because I'm a poor student ...

J(9): Maybe a different joke would be better ...

P(13): OK, one more. It's a knock, knock joke. When I say, "Knock,

knock," you both say, "Who's there?" and then later, "Blah blah who?" OK, ready?

J(10)/A(12): (together) Ready!

   P(14): "Knock, knock ..."

J(11)/A(13): "Who's there?"

   P(15): Abie.

J(12)/A(14): Abie who?

   P(16): A, B, C, D, E, F, G ...

   J(13): Hmmm, that's a little better. I think the students would get it and laugh ...

   P(17): Oh! How about this one? "The student asked the teacher: Would you punish me for something I didn't do? And the teacher replied: No, of course not! The student said: Good, because I haven't done my homework."

J(14)/A(15): (both laugh loudly)

   P(18): OK ... I have decided ... I will tell jokes.

   A(16): Great! I can't wait!

   J(15): Me, too ... I think it will be fun!

---

3 和訳 ▶p.104   ◀))38

(**A**: Axel **M**: Mei **B**: Barry)

   A(1): Hi, Mei!

   M(1): Huh? Oh. Hi, Axel. ...

   A(2): Hey, what's wrong? You look worried.

   M(2): Oh, it's probably nothing, but ... I've been trying to get ahold of Nami all weekend, and I can't. It's like she's disappeared off the face of the Earth or something. I've called again and again, but no answer.

   A(3): Did you leave a message?

   M(3): Of course! Like, so many times! And I've texted her and texted her, but it looks like she hasn't even read the messages. It's so not like her!

   A(4): Weird. Did you try calling the fitness club? I bet she's working there today. I know that she's been taking a lot more hours lately.

M(4): I just called. She's off today.

A(5): Oh. Well, maybe she's on one of those long hikes she likes to take, and she just forgot to take her phone. She loves her hiking!

M(5): Well, I just called her roommate, Kathy. She says that Nami's hiking boots are still in the closet. So, that's not it. And the thing is, Nami doesn't go anywhere without her phone. It's like a part of her body.

A(6): Really? Well, Kathy must know where she is. I mean, she is her roommate.

M(6): You won't believe this. When I called, Kathy had just gotten back from a two-week vacation in Hawaii. So she has no idea where Nami is.

A(7): Hawaii ... sounds nice. ... Oh, I know! I bet she's at her parents' place! She doesn't have a washing machine, and you know how she doesn't like laundromats. Germs. ...

M(7): Laundromats? ... Oh! You mean the place with coin-operated washing machines? Yes, I thought the same thing. But when I brought up that theory with Kathy, she told me that they just bought a new washing machine. So, that can't be it. And you know what?

A(8): What?

M(8): I was starting to think about how sometimes I see a creepy-looking guy just sitting in his car outside her place. What if that guy's a stalker? What if he finally went ahead and kidnapped her or something?

A(9): Wait a minute. Does he have an eye patch?

M(9): Yes.

A(10): And a scar on his left cheek?

M(10): Yes!

A(11): And a long beard and a giant tattoo on his arm.

M(11): Yes, yes!

A(12): That's her uncle!

M(12): What!?

A(13): Yeah, they're really close. She and her uncle often go fishing together. He was probably just waiting to pick her up.

M(13): He looks so scary!

A(14): He's actually a super nice guy. You should meet him! Hmmm. I hope she didn't get into a car accident or something.

M(14): Well, fortunately, that's not something we have to worry about. ... She doesn't drive!

A(15): Yeah, but maybe she was hit by a bus or something!

M(15): Oh, that's true. Maybe she's been in an accident. That's got to be it!

A(16): Should we call the hospitals?

M(16): All the hospitals? And what about her parents? Do you know their number?

A(17): Oh, my God, what are we going to do?

B(1): Hey guys!

A(18)/M(17): Aaah!

M(18): Barry! You scared the heck out of me!

A(19): Yeah, don't sneak up on us like that!

B(2): Sorry, guys. Say, have you seen Nami?

M(19): No. In fact, I've been trying to contact her all weekend!

B(3): Oh. Cuz I need to return her phone to her.

A(20)/M(20): What!?

B(4): Well, we were at a nightclub Friday night. And my phone went dead, so I borrowed her phone to make a call. When I tried to give it back to her, I couldn't find her. I guess she went home having forgotten that I had borrowed it.

M(21): I've been texting and calling all weekend! Why didn't you answer it?

B(5): Oh, I didn't notice the phone was ringing ... sorry.

M(22): Huh? Okay, whatever. Anyway, now I'm calling the police.

A(21): Hey, wait a minute. Isn't that her?

B(6): Oh, yeah! Hey, Nami! Over here!

A(22): Well, she looks as happy to see us as we are to see her.

M(23): Or she's just happy to see her phone!

4

[1] Have you ever lied to anybody? No? Then I'm afraid you're lying. In fact, lies are a part of our daily life. For instance, you might have made up an excuse for being absent from a class or you might give a compliment to a friend about a bad haircut. In fact, a key study in 1996 by a social psychologist, Bella DePaulo, and her colleagues, revealed just how often we tell lies. They found that their adult subjects lied on average once or twice a day. While most lies were not offensive, they also found later that adults tell one or more serious lies at some point in their life. How about children? Another researcher, Kang Lee, a psychologist at the University of Toronto, more recently conducted interesting studies about children's lies. Today we're going to explore lies by looking at Doctor Lee's child development studies. They can reveal a fascinating and surprising aspect of human nature.

[2] When you were little, did your parents tell you not to deceive others? I guess so, because most parents worry if their children lie to them. Lee said that there are three common beliefs about children's lies. First, preschool children don't lie. Second, children are bad liars, so it's easy to detect their lies. Third, if children lie when they are very young, they must have a character defect. Lee's research suggests that these three beliefs are wrong.

[3] The research was based on an experiment, in which children play the guessing game with an examiner. If they correctly guessed the numbers on cards, they would get rewards. But during the game, the examiner left the room with an excuse, telling the children not to peek at the cards. There were hidden cameras in the room to record the children's reactions. Surprisingly or perhaps not, more than 90% of the children looked at the cards. Then, when the examiner came back into the room, she asked the children if they had looked. No matter what their gender, nationality and religion was, about 30% of 2-year-olds lied, saying that they hadn't looked at the cards. At 3 years of age, about 50% lied. And at 4, more than 80% lied. Thus, the common belief that preschool children don't lie was disproved.

[4] Lee conducted a follow-up study by showing some of the videos of the

research to adults of different backgrounds. In these videos, half of the children were lying, and the other half were telling the truth. The adults were tested on whether they could tell when the children were lying. The results showed that adults such as social workers, who work closely with children, couldn't detect the children's lies. Others, such as judges or police officers, who often deal with liars, couldn't either. Even parents of the children in the videos couldn't recognize their own kids' lies. Therefore, the second common belief that children are poor liars was not supported.

[5] How about the third belief? The children who lie at an early age have a character defect. Lee says that parents should actually celebrate the emergence of lies in their children because it's a sign that the children's cognitive development is right on track. According to him, one of the requirements of lying is a development of theory of mind. Theory of mind is the ability to understand that our knowledge about the situation is different from the knowledge of others. Lee says, "I can lie because I know you don't know what I know." According to Lee, theory of mind is fundamental for us because we need to understand other people's knowledge and intentions to function well in society. So, as lies seem to reflect an important stage in our cognitive development, the third common belief also seems to be rejected.

[6] However, other researchers are not so optimistic. For instance, Victoria Talwar and her fellow researchers say children's frequent or inappropriate use of lies could be problematic. If children lie often, that might indicate poor development of conscience.

[7] Today we looked at lies through child development studies. Studies of lying would reveal more features of this complex and interesting behavior. In the future, for example, we might be better detectors of children's lies and better able to understand their behaviors. So, based on what you have learned in today's lecture, do you think we should discourage children from lying?

---

1 和訳 ▶p.112   ◀ﾘ) 40

[1] I'm sure at some point you've all thought about what kind of job you want after graduation. But have you actually thought about how companies select their employees? You probably think that having the necessary skills and qualifications

will be the key to your success. And you will be correct in thinking these two things will be very important. However, in addition to skills and qualifications, knowing about a company's recruitment procedure will also be crucial to improve your chances of success. Therefore, you need to be aware that a lot of major companies have started to use technology when deciding who they hire. They do this both to save time and because they think that using certain technologies can be an effective way of finding the candidates who will best meet their needs. So today, I'll introduce three technologies that many multinational companies have adopted. I'll then move on to explain briefly one of the concerns that has arisen as a result of the spread of the use of these technologies.

[2]　One very common approach is to use special computer programs to check résumés. Companies use them to scan the résumés for keywords that match the potential employees' criteria. If a résumé does not contain these keywords, it will be discarded. Victoria McLean, founder of a career consultancy company, estimates that these computer programs reject 75% of résumés before a human even sees them. This can save companies a huge amount of time. Let's imagine that each résumé a company receives takes about five minutes to be reviewed by a member of a company's human resources department. That might be okay if the company only gets a hundred responses to a job ad. But what if a company receives tens or even hundreds of thousands of applications? For example, in 2016 Goldman Sachs, a multinational investment bank, received a quarter of a million job applications. If humans had reviewed all these résumés it would have taken hundreds of hours.

[3]　Another way that technological advances have modified the traditional recruitment procedure is through the use of video interview services. Rather than talking to a person, in these interviews, candidates' responses to questions are recorded using the camera on their computer or mobile phone. These recorded responses are then analyzed by an AI program. Surprisingly, not only the content of the applicants' answers, but also less obvious aspects are evaluated such as minor changes in their sitting position, facial expression, and tone of voice.

[4]　Lastly and perhaps most interestingly, there's the use of computer games. Advocates of this technique such as IBM and Marriott Hotels argue that games are a very efficient way to learn about an applicant's skills and traits. One such game is called "Wasabi Waiter." In this game, the applicant plays the role of the server in a sushi restaurant and has to decide what kind of food a customer wants

based on their facial expressions. The developers of this game claim that it allows companies to know how quickly and accurately applicants can react to the expressions. More importantly, they claim that as the applicants become more involved in the game, they are more likely to show their true character. For example, the developers claim that it can show how a person reacts to a task when it becomes more challenging.

[5]　Okay, let me finish by highlighting the concern that the use of technology in recruitment can discriminate against certain types of candidates. Some argue that using AI to screen candidates can reduce the diversity of the people who are recruited. This is because the technology has been trained to make its decision based on data collected from successful employees who currently work for the company. As a result, candidates who are selected tend to possess similar characteristics to existing employees.

[6]　Another problem is that using computer games in the selection process may discriminate against older people who may not be so comfortable with them. However, supporters of the use of technology in recruitment would probably argue that there has always been bias in the recruitment process and that it is easier to correct this bias in computers than in humans. Clearly, this is a complex issue which is very much related to the broader question of how much humans should hand over decision-making to technology. This is something that we will come back to again later in the course.

2　和訳 ▶p.118　　　　　　　　　　　　　　　◀)) 41　

[1]　The Wright Brothers made the first human-powered flight in 1903, on the beaches of Kitty Hawk, North Carolina, but for most of the past 100 years, a city at the other end of the United States has been more closely associated with "flight." That's because in 1916, Pacific Aero Products Company opened in Seattle — but just a year later, the name was changed to Boeing Airplane Company, and for the rest of the century, Boeing was the biggest name in aircraft manufacturing.

[2]　But William Boeing wasn't the first person in Seattle to reach for the sky. That was Lyman Cornelius Smith, who had made his fortune manufacturing typewriters. In 1914, he built Smith Tower, the tallest building in the entire

western United States.

[3] Today, Smith Tower is made to seem small by the buildings to the north of it in downtown Seattle, but that doesn't mean there's no longer any reason to go up to the observation deck on the 35th floor. There are still good views: westward across Puget Sound to the Olympic Peninsula, southward to 4,392-meter high Mount Rainier, eastward to the Cascade Range and northward into a forest of newer, taller buildings. It's a great place to relax with your favorite drink (there's a bar and café up there) and watch the sun sink below the horizon.

[4] Smith Tower remained the tallest structure on the West Coast for nearly 50 years, but then came the Space Needle, which is about 25 percent taller. Built for the 1962 World's Fair in less than one year (Smith Tower took three years to build), it's still the most famous structure in the city for its unique shape: a flying saucer set on a high, curved frame.

[5] Ride one of the elevators up to the observation floor, at 160 meters, and take in the views. Everything you can see from Smith Tower can be seen a little better from the Space Needle, a result of the fact that there's nothing remotely as tall anywhere near it. Jets from across North America and Asia fly past on their approach to Seattle-Tacoma International Airport, and you can even watch seaplanes taking off and landing on Lake Union, to the east.

[6] One floor down from the regular observation floor there's a fashionable new wine bar which revolves, doing a complete circuit every 47 minutes. Most of that lower level features a glass floor, so if you're afraid of heights it might be better to avoid a visit.

[7] In 1985, the city took another big step closer to the heavens with the opening of the Columbia Center, some 284 meters tall. Most of the building consists of private offices, but anybody can go up to the Starbucks on the 40th floor, and for an admission fee, you can ride to the Sky View Observatory on the 73rd floor. Here, too, food and drinks (both alcoholic and nonalcoholic) are available. The atmosphere can't compare to that at the Smith Tower, but the views are better. You can even look down at the Smith Tower, which seems tiny from this position

[8] A slightly taller skyscraper was proposed in the early 2010s, but the necessary permits still haven't been granted and perhaps never will be. In the near future at least, the Columbia Center looks likely to keep its crown as the city's tallest building. But that doesn't mean that you can't get an even better view of Seattle, and your best option comes in the form of something that William

Boeing pioneered: seaplanes.

[9]　Many of Boeing's early planes were seaplanes, equipped with floats instead of wheels so that they could take off from any lake or slow-moving river, and his very first, the B&W seaplane, was assembled in a building at the edge of Lake Union. Today, that same Lake Union serves as the "runway" for Kenmore Air flights. Some of these flights transport passengers as far away as Vancouver and Victoria, British Columbia, but many just take tourists up on a sightseeing loop around the city of Seattle.

[10]　For anybody used to traveling on Boeing and Airbus airliners, a seaplane flight comes full of surprises. The flight crew consists solely of the pilot. There's no security check, no boarding pass and no meal service. For in-flight entertainment, you and the other nine passengers just look out the windows while the narration through your headphones tells you what you're seeing. All in all, if you're in the market for somewhere to visit that has a lot to see, you might just find that Seattle is the right place for you!

3　和訳 ▶ p.124　　　　　　　　　　　　◀))42

[1]　Farmers and plant breeders are in a race against time. According to Lee Hickey, an Australian plant scientist, "We face a grand challenge in terms of feeding the world. We're going to have about 10 billion people on the planet by 2050," he says, "so we'll need 60 to 80 percent more food to feed everybody."

[2]　Breeders develop new kinds of crops — more productive, disease-resistant — but it's a slow process that can take a decade or more using traditional techniques. So, to quicken the pace, Dr. Hickey's team in Australia has been working on "speed breeding," which allows them to harvest seeds and start the next generation of crops sooner. Their technique was inspired by NASA research on how to grow food on space stations. They trick crops into flowering early by shining blue and red LED lights 22 hours a day and keeping temperatures between 17 and 22 degrees Celsius. They can grow up to six generations of wheat in a year, whereas traditional methods would yield only one or two.

[3]　Researchers first started growing plants under artificial light about 150 years ago. At that time, the light was produced by what are called carbon arc lamps. Since then, advances in LED technology have vastly improved the

precision with which scientists can adjust light settings to suit individual crop species.

[4] Researchers have also adopted new genetic techniques that speed up the generation of desirable characteristics in plants. Historically, humans have relied on a combination of natural variation followed by artificial selection to achieve these gains. Now, breeders use gene-editing tools to alter DNA with great speed and accuracy. In 2004, scientists working in Europe identified a variation on a single gene that made a type of barley resistant to a serious disease. Ten years later, researchers in China edited the same gene in wheat, one of the world's most important crops, making it resistant as well.

[5] Gene-editing tools have been used to protect rice against disease, to give corn and soybeans resistance to certain chemicals, and to save oranges from a type of bacteria that has destroyed crops in Asia and the Americas. In South Korea, scientists are using these tools to rescue an endangered variety of bananas from a devastating soil disease.

[6] With cheaper, more powerful technology, opportunities are opening up to improve crops around the world. Dr. Hickey's team plans to use these discoveries to help farmers in India, Zimbabwe and Mali over the next couple of years, since he wants the discoveries to benefit developing countries, too.

[7] According to Hickey, we will need to combine speed breeding and gene editing with all the other tools we have if we are to meet the food security challenges of the future. "One technology alone," he says, "is not going to solve our problems."

[8] However, while basic speed breeding is generally accepted, many are reluctant to embrace gene-editing technology. They worry about unexpected long-term consequences. The benefits of this revolutionary technology, they feel, must be weighed against its potential dangers.

5

  Check Part 1 和訳 ▶p.51 ◀》43

Interviewer:
Hello everyone and welcome to 'Libertytown Today', bringing you the latest news

from our wonderful city. As you all know, the election for Mayor of Libertytown is only a week away, and joining us later on today's show are the two leading candidates, Mr Brad Peterson and Mrs Laura Hopkins. Mr Peterson is the present mayor of Libertytown and has held the position for the last fifteen years, winning four elections. His opponents, like Mrs Hopkins, accuse him of being conservative and out of touch with the needs of a modern city. Most of his support comes from older people, and from voters in suburban and rural districts. Mrs Hopkins, on the other hand, has only recently entered politics. She is a businesswoman, and runs a successful TV advertising agency. But, she says, she is angry with the conservatism of Mr Peterson's administration, and has promised 'to drive Libertytown into the 21st century'. Her policies have made her popular among younger, university-educated voters. But critics point out that she has no experience of political life, and argue that many of her policies would be unworkable in practice.

 Check　Part 2　和訳▶p.55　　　　　◀))44

（I: Interviewer　P: Peterson　H: Hopkins）

I(1): First, we'll talk to you, Mr Peterson. What are your main policies?

P(1): The key to our city's future is law and order. Young people today are increasingly out of control. They have wild parties that disturb the sleep of honest working citizens, they drink alcohol and engage in vandalism, they attend political meetings where dangerous views are freely discussed .... What I'm saying is that it is vitally important that our police be given the powers and resources to deal effectively with this increase of youthful disorder.

I(2): Let's turn to economic policy. Mr Peterson, what is your position on this?

P(2): That's easy. My policies are the policies of what I call 'small government'. In my opinion, for far too long governments have been taking money from good, productive people, and wasting it on unnecessary public projects, and on help for the lazy. All of this must stop! And for too long businesses have not wanted to invest in our city because of unnecessary and expensive environmental regulations. We must reform these regulations, to encourage investment.

I (3): Over to you, Mrs Hopkins. I think it's fair to say you disagree strongly with Mr Peterson.

H: Well, what Mr Peterson calls law and order is the right of the police to arrest teenagers for hanging around outside convenience stores, and fire tear gas at students protesting against overcrowded classrooms. And relaxing environmental regulations will allow factories to dump lots of poisonous chemicals in our rivers. So yes, I disagree with Mr Peterson.

 Part 3　和訳▶p.59　　　◀»)45　

(I: Interviewer　H: Hopkins　P: Peterson)

I (1): Mrs Hopkins, what do you believe in?

H (1): I believe in the future, and the future is youth! What, at this moment, does Libertytown have to offer young people? Nothing. Go into Old Town on a Saturday night, and it's dark, quiet, empty. A few people walking in the parks with their dogs, and the sound of soft music from expensive restaurants — restaurants only Peterson and his friends can afford to eat in. So, the first policy of my government will be the encouragement of businesses that cater to youth. Bars, nightclubs, Internet cafés, hamburger joints, youth theatres .... The young will flock to the town, and then tourists will flock after them. Because that's what tourists want to see: beautiful, spirited people having fun, being creative, not boring people wearing slippers, drinking weak beer, and complaining about their illnesses ....

P (1): For Mrs Hopkins everybody over the age of 30 might as well not exist.

I (2): Yes, Mrs Hopkins, that reminds me of one of your most controversial polices, the ending of the city pension scheme. Won't this make life very difficult for old people, who often have no income other than their city pension?

H (2): Who cares if a few pensioners have to cancel their vacations or can no longer afford to keep pets? Remember: my concern is with the future, and the old people will all be dead by the time that arrives ....

I (3): I'm afraid I'll have to stop you there Mrs Hopkins. Our time is up. But if I might just summarize your positions. Mr Peterson, you think teenagers should be arrested for standing outside convenience stores. Mrs Hopkins, you are looking forward to a time when all the old people are dead. Do I understand you both correctly?

P(2): That's outrageous. Obviously not all teenagers should be arrested. Only the delinquent ones ....

H(3): And in fact some of my best friends are old. My parents for example. But as for the fogies who vote for Peterson, well ....

I(4): I'm wondering, and I think our viewers will also be wondering, whether either of you is fit to be mayor of Libertytown.

P(3): Well, if not one of us, who else could it be ...?

H(4): Exactly ....

<hr>

1 Part 1　和訳▶p.129　　　　　　　　　　◀)) 46

(J: Jenkins　K: Kapoor)

J(1): Hello. I'm Jake Jenkins. A sculpture called *The Orbit* is Britain's largest piece of public art. It was designed by one of the country's most renowned artists. *The Orbit*, which can be seen in London's Olympic Park, is twice the size of New York's Statue of Liberty and it stands at 115 meters in height. Made of approximately 2,000 tons of steel, it also includes the world's tallest and longest tunnel slide. It was built as a permanent reminder of the 2012 Olympic and Paralympic games, and was completed in May 2012. Since then, it has raised eyebrows of fans and critics alike. And this is just one example of what Anish Kapoor considers art. Known for manipulating form and perspective, the Mumbai-born British artist has fascinated the public with his bean-shaped sculpture in Chicago's Millennium Park, turned New York's Rockefeller Center upside down with his 10 meter *Sky Mirror*, and astonished art fans with his enormous installation of *Giant*, in London. This week, on our show, we meet Anish Kapoor in Seoul, as he brings his eye-catching pieces to the East. Anish Kapoor, welcome to the show.

K: Hello. Thank you for inviting me.

J(2): You are one of the most famous sculptors in the world, and many believe that you are responsible for changing the way that people view sculpture. How do you think you've done this?

(**K**: Kapoor　**J**: Jenkins)

K(1): You say I have changed the way people view sculpture, but I don't know that I have, but, you know, we live, of course, in a world of objects. And we often have an image of ourselves and our whole life and environment which includes the objects we interact with. Sculpture can question or kind of pose problems that make us think again about daily objects, and by doing that it also makes us think again about our lives and environment.

J(1): Well, some people would say your work is very hard to explain — difficult to categorize. How would you describe your work?

K(2): I expect it is hard to categorize. What I think my sculpture is doing is helping people to perceive the everyday world in which they live from a different point of view or perspective. I want my sculpture to make people see everyday things like office buildings, cars, bridges etc. in a way they have never thought of before. Art is very good at changing the way people see and think about the world around them, you know. Not just sculpture, but all forms of visual art, like painting, photography, and dance, can make us see the world around us in a way which is new and novel, and surprising.

J(2): Anish, your background is quite fascinating. You were born and raised in India. Your father was a sailor with the Indian Navy. Your mother was originally from Iraq. Tell me about your childhood and were you creative as a child?

K(3): Yes, I was born in Bombay and grew up in a place called Dehra Dun, which is in the north of India. My childhood was pretty ordinary, really. Like all good Indian boys, I grew up thinking I was going to be a professional. You know, an engineer or something like that. Something professional in any case. And when I became an adult, in my late teens, I decided I was going to be an artist. My father was horrified. He told me I would never make enough money to survive and buy a house if I became an artist. But I sort of knew that it was what I had to do. And I never — once I knew it — I never thought about it again, and I never changed my mind.

J(3): You moved to London and started art school. And I believe that you said you felt utterly free. What did you feel free from?

K(4): You know, if only it was that straightforward. But anyway, I think I felt for the first time, I was doing what I really wanted to do. That there was a sense of discovery. A sense of adventure. And I think that's what's lived with me over these last 35 years, or whatever it is, that I've been professional as an artist. The sense that making a work is a kind of discovery. I feel the studio where I make my sculptures is more like a laboratory than it is like a factory or a place of manufacture. I spend my time inventing and discovering things that I think nobody has ever seen before.

J(4): You have lived in London since 1973. When you go back to India, does it feel like you're going home? Do you still have that connection? Or is the U.K. now very much home?

K(5): Well, I've lived in the U.K. for, you know, about 40 years. And I'm deeply connected with things Indian and I'm very proud of my Indian background and roots and so on. But in a way, I guess I feel like a foreigner in the U.K. and also a foreigner in India. So, it's become a permanent condition. I feel like a foreigner wherever I go now.

J(5): Anish, in 1990, you represented Britain at the Venice Festival. And you say it was a moment that changed your life. How did it change your life?

K(6): Well, you know, what you do as an artist, especially as a young artist, is tell a new story. As an artist you don't really just make things. What you're doing is telling a story about the things you create, whether it's a painting or a sculpture — whatever it is. You are telling a story about the world that you want the audience to understand and enjoy. And I experienced that in a very real way in the Venice Festival, when I represented Britain. I felt for the first time that the audience was understanding and enjoying the story about the world that I was telling with my sculptures. It was a moment I will never forget.

1 Part 3　和訳▶p.140　　　　　　◀»)48

(J: Jenkins　K: Kapoor)

J(1): What made you decide that you wanted to use mirrors in your sculpture?

For the benefit of our audience I should add that I am referring to perhaps your most famous work, *Sky Mirror*, an artwork that you have duplicated and have had installed in three locations, including the Rockefeller Center in New York City.

K(1): I'm really interested in the way art relates to the spaces around the art, and the artwork you are referring to, *Sky Mirror*, the sculpture itself, because it mirrors the ever-changing sky, fully interacts with space it reflects. For those of your audience who have not seen *Sky Mirror*, it's a circular mirror placed outside and pointed skyward. The effect is that it seems to pull the sky, upside down, toward the ground. I initially made one for the Nottingham Playhouse in the U.K. This first one was 6 meters in diameter. Later I made a larger version that is about 10 meters in diameter. This is the one installed at the Rockefeller Center. Because this work points upward to capture this very tall building and the sky beyond, it gives the viewer another perspective of the famous New York skyline.

J(2): One of your best-known sculptures is named *Giant*, which you finished in 2002. It was shown at the Tate Modern Art Museum in London, and was seen by roughly 1.8 million people according to the museum records office. This made it one of the most visited works of sculpture in the world.

K(2): The great hall at the entrance of the Tate Modern Art Museum, is, you know, one of the biggest museum spaces that there is for indoor sculpture. I decided to use the whole of the space. Up until then, other artists only used about one third of this space. That's big enough, but I am a little crazy about size. I really believe in large-scale projects, and I think that expanding into enormous spaces with art is interesting.

J(3): Because I'm sure that does scare off a lot of artists, using such a large space. For our listeners who have not seen *Giant*, this was truly an enormous piece of work that is difficult to describe in words. You used a combination of plastic and steel that seemed to stretch throughout the hall. The work was 150 meters long and 10 storeys high. In overhead pictures of the work, the people walking through seem antlike under this work.

K(3): Well, you know, the theory is that as sculpture gets bigger, it gets less meaningful. I'm not sure that's really true. So I think that large-scale works can have a wonderful effect. With the work, *Giant*, at the Tate, I wanted to make a work that people could actually walk into and experience from within the art. I also wanted the sculpture itself to seem bigger than the very large hall where it was installed. Some of your listeners may not be familiar with my work, so I should explain that *Giant* was inspired by an old Greek story. It's a story about how the God Apollo became jealous of someone who could play the flute better than Apollo could, so Apollo stretched the person out. This story is the subject of a famous painting by the Italian painter, Titian. It's an awful story but the idea of stretching a person, cruel though it may be, evokes the idea of large-scale suffering. However, the point is that we feel sorry for the man who was punished, so I think that the artwork also evokes sympathy on a large scale.

J(4): How does a new idea for a project like this start out?

K(4): Well, when you make large sculptures like *Giant* and others, there are no rehearsals. You know, you can make a model but a smaller model doesn't tell you very much. Not really. You never can tell what will happen when you expand your model into a large sculpture. The first time I see it finished is the first time the public sees it.

J(5): So tell us about the process. I mean, it starts as drawings and then you make small models?

K(5): Often there are drawings, yes. Drawings or models but quite often no drawings, no models. Sometimes you just have to make something. Anything.

J(6): Just play with whatever materials are in the studio?

K(6): Yes, yes exactly. I think that is often the process. I can't actually do it all myself. So I work with a team. We work together to make things.

J(7): Anish, your work, *Cloud Gate*, which is the name of one of your truly stunning and enormous sculptures, is located in Chicago, U.S.A. It is now known as "The Bean" because it is shaped like a bean. Is this an example of a large project that had an outcome that you did not intend? From your title it seems that it was intended to represent a cloud but now, for many, it represents a large bean.

K(7): Yes, and I have nothing but good things to say about the people of Chicago. They truly love their city. They asked me to make *Cloud Gate*, and in front of a group of Chicago's leaders I made a little drawing and said, "This is what I want to do." They approved it. So it is given another name, well, that is what happens with big art and sculpture. You start with one concept and sometimes something else ends up happening. And the artist at one point has no more control over how people will interpret the art. There is a kind of magic in this.

J(8): Another unintended outcome was that they had a budget of 9 million American dollars, and the price to finish expanded, like one of your sculptures, to an enormous 23 million dollars.

K(8): Yes, that was unintended, but the good people of Chicago understood and supported us. I am told now that it is so much part of the city that people could never imagine it not being there, and also it has drawn enormous money as a tourist attraction.

J(9): I should add that I think every single person who has seen "The Bean" absolutely falls in love with it. It is truly loved by the city. I understand it is cleaned every day.

K(9): That's correct. It is cleaned every day because there are thousands of people who visit it and touch it every day.

---

2 | **Part 1**　和訳 ▶p.149　　　　　　　◀))49　

(V: Vedantam, Host　G: Gopnik)

V(1): This is *Hidden Brain*, and I'm your host, Shankar Vedantam. This week our guest is well-known psychologist Alison Gopnik. Her most recent book, *The Gardener and the Carpenter*, is about the different ways parents approach raising kids. Dr. Gopnik, welcome to the show.

G(1): Glad to be here.

V(2): Your book is built around comparisons: parents behaving like gardeners, parents behaving like carpenters. Explain that for us.

G(2): Well, if you look at the dominant culture of parenting in the developed world now, it's a lot like being a carpenter. The idea is that you're working with fixed materials that can be shaped or rearranged, and if you have the right skills and follow the right instructions, then you'll be able to shape your child into a particular kind of adult. That approach is very different from what you get if you think of parenting as more like being a gardener. For one thing, a gardener never knows exactly what is going to happen because the gardener is working with partners — Mother Nature, the plants, as active factors — not with fixed objects. So gardeners try to create a rich, supportive environment in which a lot of different things can happen. Personally, I'm convinced that taking care of human beings is much more like being a gardener than like being a carpenter. It's much more about providing a nurturing space in which both predictable and unpredictable things can happen than about constructing a particular kind of desirable adult.

V(3): Hearing you describe it, the gardening model seems so natural, so, well, "organic." How did we turn into a society of carpenters?

G(3): Good question. For most of human history, the whole village has been involved in caring for children — brothers, sisters, uncles, aunts, cousins, everybody. And that meant that, by the time we had our own children, we had had lots of experience caring for children. During the 20th century, though, families got smaller and more mobile, couples had children at a later age, and, for the first time, many people starting families didn't have much experience caring for children but did have lots of experience going to school and working. So I think it was natural for people to think, OK, this will be like going to school and working. If I can just find the right manual or the right formula, I'll do the job well and produce a good product.

V(4): You also point out that, compared to most other animals, humans have a very long childhood.

G(4): That's right. We need a lot more time before we are ready to function on our own. So why are we different? One idea is that a long childhood gives you this protected period where you can figure out how to adapt to new conditions. And that's what makes it possible for humans to live in so many different environments.

V(5): It seems to me that the gardening model is a perfect match for those conditions, the lengthy human childhood.

G(5): That's exactly right. Imagine you could do the carpentering thing, you know, plan it all out, here is how I want my child to turn out, here is how I'm going to make that happen. You would have lost the whole point of childhood, which is to cultivate new ideas, new ways of being in the world, new ways of understanding the environment.

V(6): Fascinating. We'll continue our discussion after a brief break.

(**V**: Vedantam　**G**: Gopnik　**W**: Webb)

V(1): Welcome back to *Hidden Brain*. I'm your host, Shankar Vedantam, and we're discussing parenting with Dr. Alison Gopnik. We're also joined by Maurice Webb, head of a school for gifted children. Firstly, Dr. Gopnik, you've written that today's adolescents are in a very different situation from those in the past. Remind us of what you've observed.

G(1): You know, in some ways, they're doing much better than at any other time in modern history. They're achieving more, but that's partly because they're less likely to take risks. But that goes with a lot of anxiety — high levels of anxiety and fear. And I think, you know, that is kind of what you would predict from the carpenter story.

V(2): How do you mean?

G(2): Well, in the carpenter story, you're so concerned that the child comes out "correctly" that you're not giving the child the freedom to take risks and explore and be autonomous. And it's not risk-taking unless there is some chance that it could really go wrong, and I think that's another aspect of the current parenting culture that's problematic.

V(3): So, Dr. Gopnik, your argument is that by creating an environment where children can freely learn and explore, you raise children who perhaps are going to be better able to deal with what the world throws at them. But Dr. Webb, I wonder if things look different from your perspective?

W(1): Well, I think our world rewards people who can do very specific things and do them very well. Like in the Olympics, for example. People who are winning gold medals in ice skating in the Olympics, you know, those are usually kids who started lessons when they were three. And even though you might say, you know, let the child figure out what he or she might want to do, if a child discovers that she really wants to be an ice skater when she's fourteen, it's probably too late at that point to really be very good at it. That's the problem.

V(4): Right, and so I'm wondering if there could be reasonable differences here in what people might be aiming for as parents?

W(2): I suspect that there is. The question is, are we aiming for children who are well-adjusted, or for children who are successful? And I wish there wasn't a tension between those two things, but, unfortunately, I think there is.

G (3): There's no question that most parents have a sense of being in a very competitive universe. I mean, parents see their teenagers staying up until 2 o'clock every night studying to get that little extra advantage that's going to get them into the best college. That's crazy. I'm genuinely sympathetic, but there is something wrong here.

W (3): I agree, and I wish that success didn't require those extremes. But perhaps it isn't parenting that needs to change; instead, it's how society rewards and punishes success in school. A small advantage in a test shouldn't make the enormous difference to anyone's life that it currently does. Competition based on fairness and equality is valuable, but life shouldn't actually be like a contest, where there is either success or failure, and most people fail. But that's what we have to prepare children for and I think the real issue is there, not with the models of parenting themselves.

V (5): Unfortunately, we're out of time and will have to end our discussion on that note. Thank you both for talking with us today.

第2章練習問題2：Reproduced by permission of Oxford University Press from *Oxford Guide to British and American Culture* by Jonathan Crowther © Oxford University Press 1999.

第2章練習問題4："Address the vacant home problem (Editorial)" from *The Japan Times*, May 4, 2019. Used by permission.

第3章練習問題1："Life in the UK" from *podcastsinenglish.com*, August 22, 2019. Used by permission.

第4章練習問題2："Seattle reaches for the sky" from *Asahi Weekly*, April 7, 2019. Used by permission.

第4章練習問題3："Grow Faster, Grow Stronger: Speed-Breeding Crops to Feed the Future" by Knvul Sheikh, from *The New York Times*, June 17, 2019. Used by permission.

第5章練習問題1："TALK ASIA, Interview with Sculptor Anish Kapoor" December 7, 2012. Courtesy CNN.

第5章練習問題2："The Carpenter Vs. The Gardener: Two Models Of Modern Parenting", from *HIDDEN BRAIN*, NPR, May 28, 2018. Used by permission.